Contents

99696

Ministry to Muslim Women:

Longing to Call Them Sisters

Ministry to Muslim Women:

Longing to Call Them Sisters

Fran Love and Jeleta Eckheart

Editors

William Carey Library
Pasadena, California

Cover design by M. Sequeira

Published by
William Carey Library
P.O. Box 40129
Pasadena, California 91114
(626) 798-0819
inquiries@wclbooks.com
www.wclbooks.com

Library of Congress Cataloging-in-Publication Data

Ministry to Muslim Women: Longing to Call Them Sisters/Fran Love and Jeleta Eckheart, editors.
     p. cm.
Includes bibliographical references and index.

ISBN 0-87808-338-3 (pbk. : alk. paper)
   1. Missions to Muslims—Congresses. 2. Muslim women—Religious life—Congresses. 3. Women missionaries—Islamic countries—Congresses. I. Love, Fran, 1952- II. Eckheart, Jeleta, 1960-

BV2625 .M48 2000
266'.0088'2971—dc21
                                         00-031228

6 5 4 3 2 1
04 03 02 01 00

Printed in the United States of America

Preface

About the Consultation on Ministry to Muslim Women

At the Consultation on Ministry to Muslim Women, forty participants representing sixteen mission agencies gathered to share ideas about ministry to Muslim women. The sessions took place during May 1999 in Mesa, Arizona. The participants work among a vast spectrum of peoples—animists of Asia, fundamentalists of Arabia, neo-Muslims of Central Asia and Muslim migrants in Europe and America. They flew in from across the globe to join in the discussion. Mission leaders, mobilizers and professors who work on behalf of Muslims also attended. Most of the consultants were North American, but a few Latinas, Europeans and Middle Easterners also attended. Each was expected to contribute—if not by presenting an article, then at least by sharing her opinions and experiences and offering to network with others.

This book is a lightly edited compilation of the meetings. In it, you will discover insights into the needs of Muslim women, the efforts that are bringing Muslim women to Christ, and the ways missionary women are coping with life in the Muslim world. You will look into the hearts of women as they share their concerns, challenges and rebukes.

The intent of this compendium is that women who minister the kingdom of God to Muslim women will be encouraged, educated, and challenged to think strategically and prayerfully about the task to which God has called them.

The lively discussions that followed small group presentations were also taped, and comments from those discussions are presented here. You'll read about their conflicting ideas, too. Not everyone at the Consultation saw eye to eye! Where possible, the speaker's geographic region of experience is included as a point of reference for her comments. As in most discussions, questions are

sometimes left unanswered. The conversation rambles at times
along the way, the participants come up with valuable insights.

The questions following most articles demand the most ca
thought. They stimulate creativity about historically troub
issues and dare us to go beyond normal ministry patterns
risky, yet faith-filled ventures. Reading the articles and discuss
will inform you. The questions will stretch you.

Those who were invited to participate in this consultation were
some of our day's missionary "stateswomen" in outreach to Muslim women. Yet you will listen in as they confess their weaknesses, fears, and shortcomings. The words here represent more
than theory; they are the reports of the everyday lives of women
seeking to bring glory to God by extending his kingdom on earth.

Postscript to the Consultation

This consultation was designed to stimulate discussions and
ongoing dialogue among the participants. At the Consultation on
Ministry to Muslim Women, our purpose was to discuss the issues
relevant to ministry among Muslim women and *apply what we
learned.*

Tools

Behind each of the women who attended was a sending organization dedicated to recruiting, mobilizing, and serving missionaries.
Many organizations develop and provide tools and resources necessary to accomplish the task. We asked:

- Are missionaries receiving adequate tools to do the work?
- What tools still need to be developed?
- Some missionaries are developing tools, such as indigenous
  Bible studies, but should it be necessary for every missionary
  to develop her own tools?

Each organization and missionary represented was asked to recommend tools and resources that they have found effective in
reaching Muslim women. This compendium suggests some of
those resources. It is essential that each of us consider how we can
advance the kingdom by developing the means by which to share
these resources. Sending agencies need to explore new ideas and
fervently pursue opportunities to multiply the efforts of our workers. This is good stewardship.

Mobilization

Each missionary at the Consultation works with Muslims as the result of a felt calling. God has richly touched our hearts through an event, a book, or another person. As goers, we understand the elements that prompted us to go. But the time has come to find ways to draw in many more women who are passionate about reaching the hearts of Muslim women with the gospel.

- What will it take to draw from the wealth of resources on our college campuses, sift out women from the work place and integrate mothers and daughters into this ministry?
- Who will reach our dear friends in Islam?
- Who will join us in our pursuit of a holy fellowship of believing women from Muslim backgrounds?
- How can we pass on our own vision and passion?

We need to find a way to tell them that God is calling women to stand up and make a difference in the Muslim world. This is a worthy calling.

Training

Historically, schools and universities have been the primary choice for training and preparing missionaries for service. However, work with Muslims in limited-access environments or developing countries often requires additional or even alternate training methods. Over the years, a number of specialized courses have gained popularity.

It is also important that we address the issue of training through the sending agency or sending church. Incorporating new training ideas into missionary preparation makes us wise master builders (1 Cor. 3:10).

Task Forces Continue after Consultation

As a result of the Consultation, several task forces developed to answer the needs for greater cooperation and internationalization in developing tools, mobilizing the harvesters and training the workers. May God grant that these worthy activities result in transformed lives of Muslim women.

Terms

By and large, the Muslim world resists Christian missionary activity. For the security of those involved, most of the names in the following articles have been changed.

In addition, for the sake of brevity, the acronym MBB is used to refer to a Muslim-background believer in Christ.

Acknowledgments

With grateful acknowledgment to Fran, whose visions birthed the Consultation on Ministry to Muslim Women; Cookie, who knocked herself out to plan it; our anonymous benefactor, who believed in the vision and funded the meetings; Mary Ann and Debi, and their organizations, which cosponsored it and hope to carry on and broaden the vision of the Consultation; all the authors, who shared their experiences and ideas, with no hope of monetary recompense; Becky, who authored the thought-provoking questions following each article; the consultation participants, who allowed us to tape their discussions (and with regrets for the unavoidable occasions on which the editing process misconstrued your ideas); Valerie, who painstakingly transcribed the tapes; and Nelda, who loved me and cared for my kids, as usual.

JELETA ECKHEART

Introduction:
God's Passion Released through Us

Fran Love

The title for my talk this evening, "God's Passion Released Through Us," was given to me by a very dear friend. The dictionary describes "passion" as a powerful emotion or feeling that compels a person to take action. Time and again, this friend has told me that one quality revealed through my ministry is a passion to help women minister to and with Muslim women.

In reading the articles prepared for this Consultation, I experienced the emotional part of passion; I alternately wept with pain and burned with anger when I read your stories and experiences. But tonight I want to talk about another part of passion—my convictions. In my years as an overseas worker and now as home staffer, I have grown in passionate conviction about three things that I want to share with you. First, I am passionate about God's goodness. God's goodness is the foundation that will enable us to identify with Muslim women. Second, I am passionate about God's word. God's word is the guidebook that will equip us—and Muslim women—for every good work. Third, I am passionate about God's people. God's people are our family, who will enrich us and Muslim women.

Passionate about God's Goodness

God's goodness is the foundation that will enable us to identify with Muslim women. Psalm 67:7 says, "God, our God, blesses us. God blesses us, that all the ends of the earth may fear him."

Fran Love, a co-editor of this volume, played a leading role in organizing the Consultation on Ministry to Muslim Women.

We have a "God connection" that helps us bless Muslim women. God's blessing means that all his goodness is given to us in order that we may bless Muslim women.

This passion took root in me about eight years ago when my husband and I were doing church planting work in Southeast Asia. To be honest, it was not the work itself that gave me passion; neither was it our team's goal to plant churches, nor did Muslim women themselves fire this passion within me. Most often, the heavy responsibilities left me frustrated that these Muslims weren't cooperating with my church planting plans! Every time I saw another acquaintance begin to wear the Islamic dress and head covering, I would despair at the huge gulf widening between us. The joy of my salvation was dimmed by the daily reminders that Islam was gaining power in the lives of Muslim women. Rarely did I see these women as God-seekers, hungry to experience his approval. Rarely did I see these women as truth-seekers, desperate to behave in a manner worthy of their religion. More often I saw them as my enemies—women who did not want my religion, my Jesus. But I *couldn't* give up. After all, I was the missionary sent out by my mission agency and my church to plant churches among Muslims!

Over time, I found that while my mind was gaining understanding about the religion of Islam, my heart was being hardened against the people of Islam. My frustration drove out God's love. How can light and darkness dwell together? How can one say, "I love God whom I cannot see," yet hate her sister whom she does see? God's passion and our hate cannot exist in the same heart.

What changed me? Simply, God's goodness. Some would call it his grace, others his glory. The verse "for God so loved the world" doesn't mean that he loves Christians but not Muslims. I claimed that God loved Muslims, but inside, like the elder son in the story of the Father and the prodigal son, I couldn't fathom how he could love a Muslim woman to the same degree he loved me. This was not fair. But his goodness is not like ours. David proclaimed, "Good and upright is the Lord; therefore, he instructs sinners in his ways" (Psa. 25:8). Upon whom does God lavish his goodness, according to this verse? To sinners! To me. To Muslim women.

In the book, *Fields of Gold*, a story of church planting among the Muslims of Kazakstan, the author tells a remarkable story about one woman's search for truth.

In the last days of the Soviet Empire, Nurjan started earnestly seeking God. In those days, the only religious people she knew were the tauips and the Islamic leaders. After observing their hypocritical life-styles, she became cynical about the teachings handed down from her elders. In desperation she sincerely prayed, asking the true God to reveal himself to her. For over two years she continued to pray, asking God to show her the truth. The day she met me, hope leaped in her heart that perhaps God sent me in answer to her prayer. The Holy Spirit specifically prepared her heart to lower her prejudices against "white" people. In several of her dreams she saw white, Russian-looking people speaking Kazak, preparing Kazak tea, and identifying with Kazak culture. When white men and women first appeared in the dreams, she was frightened, but then they began to speak Kazak to her, disarming her fears. She felt these persons could be trusted to help her find the way of life.

The story astounded me. Embedded in a people cut off from the gospel, missionaries, scripture, everything, a woman cried out to know the one, true God. He heard her. A shocking truth dawned on me that night. *Those who are members of God's church may not be the only ones who importune him to send workers into the harvest. They may be persons who themselves are a part of the harvest* (Coody 1988:87-88, italics added).

Nurjan, in this story, is not the only Muslim woman hungry for God's goodness. Jihan Sadat, wife of the late President Anwar Sadat, in her wonderful book, *A Woman of Egypt*, speaks openly about her passion for her country and for her religion. And under-neath these twin passions lies her passion for God, fueled by two events early in her life. The first was her contact with Sufi Islam, of which she wrote, "I would come to admire, even envy, the inti-mate relationship the Sufis had with God. Unlike the religious fanatics who obeyed mechanically the rules and regulations of Islam, the Sufis looked on God with love and emotion" (1987:44). The second was the death of two relatives. "I felt the need to understand these deaths, to look for the answers in the Quran. I already loved the musical language of the Holy Book, having heard five times daily the call to prayer, and having listened to the cadence of the Quran on the radio. The beautiful language of our Holy Book had inspired me, as it did many Muslims. Now I sought out my religion for solace" (1987:58). Mrs. Sadat writes so naturally about praying to God, something she did all the time, not just during the five daily calls to prayer. At one critical moment when President Carter, Anwar Sadat and Menachem Begin were behind closed doors discussing a peace treaty between Israel and Egypt, Jihan Sadat and Rosalynn Carter were praying together. As the men emerged, President Sadat told the women that an agreement had been reached. Jihan's reaction was "I must have cried out. I must have hopped up and down with joy. I cannot remember, the moment was so blinding. I turned toward Rosalynn, but we could barely see each other for the tears in our eyes. 'God has heard our prayers!' I said to her" (1987:404).

A peasant Kazak woman, an urban elite Egyptian woman, and we who sit here tonight—all thirsty for truth and goodness. When I realized just how good God was to me, I repented of my unbelief. From that moment on, the truth of God's goodness was staked in my heart. The frantic fury of having to make Muslim women see things my way disappeared, to be replaced with a calm compassion. I believe with all my heart—and this is something I am passionate about—that in order for Muslim women to experience Jesus' love through us, we must first of all allow ourselves to identify with them. Jesus was identified with the transgressors. He took our sins upon himself; he became one of us. I deeply desire for us to identify with Muslim women to such a degree that we can enter into their sufferings and joys. Through moments of intercession during this Consultation and through our personal testimonies, we will be able to weep with those who weep and rejoice with those who rejoice. We will also have a time when we talk about the suffering and persecution of believers. We may hear stories of incredible suffering, for which we have no answers. If we are not convinced of God's goodness, the pain will be too hard to bear. We might get bitter and think that it is just not worth it, that our ministry is too hard. Do we have this passionate conviction about God's goodness that surrenders itself to the fact that when we bring Jesus, we may be bringing death? Oh, women, let our hearts break for these things.

Passionate about God's Word

God's Word is our guidebook that will equip us—and Muslim women—for every good work.

Paul reminded Timothy, "All Scripture is God-breathed and useful ... so that the man and woman of God may be thoroughly equipped for every good work" (2 Tim. 3:17). My passion is to see missionary women use the Bible as their ministry guidebook. Where we ministered in Southeast Asia, the believers would be suspicious of everything we said until we showed it to them in the Bible. They have a deep respect for God's word. The Bible was written by and for people of a Mediterranean culture, which was so similar to today's Islamic cultures, whether Asian or Arab. While we can learn a lot from each other during this Consultation, the thing that excites me most is for you to read the Bible through the cultural eyesight of a Muslim woman in order to find new meaning for her, as well as for yourself. When Lydia and her whole household (the account mentions no men) are baptized, we can imagine what this would mean in our context. When Jesus forgives the woman caught in adultery, we can find answers to a woman's sense of honor and shame. When Priscilla risks her life for Paul and other women go to prison for their faith in Christ, we can find strength to suffer with and for new believers.

During the candidate schools for our mission, I give candidates a Bible quiz on the lives of women in the Bible. I give a brief description of what each Bible character did, followed by the question, "Who am I?" For example, "I was the first person in the Bible to give God a name, a name that described my personal encounter with him. Who am I?" The answer is Hagar, the mother of the Arab people (Gen. 16:13). This quiz is designed to show us how inadequately we know the stories of the women in the Bible.

Reading books, listening to others speak, and writing articles for a compendium are important ways to increase our knowledge of Muslim culture and peoples. Yet personal study of Scripture remains essential. When you look at the Bible through the eyes of a Muslim woman, the power it has to answer and meet her needs is simply mind-boggling. The Bible, for me, is the bestseller on the method and the message of our ministry. One of the topics addressed in this compendium is the medium of storying the Bible. This is such a simple way of discipling because it is entirely reproducible. The author has provided a number of references to articles that can teach you how to use this method of sharing God's word. Don't pass up the opportunity to learn more about how the Bible can be an integral part of the lives of Muslim women.

Passionate about God's People

God's people are our family who will enrich us and Muslim women. Paul makes an amazing statement to the believers in Ephesus. He says that the saints of God—that's us—are this vast, rich, glorious inheritance. What is an inheritance? It is something valuable. Since we are God's inheritance—he owns us—we are also each other's inheritance. Next time you're in a gathering of believers, look around and recognize that the woman who sits across from you, behind you, in front of you—these women are your inheritance. They are part of God's gift to you.

Do you know what drives me in my ministry at my desk in my office here in the United States? The driving force behind my ministry on behalf of Muslim women is this passion to take hold of my inheritance. I want a big inheritance, so I want to be able to count many, many women as my sisters in Christ. And when it comes to Muslim women, I have an aching desire to see them brought into fellowship with us. John writes, "What we have seen and heard we proclaim to you, that you also may have fellowship with us" (1 John 1:3). Why do we preach the gospel to Muslims? So that they can be part of our inheritance, that we can fellowship with them. Do you, when you look at a Muslim woman, view her as a person who can be a new sister? How exciting if you do!

I want to see Muslim women and their families become part of the family of Christ. In our mission, we call this church planting. But it could just as well be called creating new families or Christ-centered communities. We have to believe that the day of individual and isolated conversions will soon be over, and that God dearly wants his precious children loved and cared for in their new spiritual families. At this Consultation, we will listen to women who have seen the birth of these new Muslim background believer families or communities. Their experiences have taught them a lot, but I know that they long to see God move even more powerfully to usher whole family units into his Kingdom.

I expect that among the readers of this compendium are women who are searching for the simplicity of ministry. At first, we were ignorant of what it would take to minister to and on behalf of Muslim women. To compensate, we then plunged into the complexity of learning all we could by reading books, attending classes, graphing charts and creating strategies. But soon we became tired, wondering whether in making ministry complicated we lost the simple joys of life. The good news is that on the other side of ignorance and complexity is simplicity. I hope this compendium helps you see the simplicity of our calling. I hope you are surprised when you discover on these pages how God is using women just like you, sisters in the family of God.

A Ministry of Glory

In his second letter to the believers in Corinth, Paul spoke about the ministry that you and I share in today. Do you know what he called this ministry? He called it a "ministry of glory" (2 Cor. 3:7-11). Do you know what that means to me? It means that I have a ministry, that you have a ministry, about which we can be passionate, not just with our emotions but with our convictions. Our ministries to Muslim women, while often painful, can be sustained and enriched because of God's goodness, his Word, and his people. It is ministry that is doable and pleasing to God. Is this the way it is for you? Do you long to have it this way?

Several times, I have mentioned "my passion." Yet the title of this article is about God's passion. Whose passion is it—mine or God's? I will simply state it this way: God's passion has to become mine. Often I don't know where God's passion ends and mine begins. All I know is that I cannot affirm God's passion for Muslim women when I feel none of it in my own life. God does not delight in the death of the wicked. God desires that all people come to know him. God's free gift of salvation in Jesus Christ is for all nations and both genders! And yes, God's wrath, his intense passion for justice, will be poured out. This is the passion that must pulsate in my head and in my heart and in my will. To be passionless for our ministries among and on behalf of Muslim women is to be dead to God's passion. It matters not whether you sit at desks in comfortable home offices, develop camel-knees of prayer for the salvation of the nations, or stand in clinics in remote rural villages. We all must be passionate about this ministry of glory.

SECTION 1

The World of Muslim Women

Current Issues Affecting Muslim Women

C. M. Amal

The majority of Muslim women live in developing countries, areas of conflict, war zones, or countries prone to catastrophic natural disasters. The overwhelming masses of Muslims live in abject poverty, which is aggravated by high birth rates. A large number are refugees. In 1994, estimates indicated that 18 million of the world's 23 million refugees were Muslims. In 1995, 300,000 Muslims fled Chechnya, and 5.7 million Afghans fled to nearby countries . More recently, Muslim refugees poured out of Kosovo to escape ethnic cleansing. The oldest and second largest group of people still wandering the world as refugees are Palestinians, who now number about 2.5 million. There are also 200,000 Bihari Muslims trapped in Bangladesh who are citizens of Pakistan and speak Urdu. International relief groups recognize that women refugees suffer heavy burdens.

Muslim women live in a kaleidoscope of political systems, from brutal dictatorships to constitutional monarchies. But the *umma* of Islam is spiritual, and this allegiance transcends national boundaries. A plethora of recent Muslim articles deal with the deep-felt anguish of Muslims who face a crisis because of the influence of modernism on Islam. It is one of the main themes intellectual Muslims are writing about. This is similar to Christianity's crisis in the last century, which resulted in the growth of both fundamentalism and liberalism. Whole populations are dissatisfied with governments perceived as un-Islamic and concerned that God is punishing them through these global problems for not living as good Muslims. This has led to various attempts to

C. M. Amal has lived for 24 years in the Middle East and North Africa. Her work has included church planting and literature ministry among urban Muslims.

11

return to the mores and systems of the past in order to better follow God and bring blessing on the country. On the other hand, alternative movements in Jordan, Egypt, Turkey, Algeria and Iran attempt to re-interpret Islam to the present age, an approach consistent with the Islamic doctrine of *ijtihaad*, or "endeavor." The religious tension between trying to return to the past while accommodating to the present was expressed as a real problem of Muslims by the workers I asked to survey the felt needs of Muslim women. They are as worried about the effect of materialism on their children, for example, as they are about the general pressure to be more religious.

Apart from the problems within, there is a serious problem pressuring Islam from the outside. Since the decline of Communist regimes, the West has targeted Islam as its new enemy. A part of this campaign has been systemic, negative, hostile and vengeful stereotyping of Arabs and Muslims in the Western media. Muslims are very sensitive to being portrayed in the West in negative and unsympathetic ways, and this ties in to their growing repugnance toward and repudiation of the West—its values and religion. "Newspaper articles make me feel like a walking tent with a vacuum under my scarf—which should only be filled with western ideas" (Deen 1995). They are upset with labels, especially "fundamentalism," which they believe is applied to every Muslim the West does not approve of. "We repeatedly feel deep regret every time we are reminded that non-Muslims feel hostility towards Islam" (Deen 1995:157).

Women find themselves on the front lines in this issue. Muslim women, chronically perceived by non-Muslims as victims, complain, "Western women are always trying to save Muslim women. We want empathy, not sympathy" (Deen 1995:124). Muslim women are showing a strong desire to solve their own problems their own way. The feminist movement is attempting to empower women while remaining Islamic.

With all these problems, we might expect to find that the issues that trouble Muslim women are those that receive wide media coverage. However, I surveyed women missionaries across the Muslim world, asking, "What are the major issues facing Muslim women in your place of residence?" Surprisingly few of them referred to the headlines. Is this an indicator that Muslim women do not care about the wider religious/cultural issues? Or are Christians not opening these subjects with their Muslim friends, not talking at levels deeper than the daily family problems? Or do Christians not have friends in the educated circles who talk about these subjects?

I suspect that wider religious/cultural issues do deeply affect women's lives, but at a grassroots level, they are not discussed as an intellectual topic. The thinkers are analyzing and discussing; the rest of society is simply living with the problems.

Instead, according to the responses gleaned in my limited survey, women's greatest felt needs are those that affect the home. Women are mainly concerned with how social problems touch their families. In fact, the women's anxieties for their families mirrored the international issues. They do struggle with their changing cultures, Westernization, armed conflict, refugee life and crushing poverty. But overwhelmingly, the women focus on their daily life and family relationships. Women return to the bottom line: How does this affect my family? Muslim women in China, Indonesia, Arabian Gulf, North Africa, Afghanistan, Maldive Islands, Kazakstan and the West all identified these same subjects of concern:

- finding and keeping a husband
- raising children
- addictions of the husband—mainly to alcohol
- financial struggles
- crises
- feeling powerless
- pressure of society
- conflicting demands of employment vs. home /family

How Different Are We?

Women want to bring harmony and healing to the world, beginning with their closest relationships. The issues raised by Muslim women worldwide are no different from those that concern my neighbors in Melbourne, most of whom are White Anglo-Saxon Protestants.

Recently, I was talking with a young Arab couple in Melbourne who had decided to return to Lebanon. The husband is an Iraqi refugee, and refugee issues complicated their life. They expressed concerns about raising their young family in the West with its negative, ungodly influences on their children. They were worried that the pressure of a secular society would undermine their religious influence. They feared for their children's future and the quality of their family life. When the husband failed to find work after eight months in Australia, he could not cope with the effect on his self-esteem. It placed a pressure on their marriage relationship. They worked through it but agreed that their family had a better future in Lebanon, and they have now returned to Beirut. Most of the issues identified by the Muslim women in my survey were reflected in the lives of this couple. However, they are Baptist Christians.

I suggest we change our focus in this discussion from thinking of challenges facing *Muslim* women to those facing *women* in today's Muslim world, or even women in today's global village. Muslims, Christians and all other women are concerned about the stuff of daily life. Women think and act and react like women.

It's difficult for women to shut the doors of their homes and leave family worries behind when they go out to work. Men have a greater capacity to compartmentalize their family life and focus on their jobs. We can probably all relate to instances when, after a fight, the husband goes to work. He is blessed with a temporary memory lapse until he returns that night. Meanwhile, the wife replays the movie a million times during the day and is emotionally distressed until the problem is resolved and harmony is restored. Women shut the door of the house, but we carry the occupants' problems with us like shadows in our bloodstream.

We are women together in the struggle of life. I want to suggest that we don't look at Muslim women as "the other" on a different side from us, an opposing side who cope with life in weird ways. We are women, made in the image of God and sharing women's outlooks and perspectives. Many of us probably recognized how the book *Men Are from Mars, Women Are from Venus* (Gray 1992) captured truths about the differences between the male and female perspectives on life. The book didn't need to differentiate between religious affiliations. Men are men, and women are women—wherever they are found. So we have a common bond in life with Muslim women. We face the same problems in different settings. It's where and how we look for the solutions that has more relevance to religion.

Muslim women represented in my survey expressed a lot of insecurity and fear and a sense of powerlessness. However, we need to be careful that we do not stereotype Muslim women as being insecure and fearful simply because they are Muslims. Some Christian literature focuses on this, portraying Muslim women as miserable prisoners in a life of bondage. Terms such as "the shroud of Islam" are bandied about. This miserable picture of a deprived life is probably close to the truth in today's Afghanistan, where Muslim women themselves are describing their lives in these terms. In this situation and others like it, we can join with them lamenting the circumstances and try to help them find solutions. But we need to beware of pasting our labels on the lives of Muslims and summing up their circumstances in ways they do not agree with. Many women whom Christians have described as miserably unhappy and prisoners in *purdah* are in fact happy and content with their lives and would not trade their lives for a Western woman's style of life. In fact, they feel sorry for the Western woman, who they perceive has lost the most precious possessions in life—faith in God and close family ties. Remember the women asked for empathy, not sympathy.

I have many times been asked for stories about the lives of Muslim women, but the request has been loaded. The stories were required to fit the person's preconceived ideas of the bleak and miserable lives of Muslim women. The people asking me had no experience of life in Muslim countries, but they "knew" the women were wretchedly unhappy. They based this on one idea: Muslim women do not know Christ; therefore, they are unhappy. Yet we all know there are Muslim women who are totally content in their faith. They feel sorry for us and so long for us to have their experience of God that they keep trying to convert us.

Many people who do not know Christ are happy. Let's be careful of blanket generalizations about the unhappiness of Muslim women. Besides, fear and insecurity are not endemic to Muslims. Fear, insecurity and anxiety are rampant in our century. In my experience, Muslims' felt needs and pressures are mainly due to their political situation, whereas in the West our problems are not political but due to the breakdown of our society. Most Christians would lay the blame for this in the West's rejection of God and loss of values. Sociologists speak of the loss of a collective conscience that provided people with a clear idea of how they should think, act and feel and see this as the result of the loss of a strong communal life through the industrial revolution (Durkeim 1998). Muslim society typically still provides a strong communal life that enhances security, which we do not experience in the West.

Whatever the reasons for the breakdown of the family unit in the West, one factor that compounds fear and insecurity is loneliness and isolation. The West has a greater incidence of mental and nervous disorders and a higher suicide rate than the Muslim world. However, isolation is an increasing issue in Muslim society today, and it's a new issue. Women activists want to improve access to education and employment for women, but when they achieve this goal, they find it brings new problems. It is becoming more common for both parents to work full-time and for the nuclear family to live together without the traditional help of older women to oversee chores and childcare. Just like Western women, modern Muslim women are experiencing stress as they try to balance their roles, particularly as men have not taken up an equivalent share of household tasks to help the working wife. This stress is compounded by women's desires for husbands to be their companions, especially if they no longer live within an extended family. But many husbands still follow the conservative model of not having a deep level of companionship and sharing with their wives.

Nonetheless, as we approach the beginning of the third millennium, if we compare culture to culture, I believe Islam is coping better than Christianity. Here Christians usually protest: But not all the West are real Christians. Ah yes, but not all Muslims are faith-filled Muslims, either. So if we are going to talk in generalities about the Muslim world, then we must talk in generalities about the countries that call themselves "Christian." We know that a Muslim woman with deep faith generally copes better than a Muslim woman with only surface belief. So if we are going to draw comparisons, we should try to keep them balanced: Muslim and Christian women with faith compared to Muslim and Christian women with no faith. So as we highlight certain problems expressed by Muslim women, I want us to keep in mind that I am not claiming that women have these problems because they follow Islam. They have these problems because they are human beings in today's troubled world.

What Issues Concern Them?

Finding and Keeping a Husband

Husbands were the first concern mentioned in my survey—especially how to find one. This reflects changes in the cultural pattern from arranged marriages to a more Western model. Women expressed tension about needing to find their own partners. This made them feel insecure.

Keeping a husband was the next concern, especially in some

countries where men were taking concurrent wives. Women expressed a lot of anxiety about this, and it affected their relationships with other women. It's a major factor in the lack of trust in some societies. But is monogamy a better system? One of the countries where I have lived outlawed polygamy, so men took mistresses instead.

Fear of Gossip

Women from most countries in the survey expressed a fear of gossip. Are we so different? Do we fear what people will think about us, especially if they really see behind the outer shell? How free are we from others' opinions? Muslim women's concerns in this matter are related to honor and power—keeping an unsullied reputation and not giving another person power over you by putting the weapon of gossip in their hands.

Conflicting Demands of Employment vs. Home/Family

Women who are not in crisis situations feel stressed from overwork. They are pulled between full-time employment and the demands of homemaking in cultures where the woman is typically solely responsible for the home, and husbands do not see their role as house helpers. This is also a problem in the West, but Muslim women are struggling more because their society is in a process of change and is not as egalitarian as the West. Again, we need to be careful not to stereotype Muslim men. I know a number of Muslim men who help out with home entertaining. One usually bakes the dessert!

Lack of Forgiveness

It is especially important for us to recognize the expressed concern of women in Muslim society about their struggle with the lack of forgiveness in the family and society. One of the most common responses I note Muslims making to Christianity is their astonishment about our teaching on forgiving and loving everyone indiscriminately. In Morocco, women who heard the Lord's prayer—"forgive us as we want to be forgiven"—were immediately attentive. It was such a beautiful idea. It was so radical. They recognized what marvelous places our homes and countries would be if we lived this way. How wonderful it is to be forgiven, and how hard to forgive.

Their response continues to challenge and convict me. Do I really believe that I will be forgiven as I forgive others? How does this tie in with Christ's finished work on the cross? Does God really need me to forgive before he can forgive me? This can be one of the areas where Muslims watch and accuse us of practicing cheap grace. We can do anything because Christ forgives all anyway. Do we believe it is necessary to forgive in order for God to forgive us?

An Iranian in Australia saw a scripture verse on the wall in a public place. After questioning colleagues, he discovered it was from the Bible. He purchased a Bible and was captured by it. He told a Christian colleague, "Do you know it says to love your enemies? That is really amazing, and it has deeply challenged me." He had enemies in the Iran-Iraq war and is looking into his heart attitudes. I have also seen Muslims astounded by how Christ forgave his enemies and heard them say, "This is the difference between Islam and Christianity." Similarly, E. Stanley Jones asked Ghandi how Christian missionaries could be more effective in India. Ghandi told him the most effective method of seeing the church grow was to put their faith into practice.

Lack of Trust

Lack of forgiveness is connected to another great concern in Muslim countries, lack of trust. Primarily, I think this stems from the political systems they live under. Trusting anyone with information about you literally puts the power of life and death in their hands. In oppressive regimes, people can be tortured until they reveal secrets, or at least until they make up the expected stories in order for authorities to have an excuse to arrest someone. We should not forget the powerful fear that living in this type of system generates. Many of us have experienced its paralyzing effects. So not trusting people is partially rooted in the political systems of the countries where most Muslim women live. I mention this because we need to be careful that we do not put the blame on religion for all of society's ills.

How Are Muslim Women Coping?

They cope the same way we cope. They turn to help outside themselves in religion, magic and education.

Through Religion

First, they look for salvation in God's mercy. Muslims have an incredible official belief in the mercy of God. I think we overlook this. The Quran teaches the road to God's forgiveness is through repentance. God forgives the person who repents because God is merciful. This is one of the reasons Muslims have trouble with Christ being presented as an intercessor. God's mercy is so great that we don't need an intercessor between God and humans. The idea of an intercessor puts a limit on the great mercy of God. How many times a day does a Muslim call to remembrance the great mercy of God? *Bismallah al-rahmaan al-rahiim*. In the name of God, the merciful and compassionate.

The desire for rebirth and beginning anew in this life is an important faith issue always connected with the *hajj*. Women tell of feeling reborn and returning to their lives with a new energy and new, revitalized faith after feeling very close to God on the *hajj*.

Through Magic

Second, they look for help through harnessing the spiritual powers to work for them. This includes the quasi-Islamic magical practices connected to the mosque, such as writing charms. These practices are rejected by official Islam yet embraced by lay practitioners and mediums in the occult. In Egypt, al-Azhar University will not perform exorcisms, so lay practitioners who believe it is part of the faith offer their services to the public. They exorcise demons and treat unresponsive illness by the reading of the Quran. Cures are effected. Certain *sheikhs* are perceived as being close to God and therefore having the power to heal.

Recently "Ya Hala," a program on an Islamic station in Australia, held a forum on exorcism and similar spiritual practices. The panel on the show represented beliefs across the whole spectrum, from those who professed that there is no such thing as evil spirits, to practitioners who exorcise them. Many Muslims believe that only the powerful word of God—the Quran—is able to cast out demons.

Women also turn to the occult practitioners that are not approved by orthodox Islam, such as mediums and those who practice "white magic," which includes placing spells and curses on others and making animal sacrifices. These practices are carried out to heal mental and physical illnesses, to keep a husband's love, to keep him away from other women and to place curses on enemies.

I was first exposed to this type of magic when I lived in a Muslim country. Yet in a recent issue of a mainline Australian women's magazine, I found that the "Dear Abby" page covered how to place spells to solve problems.

Through Education

Third, people also look for salvation in education. This may not be stated as a belief, but it is practiced. Families will expend great effort and make great sacrifices to provide a good education for their children.

Vulnerability and Honesty Open the Way

Happiness in the home, raising children, relationships with husbands, finding the right husband, coping with financial stress, coping with illness and disasters, concerns for good education for children, concerns about influence of materialism and secular culture on children, struggling with numerous demands on time, desire for rebirth and power for living God's way in today's world. These are the issues concerning Muslim women in today's troubled world. These are also the issues concerning Christian women.

These similarities between us provide a meeting place for women of both faiths to come together in honesty and vulnerability and share our common concerns and our search for the "right path." When we step beyond the -*isms* and the theology to expose our human side, our common bond as God's creation, made in the image of God, then we can touch each other's hearts and unite in our common search and journey on the straight path and the goal of a love relationship with God.

Jalaldin al Rummy, a Sufi poet, wrote this about the image of God in women:

> Woman is a ray of god, not a mere mistress.
> The creator's self, as it were, not a mere creature.
> (Quoted in Deen 1995:139)

Muslim Women in Crisis

Debi Bartlotti

Four critical issues facing Muslim women in crisis—abuse, divorce, polygamy and displacement/refugee life—will be the focus of this paper. I will draw some general conclusions about their needs, then suggest a model for ministry and a few ministry principles.

Abuse

Abuse takes many forms, ranging from neglect to verbal abuse to beating—most of it unseen by the outside world. As a nurse clinician and midwife working for an Afghan clinic and hospital, I have seen gross examples of physical abuse and neglect.

A large nomad woman dressed in a colorful velvet dress flowing down to the floor came for an antenatal exam. As I listened to her chest, I noticed huge black and blue marks all over her back and buttocks. Through the small braids ringing her face, I heard a quiet voice utter one word, the Pashto word for "brick."

On another day, I noticed a lot of commotion at the end of the hall. There lying on a stretcher was a small and frail woman with extensive injuries to her vaginal area, where her husband had kicked her. We rushed her to surgery for repairs.

A wedding night can be a frightening time anyway for women who have no idea what to expect sexually even in the best of scenarios. Several times in the middle of the night, the gate bell to our clinic has rung frantically. Outside are a bride's in-laws and the groom. Standing there with them is a bride, with bloodstains all

---

Debi Bartlotti lived and worked for 13 years among women on the border between Pakistan and Afghanistan.

21

over her dress, head hung in shame, tears flowing down her face. On exam, she has deep lacerations of her vagina, requiring stitches and repair work.

Neglect is also common. Men's and children's needs always come before those of women. At meals, women eat whatever is left. In the strict *purdah* of our area, women may not be permitted to go out of the house at all. All contact with the outside world is through the male family members. In this restrictive environment, a new form of social life has emerged where sickness—real or imagined—becomes an excuse to dress up and enter the bright, lively world of chatty clinic waiting rooms, medical labs and bazaars. On rounds one day in our clinic, I happily told a lovely young woman that her bleeding had stopped and she could go home. Shocked, her face dropped. She begged me not to send her back to the horrible home of her in-laws, where she was made to work day and night. Once a relatively free urban woman, she had found her life dramatically changed both by the rigid version of Islam recently imposed on her country, and by the conservative family into which her family had married her.

One particularly horrible form of abuse is wife burnings. A common scenario is that of a woman innocently cooking in the kitchen when a husband or mother-in-law, embittered over the amount of the dowry or some other misbehavior, pours kerosene over her body and sets it aflame. The woman usually lives a few days in pain and silence, refusing to shame her family by accusing her husband, finally dying a horrible death. The few women who have spoken out tell other frightful stories of being locked in rooms and set afire while the husband coolly sits by and watches.

Notice that in this environment of abuse, the woman has few defenders and generally little or no access to a protective legal system. In addition, social norms shame the woman and endorse the authority of men, family and culture. She is thus disempowered to effect change in her circumstances.

Divorce

The practice of divorce differs greatly, depending on social class and ethnicity. It might be helpful to imagine Afghan and Pakistani Pashtun culture as a pyramid. The bottom is composed of village women—simple, uneducated and traditional. The middle layer is made up largely of the middle class—teachers, nurses, etc. The top level is the smallest, composed of the wealthiest, most

Western, educated urban women. Divorce is generally unheard of among the lower class; when faced with being beaten, the only recourse for these poorer women is to leave the husbands and return to their parents' homes.

Fatima and Jamil had three lovely children. Both had become believers and attended discipleship meetings. On the outside, they appeared to have a perfect marriage, until one day Fatima burst into tears, saying Jamil was beating her in fits of jealous rage, and hurling accusations of infidelity at her. Counseling and deliverance were unfruitful. The only recourse was for her to return to her father's home in the village.

I have heard other stories of women who have been unjustly accused of adultery or insanity so that the husband could divorce her and receive all her money. The women end up spending the rest of their lives in jail or mental hospitals.

Toni belongs to the Pakistani upper class. On her wedding night, her husband looked into her eyes, laughed and told her that he detested her and now had finally gotten what he wanted—her money. Horrified, she kept quiet, hoping things would improve. Eight months later and pregnant, she started to bleed heavily. Her husband, a doctor, refused to take her to the hospital. Toni secretly called her parents, who came from a distant city and rescued her. She received a divorce and custody of her daughter— something she says would not have been possible if her child had been male, or if she had not been from the upper class with ready access to a lawyer. Absorbed back into her parents' home, she lives a life of strictest *purdah*; her greatest fear is gossip and slander. She now receives protection from her father, in exchange for her loss of freedom and independence.

In a recent notorious case, Sammi, after four years of separation from her husband due to abuse, filed for divorce in hopes of marrying another man. While she was sitting in a legal aid office related to the Human Rights Commission of Pakistan, her mother and a driver walked in. The driver shot and killed her; the mother escaped with a waiting accomplice. The father, a prominent businessman in the province, defended the murder of his own daughter on the basis of "honor."

Notice here that a Muslim woman's essential identity is determined by her relationships with men—her father, her husband, and her family. She is not defined autonomously, but in relationship to males, for whom she functions as a symbol of both honor and of Islam. Just as a Muslim man relates to Almighty God and his decrees—with submission, meekness and obedience, his life directed toward a Divine center and revolving around Allah—so a woman is to relate to a man: with submission, obedience and meekness, her life circling his. In this sense, Muslim women symbolize the essence of Islam—and in this we find the roots of their social vulnerability.

Polygamy

My heart has burned as I have heard women recount the pain of sharing a husband and home with another wife. The Prophet of Islam allows up to four wives, while he himself had eleven. This has given men the freedom, on various pretexts, to buy another wife. In our area, polygamy is generally not encouraged, although it is certainly practiced. No hard data is available as to how common this practice is.

Yet in discussing it with my Afghan neighbors, I gained new insight on how women themselves view the practice. Two wizened old women dressed in black are the matriarchs of our neighbor's family. These women and a third woman now dead shared one husband. The products of that mixed family were before me, three daughters, each with a different mother, each now with her own husband and children. They were shaking their heads in disbelief after hearing that in the West men would be put in jail for having more than one wife. They looked wide-eyed at one another and at me and spoke with sincere logic: "What if the husband is unhappy with his wife?" "What if she can have no children?" Then in a gasping finale, "What if she can have no sons?"

Across from me in the clinic sat a well-dressed Afghan woman. She explained the presence of her husband's other wife with the words, "I have a crooked nose." She was, in fact, beautiful. Jealousy and fear abound in such situations.

While I was taking her medical history, a threadbare little woman burst into tears and told her story. Her last pregnancy was going well until one day she started to bleed heavily. She called out for the other woman in the house, her husband's first wife. The woman came in, saw what was happening, laughed and, while closing the door, said, "Now you and your baby will die." The door bolted shut from the other side. Alone, the woman delivered her own baby, now dead. After telling me the story, she looked deep into my eyes and said the first wife had cursed this pregnancy as well, vowing that this time both mother and baby would surely die.

Zamina, my language teacher and dear friend, was a widow. Her husband had died four years earlier in a rocket attack. Vulnerable, living with her brothers, she walked a fine line between freedom to practice her profession and the protection offered by *purdah*. After a while, her brothers started to hear gossip and slander about Zamina, accusing her of prostitution. Afraid of shame being brought on the family, they sought for a solution. Habib, an uncle enamored by Zamina's sophistication and urbane ways, offered to marry her. He wrote her letters of undying love and devotion, even threatening to kill himself if she refused his offer of marriage. She was both charmed and afraid. Habib was already married and had ten children. He promised her a separate house. Zamina did not trust him and came to me desperate for a way out. On the night before her wedding, she took pills to try to end her life, but as Providence would have it, five Tylenol were not enough to kill her. After the marriage, her worst fears were realized. The educated lady now shares her home with a kind but illiterate first wife and ten children ranging in age from one year to fifteen. A drainage ditch filled with dirty water and garbage runs down the middle of the indoor courtyard. She is unable to conceive, due to a pelvic infection that she contracted when she first married at the age of twelve. Her present husband has isolated and rejected her because of her complaining and tears. She is now enrolled in a five-year program of Quranic memorization in a distant city.

Displacement and Refugee Life

The area where I live has seen many crises and a large flow of refugees and displaced persons. First came the Soviet invasion and war, then internal civil war, and now the oppression of a rigid Islamic regime. I have seen firsthand the pain, fear, loneliness, poverty and despair felt by displaced Muslim women.

Fauzia fled Afghanistan with her husband and five children when the Russians bombed their village. They crossed the mountains on foot, sleeping under rocks in the day and moving quietly at night to avoid being spotted by helicopter gunships. Her husband has found steady work while they live in a mud house with ten children in a refugee camp. This poor woman's life here is more restricted than it was back home in her village; in reality, she is not "at home."

Samina has been here for the past two years. An educated urban woman married to a former communist from the capital city, she finds life here in Pakistan intolerable. She fled the fundamentalist Taliban in search of some sort of future for her daughters. But the Pakistani government has closed the educational facilities for refugees; the government is tired of refugees, wants them to go back home, and threatens to force them to do so. Samina and her family live in one room with a shared kitchen. She badgered her husband until he agreed to leave the country illegally in search of economic gain. He left for Europe ahead of them, taking with him all of their savings. He is now stranded in Moscow, without money or a way out. She is alone, angry and in pain.

Khadija is a young Afghan woman doctor who arrived recently from a relatively free northern city in the neighboring country looking for work. Being Hazara, a despised ethnic group, she and her family were fleeing ethnic strife and fighting. She hates the heat, oppressive poverty and purdah of Pakistan.

Each story tells of fear, pain, danger, loneliness and often death. Families have become fragmented, with many of the nation's best minds emigrating to the West. Among these women, there is a desperate desire to find a way out, a way to prosperity and a better future. Feelings of hopelessness and despair lead to many symptoms of depression. No real political solutions are in sight. In the meantime, women remain at the mercy of powerful social-political forces that shape their lives and press in on the most intimate parts of their hearts. This has led some women to disillusionment, perhaps the most essential first step to finding a new Path to Life.

Emotional Issues and Needs

Each of these four sample issues represent crisis for the women involved. What are the common threads that tie their stories together? How do these women experience crises? As we listen closely to their talk, we can discern several themes or emotional issues. I would like to point out three.

One is a sense of powerlessness in the face of male control, or the larger social forces and political currents surging around them. In reaction, some women look to the darker side of Islam and go to shrines to buy amulets, or pronounce curses and thereby gain power.

Second, life often has a strong undercurrent of fear. Fear of gossip, of slander, of evil spirits and the evil eye, of shame and dishonor, even of death at the hand of a family member—all control much of the behavior of Muslim women.

Third, there is the issue of identity. As we have seen, a Muslim woman's identity is derivative—based on dictates of culture and religion, not her essential and uniquely beautiful self as created by God. As symbols and representatives of honor and of Islam, women pose the greatest risk to Muslim men and to Muslim culture. And the men know it.

Paraclete Ministry to Women in Crisis

In a situation where we can't change the social system or structure, what are we called to be and do as followers of Christ who came to "set captives free"? I have come to depend entirely on the Holy Spirit, the Comforter. He is the one who has opened up these women's hearts to trust me and share their deepest fears and pain. In prayer, I ask each day for a special anointing to minister in his power.

I would suggest what could be called a "Paraclete Model" of ministry. Whereas fully "incarnational" ministry to women is sometimes constrained by the closed-in social system and family, a paraclete ministry is based on the work of the Holy Spirit. A paraclete is "one called alongside to help," a comforter and encourager. He is always there, but manifests his anointing most during times of need. In some sense, we are called to be like him.

For starters, I would suggest three ministry principles that flow from the paraclete model. The first is **empathy**. The Holy Spirit enables us to feel their heart pain and sorrow. This is basically a ministry of shared tears.

The second is **availability**. I make myself wholly there for them, especially in times of need. This includes being vulnerable myself as well. Sharing my struggles and fears seems to release women to trust me enough to share their own pain. And then I really listen. I call this a ministry of time and touch.

The third is **presence**. Although we cannot always be with these women, the Holy Spirit can. And we, in our moments with them, can introduce them to the wondrous feeling of being in the presence of One who truly loves them. All of us as women are left "*in* the world," a world we sometimes can't change, but we know the One who has "*overcome* the world." I call this the ministry of tenderness.

As I "come alongside" women in crisis, through shared tears, through time and touch and tenderness, I myself feel powerless to change their circumstances. But I can walk with them and bring them a few steps closer to Jesus, the one who says, "Come to me all you who are weary and burdened, and I will give you rest" (Matt. 11:28). And "The Spirit of the Sovereign Lord is upon me, because the Lord has anointed me to preach good news to the poor. He has sent me to bind up the brokenhearted, to proclaim the year of the Lord's favor and the day of vengeance of our God, to comfort all who mourn, and provide for those who grieve in Zion—to bestow on them a crown of beauty instead of ashes, the oil of gladness instead of mourning, and a garment of praise instead of a spirit of despair" (Isa. 61:1-3).

Participants' Discussion

From Central Asia—I have seen the effects of physical abuse brought on by rampant alcoholism. Many of the single women I worked with were beaten by their fathers and brothers. We also saw numerous cases of rape. Of the four women that I discipled closely, two had been raped—one of them after she had become a believer. I ministered in tears, yet I saw her trust the Lord through it. Now, as one of the strongest leaders of the cell church, she ministers to others who have gone through the same thing.

I knew of another man who was trying to kill his wife. She told him, "You don't have to kill me, I'll jump." She jumped out of the window of her fourth story apartment and ended up in the hospital for a month. While she was there, she told me that Jesus appeared to her. I had brought her scripture and worship tapes in her language. And then Jesus came and met her. If she hadn't jumped, would the Lord have appeared to her some other way? I don't know, but God used her crisis anyway.

From the Maldives—Not one girl that our team knew had escaped sexual harassment. Most had been raped even before they were teenagers. After a 15-year-old girl came to believe in Christ, we learned that her father abused her. What shocked me most was that she didn't even feel that something unjust had happened to her. Everyone knows about it, but does nothing. The fact that the young girl didn't see herself as being violated made it difficult for me to understand how to help her.

From North Africa—Working among the Pulaar, we most

often see economic crises related to divorce, which is epidemic. When the husband abandons a wife with two or three preschool-aged children, they are left with no way to support themselves, which forces them into prostitution. How else can they provide for their families? I think about the parable of the sower, about how the young plants are choked out by the cares and worries of the world. When they are looking for their next meal, how can they even care about spiritual things?

From China—I knew a 19-year-old who was the mother of two. The first time I met her, I assumed she was mentally ill because of the way she neglected her children. She let her youngest baby crawl in the street. It turned out that her husband had been beating her. So she locked her kids in a room and left for two days. Her baby died, and she was blamed.

We met with her father-in-law and told him it was wrong for his son to beat her. He replied that he hoped his son would beat her again because she had dishonored their family. How do you break that cycle?

Question—Is there anything in their culture or in the Quran that we can use to appeal to them to care for these women?

From Kazakstan—Most of the women I deal with have never read the Quran. I show them in God's Word how God looks at them, especially using Psalm 139. I affirm that he grieves over the things that have happened to them. I show them that God will judge the wicked and that he offers forgiveness. I try to tell them, "Yes. This is awful. What happened to you isn't right. But God's still bigger than this." It doesn't provide all the answers, but it seems to help.

From North Africa—I also prefer to turn women to the Word. The Gospels provide so many stories about Jesus reaching out to women: the woman with the hemorrhage of blood, the woman at the well, the widow whose son Elijah raised back to life. These provide powerful evidence that God cares for women and their needs.

Praying with them is also helpful. As I gained spiritual vocabulary in Arabic, I grew more willing to pray for my friends—even in the semipublic setting of their homes. I think it is important to publicly affirm the power of prayer.

From a mobilizer in U.S.—Scripture recognizes that suffering is normal, but it is outside the realm of typical Western experience. We are so far away from their reality, but we have to recognize the biblical truth that suffering is normal. God will be with us in our suffering. This must be the truth that we share with our friends.

From a U.S. missiology professor—Our job as missionaries is not to rearrange everything in their culture. God is in control. The best we can do is come alongside, cry with them, and point them to what God said.

From Indonesia—When I watch the injustice people face, I get to the point where I harden my heart because I don't want to see it or hear about it anymore. But I must realize that God can give them the grace they need. Sometimes it is harder to believe that for them than it is for myself.

From Central Asia—God has been teaching me to enter more deeply into intercession for these women. If I'm holding back saying, "I can't handle any more of these sad stories," then I'm not trusting God. If I can't go to the authorities to protest injustice against these women, I can still go to God.

Thinking through the Issues

1. *How our hearts weep for the abused women in Islam! There are so many more incidents of abuse among them than in the West—with much less legal recourse! What physical or emotional abuse have you seen in your area? What is the abused woman's usual response? How have you seen the community or woman's own family respond to abuse? What does the community, especially the other women, think of these abuses?*

2. *In your area how widespread is divorce among each of the three classes: poor, middle class, wealthy? What factors precipitate divorce? What happens to divorced women in your culture? Do the women ever get to keep their children? Who supports them? Are they able to gain respect in the community?*

3. *How does the Islamic view of women's sexuality fuel male suspicions, jealousy, and divorce?*

4. *The author describes the "family honor" as being defined by the behavior (and control) of the women. Does this extend to the behavior of the men as well, or not? What things are perceived as bringing the most shame on a family in your culture? What values or needs do these represent?*

5. *Do you agree that a man's life is "directed toward a Divine center and revolving around Allah," while a woman's life circles around the*

man's? Why or why not? Do you believe that the women symbolize not only the honor of their families, but also the honor of Islam?

6. Is polygamy common in your area? Do more rich or poor people practice it? Do the women find it threatening, or do they view it as a positive thing? Considering the Old Testament record of polygamy, should you take a harder stance against divorce, which God "hates," than polygamy? What underlying issues or strongholds may need to be addressed first?

7. How should you respond to women you know who are being abused? Can you approach this problem through spiritual warfare? … through cultural or legal means? … through medical means? What is your biblical responsibility toward abused people?

8. How should you respond to impending divorces? Is it possible to have a special ministry to divorced women? How could you gain access to them? What needs would you seek to meet? How could MBBs [1] reach out to divorced women?

9. How can you help women who are isolated within their homes? Is there some role other women could play that would give them access to these women?

10. Wars that displace whole communities greatly add to the sense of hopelessness, powerlessness, and fear of these women. These same emotions are also greatly increased in the men, who further take it out on the women. You may experience similar feelings as you enter into the difficulties of their world. What biblical passages deal with people in these types of circumstances? What encouragement or direction does the Bible offer?

11. The author proposes a "paraclete model" of ministry involving (1) empathy, or "shared tears," (2) availability, or "time and touch," and (3) presence, bringing the presence of the Holy Spirit through "tenderness." What type of healing would this provide these women? How could a spiritual warfare ministry complement the paraclete model of ministry to help achieve "freedom for the captives and release from the darkness"? Since you cannot usually set the women free from their situation, what is the freedom you are proclaiming to them?

---

[1] The abbreviation MMBs refers to Muslim background believers in Christ and will be used throughout this book.

12. *What power can you legitimately offer these "powerless" women? What identity can Christ give them in exchange for the false identity their culture has given them? How can you help them understand their identity in Christ?*

13. *If you use chronological Bible storying[2] with abused, divorced, or refugee women, what stories could speak best to their deepest needs including freedom from fear of man and circumstances, freedom from hurt, and freedom from the occult and deceitfulness? Can you demonstrate to these women that God is not like the men they know and is ready and able to help them?*

For Further Study and Reflection

•   *Do you find yourself taking on the fear, hopelessness, powerlessness, and anger of abused or destitute women? What passages of scripture and/or modes of intercession can help you maintain faith in God's power and willingness to intervene?*

•   *Islamic women often know God is all-powerful but see him as inaccessible. How can you use their own concepts of clean/unclean to explain how Christ provides cleanliness and direct access to God's presence, power, and help? What parables or stories could help them understand the cleanliness of hearts? ... or understand God's unsurpassably great power on behalf of those who believe?*

---

[2] See related article in Section 2.

Muslim Women and the Occult: Seeing Jesus Set the Captives Free

Julia Colgate

Introduction

In the last two decades, increased attention has been given to the presence of the occult within Islam. Bill Musk's book, *The Unseen Face of Islam*, exposed the powerful mixture of Islam and occult practices found throughout the Muslim world. Several missionary training centers now offer folk Islam courses. I write this article as one privileged to watch God at work among folk Muslim women. Though I have not read widely on the occult *per se* (or taken a course on folk Islam), I have had help from colleagues in our region as we have learned from each other. The best teacher has been the Lord himself! I have learned so much simply by walking with Jesus throughout my neighborhood.

When I moved from a community of "middle-class mosque-going" women to a neighborhood of lower-class truly folk Muslim women I had to make some major adjustments. Many of the women I now rub shoulders with are functionally illiterate and poor. They live in constant interaction with the dark spirit realm. As I have learned to love these women, I have had to face my own fears and unbelief, and I have had to accept a new paradigm from the Lord for ministering his kingdom among these women. Some of this "shift" has come as I have interacted with other women in what we call the "Women's Forum."

About a year into its existence, this forum includes 35 women from nine mission groups who meet bimonthly. The idea for the

Julia Colgate has spent nine years living among a Southeast Asian people. Her experience includes church planting, intercession and mentoring.

forum came as a colleague and I shared our hearts regarding the Indah people among whom we worked. One gifted missionary evangelist had told my colleague, "It's really not that difficult to lead these people to Isa [Jesus], but to see them truly set free from the dark powers ... that is our big problem!"

We began the Women's Forum by inviting fifteen of our colleagues to gather and discuss a paper I had written on the stages of friendship between Indah women. The ensuing discussion was rich with personal experiences, and it was obvious God was motivating us to look deeper at our relationships with Indah women. He was also moving us into new realms of believing, listening prayer. In the months that followed, we were led down new paths of exploration. Those paths themselves form the structure for the first part of this paper.

Along the way, the Lord has led the women into different avenues of involvement, depending on their spiritual gifts and interests. The "point guards" are the intercessors. They are not organized into a large group with printed prayer requests; rather, they seem simply to find each other and gather in groups of two or three. As they intercede, they are also listening to God's heart. As one of them described, "We are learning to allow God to draw us into his caring heart of love for the Indah women we know ... and in that place he shows us things!"

The "practitioners" form another group. These are the ladies who have face-to-face contact with Indah women throughout the day. They take the ideas that the group is discovering and wait for the Lord to open a window of opportunity with one of their Indah friends. Then they write notes on how the window opened and what the Lord directed them to say. I am one of those "practitioners," and I will share a "window" that I experienced several weeks ago:

I went to visit my neighbor who had just given birth to her fourth child. I noticed a little sack near the baby's head. Because of studies the Women's Forum had done on birth rituals, I knew that the sack probably contained a pair of scissors with garlic and the dried umbilical cord, which are meant to protect the baby from the danger of evil powers. I was able to knowingly ask a few questions regarding these things. Suddenly, Carrie asked me, "You do not take these precautions with your newborns, do you?" I answered quietly, "No, we do not." I let several moments pass, listening in my heart for the Lord's guidance. Carrie was so gentle and seemed receptive, so I went on, "Actually we believe that the sacrificial blood which Isa al-Masih shed is all that is needed for our protection from harm." I explained in a few more sentences how Christ's death defeated demonic powers. Later, I made written notes on this encounter to share at our next Women's Forum.

Another group of women are involved in "deep research." They are doing ethnographic interviews, tape-recording them, transcribing them and submitting them to a colleague trained in anthropology for data analysis using Spradley's twelve-step model (1979:76). This is our "scientific" attempt to discover worldview, but we are also fully expecting the Lord to give us "shortcuts" involving insights into worldview that this process will verify. These various forms of data will eventually be compiled in a database that we plan to make available to the Women's Forum through the Internet.

My purpose in sharing about the Indah Women's Forum is to encourage women in other regions to try this approach. It has been an adventure. The following outline describes our journey from observation of occult activities to the discovery of how the enemy keeps a people in bondage through the assumptions of their worldview. In this model, I emphasize the role of intercession because we have seen how effective research is when it is linked to listening intercession.

Our Journey into Spiritual Warfare for Muslim Women

The chart on the following page illustrates our journey into spiritual warfare for Muslim women. Our group's experience has proven the effectiveness of these steps of observation, examination, analysis and discovery—each vitally linked with intercession. As church planters and intercessors, it is not we ourselves but God who unlocks the mysteries that become our clues for strategic warfare prayer. Our job is not simply to observe and comprehend the power of the occult over a culture; our job is to demonstrate the eternal supremacy of Jesus Christ over the kingdom of darkness!

One last note: to pursue the subject of the occult takes courage. Our experience has been that as we approach the core issues of worldview, our personal response crescendos because our hearts discern the power that is there. We intuitively know that we are close to Satan's strongholds, and for each of us, the choice we face at that moment is whether to fear the enemy and be immobilized, *or* to fear God (submit to his overarching authority and power) and press on to free captives. In this paper, we will later consider a biblical foundation for fearlessness that can make a difference for us personally as well as for the women of Islam.

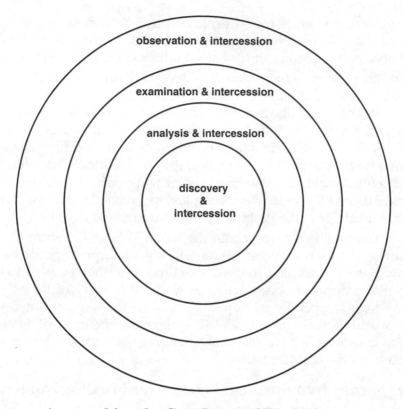

Approaching the Core Issues of Worldview

Part 1

Research and Intercession: An Adventure That Readies Us for Seeing Captives Set Free

Observation: A Starting Point for Our Journey

Our starting point is what our senses observe about Muslim women and the occult. As you read about our discoveries, you will probably be able to identify your own folk Muslim friends.

In the Women's Forum, we felt that God wanted to lead us down a path so that we would begin to understand the influence of the occult. We began by asking ourselves, "What are the signs that point to the fact that Muslim women feel vulnerable?"

The first sign of vulnerability is that Muslim women themselves confess that they are fearful! Women in my region are terrorized by trips to the bathroom at night, even when lights throughout the house are left on. They are terrorized by the need to pass by wet rice fields in the heat of the day. They do not hesitate to confess fear, and their behavior exhibits fear. They feel very vulnerable.

Second, folk Muslim women confess that they are powerless. An example is my friend Nancy. She is bewildered by her teenage daughter's unusual aversion to chili peppers, which is a main ingredient in cooking.

"What do you think caused this?" I asked. She answered quietly, "I can only imagine it has something to do with the chilies that hung by her head when she was a newborn." She was resigned to the thought that her daughter's condition would continue indefinitely. She had no hope of overcoming this strange situation. When I look at Nancy and my other Muslim friends, I realize that most of them live in a gray fog. They are resigned to a pervasive sense of powerlessness.

A third evidence that Muslim women feel vulnerable is that they actively seek spiritual power to meet their felt needs. What are the felt needs of Muslim women? In *The Unseen Face of Islam*, Bill Musk lists ten (1989:76): Fear of the unknown, fear of evil spirits, powerlessness before shamanic power, fear of the future, shame at not belonging to the in-group, disequilibrium, sickness, helplessness in crisis, meaninglessness in life and vulnerability of women

Dr. Marguerite Kraft's dissertation studied the dynamics of felt needs and spiritual power. Although she did not focus specifically on Muslim women, Kraft postulates that the felt needs that motivate individuals to seek spiritual power are similar across cultures and can be grouped into six categories (1990:10-11). She explains that these are "common human needs that cause people to seek spiritual power, insight and direction, to mend their erring ways, to repair relationships with people and spirits and to gain protection and blessing." This list is not exhaustive but is the result of her research (1990:14).

- Power needs
- Perpetuity needs
- Prosperity needs
- Health needs
- Security needs

- Restitution needs

I have expanded the above list to include Kraft's explanation and examples from the lives of my Muslim friends.

Power Needs. "Human technology suffices in many areas of life, but there are areas of life where people have no control" (Kraft 1990:11).

In my community, gossip is a vicious weapon. Women wield this weapon to bolster their own names while destroying the names of others, to gain control, to establish justice by punishing offenders, and to maintain a balance of power. Not all my neighbors have the money to acquire power through magic at the hands of a shaman, but the power of gossip is free and available anywhere. (By the way, my colleagues and I have used gossip for the advantage of the gospel. We have intentionally told testimonies which glorify God and prayed that the winds of gossip would carry these gospel seeds far into the community to homes we wouldn't think to visit.)

Perpetuity Needs. "...felt needs that are related to maintaining the lineage, tribe, and people. A very common reason people seek spiritual assistance is barrenness." Fertility is related not only to human reproduction to maintain its people, but also to land, crops and livestock (Kraft 1990:11).

My friends contact their ancestor spirits in an attempt to guard their perpetuity. For example, our neighbors burn incense to keep the living connected with the dead for the perpetuity of family and clan. Nancy has told me that incense is like a telephone; it ensures that requests to God are channeled through a grandmother or another deceased loved one who intercedes directly to the throne of God. The hope is for perpetual peace, prosperity and safety, particularly at those rites of passage when families feel most vulnerable.

Prosperity Needs. "The people's need for spiritual power is evidenced in the ritual activities of life cycle events" (Kraft 1990:12).

The folk religion of the Indah includes sixteen life cycle rituals that are carefully followed in hopes of prosperity. These rites of passage are clearly times of spiritual insecurity, and this desire for prosperity and perpetuity is tied to a deep need for security. Thus, they enact special rites.

Health Needs. "The linkage [between sickness/treatment and spiritual resources] varies according to a society's theory of sickness" (Kraft 1990:12).

My acquaintance Susie's experience provides an example of this felt need. She sought help for a physical problem from a paranormal spiritual practitioner in a town two hours away. This spiritist said Susie's symptoms came from stress and overtiredness and from "being too good to others." A girlfriend who was embittered toward her and an unidentified person from out of town were also said to be responsible for the illness. He gave her a bitter herb drink that produced an allergic reaction by the following morning.

Security Needs. The need to feel secure "may involve taking precautions to contact spiritual sources before going into an unknown territory, or undergoing purification when one returns" (Kraft 1990:13). Other dangers and misfortunes call for spiritual protection.

In our neighborhood, Penny and her children refuse to move into their new little house down the path until a certain "power time" arrives next month. This means that her husband is sleeping alone in a supposedly unsafe house. In order to guarantee their security, they will undoubtedly enact the customary Indah moving ceremony when that advantageous day arrives.

Another example: My neighbors use amulets for protection and prosperity. However, they must follow special rules to ensure that power continues to flow from the amulet, such as removing the amulet before entering a bathroom or avoiding certain foods. One missionary's research on our people group has shown that if a family wants to move (or marry) on an "inauspicious day," they can do so safely only if they make a special sacrifice, such as burying a chicken head.

Restitution Needs. "[The] concept of right and wrong behavior is a part of all cultures. Each [culture] has prescribed ways to restore order after someone has broken the rules. Spiritual power is often used to restore relationships" (Kraft 1990:13).

In our neighborhood, when Andy's brand-new car was stolen by an acquaintance of his, he was crushed. In response, Andy hurried to a spiritual power holder for counsel. However, Mr. Amen, a local shaman with powers of divination, was able to give him only vague and unsatisfactory instructions. (The story ended happily: my

husband and I asked God for Jesus' sake to return the car to Andy.
It was returned in the middle of that very night, and Andy's family
gave glory to God.)

Intercession: "What Is This, Lord?"

What are we to do with what we have observed so far? It is
time to look and listen—listen to what God is saying about this
culture. At this transition point between the concentric circles
of our "journey," our Women's Forum does just that. We take
the time to allow the Lord to teach our hearts, crying out to
Him: "Lord, what does this really mean? Do you want to tell us
something we haven't yet discovered? Lead us in deeper,
Lord!"

And he does lead onward. The way we know is that he gives
wisdom and discernment just as he has promised in his Word. We
knew that the activities Muslim women carry out in seeking spiritual power are not just cultural curios fit for travel magazine coverage, but they are evidence of spiritual bondage.

A colleague shared her insight on the nature of these demonic
strongholds: "It seems to me that when we talk about seeing the
Indah people set free through Christ, we are talking about freedom on several different levels. The first level has to do with rites
and rituals that are done to their babies before they are even
born." She mentioned George Otis's book, *Twilight Labyrinth*. He
contends that people groups the world over have made ancient
pacts with Satan. These pacts are then renewed each generation
through birth rituals, automatically opening the children to the
bondage of satanic powers. My colleague continued, "There is evidence of these rites among the Indah. If this is so, it would seem
that a new follower of Isa would have to renounce these ancient
rituals as a step into Christ's freedom."

The second level of freedom has to do with all the occult activities that a person has willingly taken part in. This involves more
than the burning of fetishes and charms; it requires a definite shift
in allegiances, values and assumptions. Christ himself must pen-
etrate a person's worldview at the deepest levels. We must also
develop a Christian theology that addresses these deepest needs.

The third level of freedom involves people's wounded hearts.
This is also true for Westerners. Through trauma, abuse and rejection, Satan has gained subtle, yet powerful footholds that keep
individuals in bondage. They need to forgive, repent from using

defense mechanisms, and find healing from past hurts in order to see freedom.

Through this colleague's insights and others that were shared, God revealed the next step in our journey of discovery. We began to focus our research on the birth rituals that are practiced by the Indah. These are the first of sixteen rituals in their life cycle. The birth rituals begin at the fourth month of pregnancy and extend to the fortieth day after the baby's birth.

Examination: Going Not Farther, But Deeper Examination

As we began more focused research, we asked the Lord: "What is the lie here? We need to see that these Muslim women are truly in bondage to the dark powers. Show us their bondage, Lord! Show us how it works!" Answers came as we began to examine the observations and data compiled by the Women's Forum.

In studying the birth rituals, we observed that the Indah women's sense of safety depends on how completely they feel they have carried out the rituals. This gives them the illusion of personal power: not the power to overcome the perceived enemy, but the power to survive this season of acute vulnerability (pregnancy and early days of baby's life).

Power persons who oversee life cycle events hold these women within the system. These individuals are indispensable to the folk Muslim community. In our research of birth rituals we found the power person is usually a particular type of female shaman who serves women from pregnancy through childbirth and then later at death, preparing the body for burial and sending the spirit of the dead on its way with billows of incense smoke.

When the power person dies without a replacement, the community feels a void. In my own neighborhood, the two old women who had functioned as female shamans have both died. My close neighbor was eight months pregnant when she shared that she was stressed because there was no power person to help her. When I suggested she call one from the next neighborhood, it was clear that this was not acceptable. Later, I asked another neighbor if it was a problem now that our neighborhood no longer had its own female shaman.

"Yes, it is a big problem," she informed me. "There is no one left who knows how to properly bury the placenta. No one but the [female shaman] knows the exact combinations of spices to mix, as well as the proper proportions of other ingredients [such as the petals from seven kinds of flowers] to keep the placenta from being cruel." (Indah believe that the rituals used in burying the placenta can determine the character of the baby and its life's destiny.)

I was, frankly, quite surprised that our neighborhood would miss one of the women who had died. Isabel was not known for being a good woman, and she had died a "bad" death (with her face tense and her fingers curled). My friend told me, "She died that way because she performed abortions." Later I went to the Lord with the question on my heart, "Lord, why would a woman like this be missed?" I sensed him answering me with these words: "The children want to know that someone is in control."

The Lord also used our dreams at night to speak to us about Muslim women's bondage. The two examples I will share from my personal experience are occasions when the Lord allowed me to receive messages of intimidation from the enemy.

One night I awoke hearing a cruel voice speaking of my dear Muslim friend Anisa: "You can't have her. She is mine. Blood has been shed." This probably referred to the sacrifice of a chicken that is part of Indah rituals. On another occasion, in my dream I felt great condemnation for evangelizing my other friend, Erma. A man took his knife to the back of my head and I felt myself weaken as my blood spilled out. I awoke at this point. The very next day Erma phoned me with the news that she had been in a motorcycle accident with her boyfriend (who was involved in evil powers) and had sustained a cut to the back of her head ... in exactly the place where I had been wounded in my dream.

Coincidence? I know better! The message from the enemy was loud and clear: "You don't really want to pay the price to see these girls brought to freedom!" I smile when I recall how Satan's intimidation backfired. Jesus made me more zealous than ever for their salvation (which has not yet happened), and I was more open to sharing with other Muslim women as well.

Jesus has revealed to many of us in the Women's Forum pictures or signs of specific bondages as we have interceded for Indah women. Once the Lord showed me a sheaf of rice and a pool of blood in the home of the family that I was praying for. I later learned that these are part of rituals carried out for a fertility goddess. On another occasion I was deep in prayer for my friend Diamond when I saw a clear picture of an old man. I did not know who he was, but I felt in my heart that Diamond was keeping a secret from me and that it had to do with an unholy tie to this man. I also had a strong urge to visit Diamond at her house even though it was evening and I do not usually make visits at that hour. I was excited as I wondered what the Lord would do.

I found her with her family gathered around the television in their small living room. So that I could talk alone with Diamond, I quickly made the excuse that I needed a haircut before leaving town the next day. As I settled into the chair in her tiny beauty salon, I noticed the picture of her ex-husband (whom she hates) displayed prominently above the doorframe (because he is the father of her daughter). Then my eyes fell on another picture close by, and I was amazed! I recognized the old man that the Lord had just shown me while I was praying. "Who is that old man in the picture?" I asked her, struggling to keep my voice calm.

"He is my ex-husband's grandfather. He is a powerful shaman." As Diamond told me about him, I knew I was to take a step of faith.

"Diamond, Allah has sent me here tonight. When I was in prayer for you earlier, he showed me that you are in some kind of bondage that he wants to free you from. Is there something you want to tell me?"

She hesitated and then slowly began her story. "I have never told you this before but every Thursday evening after the last call to prayer, I experience a terrible itch. It is so bad that I am sleepless until the first call to prayer the next morning. I spend the whole night in misery, and when I wake there is no rash, no scratch marks. This has happened to me every Thursday night for the last three years!" (Thursday night is a "power time" in Indah folk religion.)

We both could see that Diamond was under a curse. Diamond was aware that the curse had come from the old man at the request of her embittered ex-husband. God had sent me to her because he wanted to free her from her bondage. Isa did set her free, and she has never again experienced that curse. That incident, along with many experiences of dramatic provisions and healings, was a key in Diamond's journey. Within a month, she became a follower of Isa. He is continuing to bring her freedom from various other bondages including dramatic forgiveness of her ex-husband.

God even reveals these bondages to intercessors who are far away. About six months ago I received an e-mail from one of my special prayer warriors in America. She told me that while she was praying for a specific Indah woman to whom I had been ministering, God had shown her some images whose meanings she did not understand. She submitted what she had "seen." When my colleagues and I were discussing the life cycle rituals of the Indah, we made the connection between what my friend had discerned in prayer and what we were discovering in our studies. We believe that God had shown this intercessor some symbols of Indah worldview, and that through her partnership with us (from across the ocean!), he was affirming that we were on the right track. We were awed by his diligence in pointing the way!

We are at another transition, crossing into the next concentric circle. What we have observed broadly has been taken to prayer. Then we have explored more deeply through case study and informal interviews, and we have verified that information through group discussion. We continue to ask the question, "What will Jesus have to do to set Muslim women really free?"

Analysis: Discerning What Is Important

The next step was to analyze the data that we had gathered through informal interviews. If the Lord would grant us special discernment, we could discover some of the meanings of the symbols we had observed and the patterns we had identified as bondages. We were at a point deep enough to get hints of their worldview—the assumptions, allegiances and values of the Indah—and close enough to see the deceptions with which Satan had imprinted their minds. We asked the Lord, "What lies has Satan used to win their hearts?" Soon he began to bring us insights.

First, God focused us on the fact that Satan had won their hearts. When we Westerners think of the occult, we assume that the average person reacts to it with "terror-fear." But those of us who live among folk Muslims know that that is not the case! Power persons (whether alive or deceased) and spirits are feared and reverenced. Folk Muslims offer these spirits a response of awe and worship. No matter how fearsome the ancestor spirit appears, or how terrible is the power of the sorcerer, he is worthy of reverence. They are bound to their spirits and gods by a power that is greater than "terror-fear." Theirs is a reverent "love-fear."

"Don't send the spirit away! We must honor the dead!" said a neighbor, when his brother was suddenly overcome by a spirit and went into a trance during a life cycle event. From the perspective of worldview, it is obvious that Satan has won their allegiance.

As I prayed about this allegiance to the Evil One, God reminded me that the Israelites also had a reverent "love-fear" relationship with evil. Ezekiel provides a summary of God's inter-actions with the Israelites; from Egypt to Babylon, it is obvious that "their hearts were devoted to their idols" (Eze. 20:16b).

What are the lies that Satan uses to win such a powerful alle-giance? God began to unfold the answers as a small group from the Women's Forum met to discuss the data we had gathered on Indah birth rituals. When I shared my observations from Ezekiel 20, one of the women spoke up:

"I have been thinking about the ways of evil for some time now, and I think I see a principle: Everything that exists in the kingdom of darkness seems to draw its power from the fact that it is a replica, a counterfeit, of some great powerful truth borrowed from the king-dom of light. So, to understand the counterfeit (How does Satan win such a powerful heart allegiance?), we must look closely at what it is from the kingdom of light that evil is replicating."

That comment caused me to reflect again on Ezekiel 20. God was longing for the Israelites to have a reverent "love-fear" rela-tionship with him. (The Bible calls it "fear of the Lord" ... sub-mission to his authority and his majesty.) "Fear of the Lord" is the beginning of wisdom, and it is the source of God's blessing for his children. At that point, it became obvious to us all that Satan's deception resulting in a "love-fear" relationship with folk Mus-lims was based on his ability to counterfeit "the fear of the Lord." This discovery later proved to be quite significant.

However, as we continued to discuss our research findings regarding the birth rituals of the Indah, it soon became clear that although there was a reverent "love-fear" relationship with evil, there was also a very strong "terror-fear" of evil spirits, especially for pregnant women. We compiled a long list of items and rit-uals—sharp scissors, garlic, chewed up yellow root, flowers, spices, specific rituals of bathing—that our neighbors use to pro-tect the pregnant mother. They say that "the terrible baby-stealing spirit that lurks near water can take on the form of a neighbor or friend, and cause the baby to just disappear from the womb."

The information we were sifting through was fascinating. Often as we shared our information, the Lord prompted us to remember insights we had gained through intercessory prayer, and this verified the research and confirmed the direction the Lord was taking us. We also began to see the meanings of some of the symbols that appear in the Indah life cycle rituals. God was opening our understanding to see the ties that bind Indah women to the occult. Our prayer was, "Where are you at work to set captives free?"

When a Indah woman is four or seven months pregnant her stomach is encircled by string. At 40 days after birth, the babies are given a necklace, bracelet, anklet and a tie around the waist. The mother receives them also. The necklace and bracelet have a bead or two strung on them. This is not simply decoration; it means something. Our discovery was confirmed by an anthropological researcher among our people, who wrote:

> The ... customary law and traditions of the [Indah] is best referred to by the [Indah] term... [that] literally ... means "a string of traditions, the image of a string implying both binding and measuring." ... From early times the people have felt it was obligatory to observe these traditions handed down by their ancestors. There are many punishments associated with the failure to complete the ... ["string of traditions"], the most fearful one being the loss of soul rest. ... Supernatural aspects of birth, life and death are kept in balance by the ["string of traditions"] ceremonies. The [Indah] believe cosmic powers are released during major transitions of a person's life and if these forces are not countered, the balance of nature will be upset. This imbalance can cause sickness and death and other misfortune (Women's Forum: April 7,1999).

Discovering Core Meanings: Readiness for Warfare Prayer

The next day, as we gathered for the larger group meeting of the Indah Women' Forum, the Lord showed how this information tied into a deep worldview assumption. [1] My colleague summarized the session this way:

> As we have discussed the various aspects of the Indah birth rites and rituals, we have been looking "face-to-face" at one of Satan's great lies that he uses to keep these women in bondage. We have discovered their worldview assumption that "harmony" is the best you can do.

---

[1] We begin these wrap-up sessions with a few leading questions. Our purpose in the Women's Forum is not to give reports on our findings. Rather, we start the session with questions to cause women to share what they have learned and experienced on the subject. This inductive approach has been a powerful motivator to make women want to be involved, and it has enabled us to learn from each other and pray for one another. In such a format, the wrapup session becomes an important time for pulling thoughts together and focusing on what is significant as well as imparting any important information that has not yet come out.

Their world is full of evil things. When you are pregnant, you and your baby are especially vulnerable to those things. The string of rituals, if carried out as prescribed, creates a tunnel or a dam of protection against this tide of evil that extends to the 40th day after birth and beyond. The best you can do is put up a defense. But if there's a hole in your defense (i.e., you forgot your sharp scissors, or you didn't do the ritual just exactly the right way) something's going to happen. You've got to maintain that defense.

The feeling through all of this is like the color gray: there's no black or white. Everything is gray … that's the color of harmony. And when you think in terms of Satan's counterfeit (What is the lie he is operating through?), the lie is this: "It's the best you can do! The only thing you can do is try and defend yourself. … Keep the wall strong and keep evil from overwhelming you." The lie says that evil is supreme … it must be kept at bay!

The interesting thing is that [the "string of rituals"] is spiritual warfare for them. What are the weapons of their warfare? Garlic, scissors, chewed up roots …

What are the weapons of *our* warfare?

Let's look at 2 Corinthians 10:3, 4. "For though we live in the world we do not wage war as the world does. The weapons we fight with are not the weapons of the world. On the contrary, they have divine power to demolish strongholds."

It is a lie that evil is supreme. Evil has been defeated by Isa al-Masih when he was sacrificed at the cross. The Lord is saying to us this day that our weapon of prayer is powerful for the demolishing of strongholds (Women's Forum: April 7, 1999).

Then she drew their attention to a story I had shared with her. It holds a powerful encouragement for all of us because it demonstrates the truth of what God tells us in 2 Corinthians 10:3, 4. Let me tell you the story.

Several months ago, I was interceding for the hillside community where I live. My husband and I had just ministered to a young family and had seen the power of God at work freeing the young man from a curse brought into the home through a magic ring. As I prayed, I was filled with zeal as I proclaimed the Lord's holiness and power over the young family's home and the surrounding neighborhood. Suddenly, I realized God was leading me to renounce the power of amulets held by all my neighbors. I prayed that the amulets would be cut off from their source and dry up and become useless and that my neighbors would become disillusioned with them. It was the first time God had ever led me to pray specifically against amulets.

My faith was very strong that day, and after praying, I left the matter with the Lord. I didn't notice any particular changes in my neighborhood until four months had passed. I was in the home of my seamstress friend Mrs. Carpenter. She said, "I just don't understand why we have had such misfortune since a year ago." "What happened a year ago?" I asked.

"A year ago we had our son, Jimmy, circumcised. We have had troubles ever since. And my husband's amulets bring him no blessing. I am wondering about that strange fish in my aquarium. My husband says we mustn't get rid of it because it has magic powers, but it is growing so big and is so ugly and eats so much. I'm very disappointed."

A week later a friend and I waged spiritual warfare from a nearby rooftop overlooking my neighborhood. After worshipping, I was interested when the Lord again led us to pray about the amulets. This time we prayed not only for disillusionment but also for a clear exposure of the real worthlessness of these power objects.

Several days later, on Good Friday, my husband and I visited the family of Mrs. Carpenter. My husband shared a story that highlighted Jesus' taking upon himself the curse for men. Mr. Carpenter heard for the first time about Christ's suffering and the connection between his death and the defeat of Satan. After the story was finished, Mr. Carpenter left the room and came back carrying two magic belts. He said, "Let's just see what is inside these amulets that have never done me any good." To his family's astonishment, he took a sharp pair of scissors and tore open the belts and laid their contents upon the table—coins, pebbles, Arabic writing on a piece of paper, a piece of animal hide. His disillusionment and his repulsion were clear, and, though he has not yet made a clear commitment to Christ, it was a very powerful testimony to us and to his family that his allegiance was shifting from the fear of the demonic to the fear of God.

God is showing us again and again that the weapons of our warfare are in the prayer closet (or on the prayer rug for those who use contextualized forms). My colleague's words sum up what God has been showing us about Muslims and the occult.

> This story about Mr. Carpenter reveals God unfolding encouragement to us. He is showing us step by step what to do, if we have ears that listen and eyes that truly see. If we spend time in prayer, listening ... listening to his heartbeat for the Indah ... he will show us how to go about doing things in this realm. Clearly, his plan for us is that we would wage powerful warfare and see strongholds demolished, because the truth is that the "gray" is not the best there

is. There is a holy power which has already crushed the demonic realm ... every demon, every person, every living thing is going to bend their knee to him (Women's Forum: April 7, 1999).

The description of the Indah woman living in "the gray" was quite sobering to the Women's Forum participants that day. At first we felt disgust and shook our heads as we considered the pitiful weapons of their warfare—forced to use sharp scissors and garlic against evil that masquerades as ultimate power. But the Lord had more for us. Before the end of our gathering that day, we realized God was using our discussion of the occult to uncover what was in our own hearts: a good deal of fear! How glad we were, after realizing our need, to learn that God's solution for Muslim women is his solution for us!

As we transition now to an examination of our own heart's response, we will see that God is drawing us, as if on a parallel track beside our Muslim sisters, out of deception into the light of true fear, the fear of the Lord.

Part 2

Our Great Weapon, Powerful for Setting the Fearful Free

A Call from Fear to Fearlessness

What is our heart's response to the barrage of counterfeits that God has exposed? In the grip of the occult, well-being and even fear itself are counterfeited. The tragic reality is that, even if it were possible to hold back the flood of evil through keeping traditional customs, Muslim women could not stem the flood of *fear* itself.

Are folk Muslims the only ones who live in the gray ambiguity of a sense of powerlessness? The only ones who wield their feeble tools in an attempt to ward off dangers?

Too often we also are drawn into the same counterfeit that ensnares the Muslim women we seek to bring to freedom. This gray ambiguity is our fear. Fear says: "There can be no decisive victory. So we will do the best we can, co-existing with our enemy, hoping that somehow we will be protected from his onslaughts."

Muslim women confess their fears. Can we? Every "terror-fear" we discover in our own hearts must be faced and surrendered, so that we can be brought fully into the "reverent love-fear" that God longs for our good and our complete protection in him.

Admittedly, many women serving among Muslims face incredible hardship and physical danger. It takes time for us to sort through perceived threats to determine which are real and which illusory. A colleague who is living among a very volatile Muslim people has, over time, been able to sort these out. At the same time, she has begun to replace unhealthy thoughts with right thinking and sound judgment based on reality. She is coming into the freedom of Proverbs 3:25-26:

> Do not be afraid of sudden fear
> Nor of the onslaught of the wicked when it comes;
> For the LORD will be your confidence
> And will keep your foot from being caught.

Are missionaries afraid? It is no secret that many are—for we admit it. We believe that as God sets us free from that fear, he will use us to set Muslim women free! But as long as we are still in bondage to fear, we cannot hope to speak freedom and minister power to Muslim women in bondage. We will not be able to hear what God longs to tell us or serve as his warriors of intercession.

God's Solution: The Fear of the Lord

God has called our Women's Forum—and is calling all of us—to turn from Satan's counterfeit and give our full attention and affection to the truth of Jesus' supremacy. We can be fearless only in the fear of the Lord! This is God's solution for both fearful missionaries and fearful Muslim women.

We are familiar with definitions of the fear of the Lord found in Proverbs 1:7, 16:6 and Deuteronomy 6:13. In Exodus 20:20, Moses said to the people, "Do not be afraid; for God has come in order to test you, and in order that the fear of Him may remain with you, so that you may not sin." Proverbs 29:25 reads, "The fear of man brings a snare, but he who trusts in the LORD will be exalted." Acts 9:31 interests me very much because of our church planting: "… so the church throughout all Judea and Galilee and Samaria enjoyed peace, being built up; and, going on in the fear of the Lord and in the comfort of the Holy Spirit, it continued to increase." The blessings of the fear of the Lord are clear!

Earlier evidence described Muslim women's feelings of vulnerability. Let's now identify some signs of fearlessness in the fear of the Lord.

Among the biblical women who were fearless because they delighted in the fear of the Lord are Deborah, Jael, Rahab, Esther, Abigail, and Mary the mother of Jesus. God wants us to believe that we, too, can minister without fear in the fear of the Lord.

I'd like to encourage you with a real life example from the struggle for my neighborhood—a story that shows women responding boldly in the fear of the Lord and not in the fear of man or unseen foe, or out of their love of an idol-spirit.

My neighbor Tracy, an expatriate missionary, lived among us temporarily while her family was learning the national language. They have since moved to their field of service, but not before Tracy invested herself in a very powerful way in the lives of many women in our community. She told me, "It is time that my bag of tears become a bag of seed." The seed was her testimony. The telling of the story of her life represented bold warfare on her part, and on my part too, actually.

Tracy was sexually abused as a little girl. Demonic visits followed on an almost daily basis. At first, these terrorized Tracy; later, they lulled her into a feeling of helplessness in the face of temptation. From early childhood, she felt overpowered by a strong sense of shame. Later, she came to know Jesus Christ, but she still felt powerless over temptation. Finally, she confessed her shame and feeling of powerlessness to her Christian husband. He knew they needed to go to spiritual battle. In Jesus' name, he offered her forgiveness for her impurity. Then in Jesus' name, he broke the power of the spirits of lust and shame. For the first time, Tracy began to resist her private temptations. And for the first time, she could totally accept and enjoy God's love. Her deliverance came because of Jesus Christ.

As Tracy requested my help to translate her story to a group of our neighbors, we knew that many of our mutual acquaintances who were bound by shame could be powerfully influenced by the gospel. Satan opposed us, targeting our children just days before we were to present this testimony; he tried to intimidate both of our families with accusations of the power of shame. But Tracy and I knew that we would be victorious in the Lord. We looked the enemy in the eye and pressed forward.

We fasted and prayed for anointing and for deliverance for

our neighbors. The event finally happened, and the presence and power of God were apparent! Several women confessed their own sinfulness and the conviction that they needed to seek God and not depend on amulets for spiritual help. There were wide, alert eyes in the group, and there were downcast eyes filled with tears.

Tracy testified to me several days later that the telling of her dramatic story seemed to be the completion of her own healing. Satan's weapon against her had been exposed and defused. Since the event, when she truly laid down her life so that Muslim women could hear of the Deliverer, she had experienced total victory over temptation! Her healing was completed by her public declaration of the power of Jesus. The fear of God made her fearless in the face of the enemy.

How can we ourselves come into the fullness of the fear of the Lord?

Repentance: Many of us need to repent, confessing and renouncing the deception inherent in our fears. When my colleagues and I repented corporately of our fears, many confessed that they had strived over years to create "safe places" for themselves; now they renounced these counterfeit strongholds in the name of Jesus. In this way, we have rejected the lies Satan had used to keep us bound by fear.

Then we come out of the ambiguity. We ask God to show us how black and white—how absolute—is Jesus' sovereign supremacy. We tell God we want to live in the freedom of it. We believe that he will help us understand the fear of the Lord, because this is his promise in Proverbs 2:1-8.

And we worship him! When our hearts are in worship, we are in the safest place we could ever be. (See Psalm 27.) When we delight in the fear of the Lord, we are no longer afraid of our "smallness;" instead, we are confident that *all* that Almighty God *is*, he will be to *us*!

The Renewal of our minds: We need to feast our hearts upon the living word of God for a fresh perspective, a new paradigm if necessary.

Not long ago, I had to search my own heart, "Do I really believe that Christ is greater than my fears?" Then God touched my heart with several scriptures that contributed to a biblical foundation for fearlessness. Here is a sampling of truths that have transformed me:

- It is true that every knee will bow to Christ (Phil. 2:9-11).
- It is true that Christ is over all creation, over every power and authority (Col. 1:16, 2:10).
- It is true that in everything Christ will have the supremacy (Col. 1:18).

All creation *will bow*. This is the *end* we know from the beginning. I observe that many missionary women and Muslim-background women accept the truth of what will happen at the end, but they are still bound by fear because they do not yet have perspective of the *beginning*.

Colossians 1:16ff testifies to a greatly liberating truth:

> For by him all things were created: things in heaven and on earth, visible and invisible, whether thrones or powers or rulers or authorities: all things were created by him and for him. He is before all things, and in him all things hold together.

All things were created …

by him .... *for* him

and *in him* all things hold together

How big is our God? How eternal is his claim on us all? Are these important questions? Yes! They affect my intercession. Many times, God has led me to imagine the community where I live now as the bare hillside it was before the Indah moved here. The hill belongs to Jesus from all time and for all time. The blood of his eternal sacrifice lays claim to the land and its people … no matter Satan's boast, no matter the blood of unholy sacrifices that has drenched its fertile tropical soil.

The discovery of Jesus' supremacy is like the hour when twilight fades to darkness: suddenly, we glimpse the measureless starry heavens—and we realize that the Creator of the universe is even bigger, for he is eternal, and all things were created by him and for him and have their being *in* him. He contains all his creation and has true, ultimate power over it. This meditation makes me fearless in Christ. It makes me cry out to him: "Give me a faith as big as *you* are!" This prayer is never in vain. Usually, he sweeps me into his activities around me, and I see his kingdom come in some fresh way.

Romans 11:36 adds to our firm foundation:

> For...
> from him .... and to him
> and through him
> are all things.
> To him be the glory forever!

Believe the truth that God is greater and mightier than his creation, including all spirits! All foes of God, whether seen or unseen, will bow to Jesus Christ. We are enclosed by his power and love and not by evil. We can do more than just survive our seasons of life.

Ministering to Fearful Missionary Women

Here is an exercise that can strengthen the hearts of fearful missionary women: Imagine in biblical detail the presence of God that is our covering—underneath, overhead, behind and before. This exercise can be fun and very enriching. Some metaphors that God has used to train my heart for fearlessness can be found in Psalm 89:14-15, Psalm 23:6, Isaiah 51:16, Psalm 63:8 and Deuteronomy 33:27.

Take hold of some biblical imagery that grabs your heart, then meditate on it until you begin to live in it. You'll know the effect of the living word of God as your faith surges! You'll feel your weak knees strengthen as you walk through the dark spots of your neighborhood. It is likely that you will cast fear away with abandon when you truly believe that God's loving gaze is upon you and that his protection covers you.

> It was not by their sword that they won the land,
> Nor did their arm bring them victory;
> It was your right hand, your arm,
> And the light of your face, for you loved them (Psalm 44: 3).

This is our God! We are discovering our one true fear.

Do you see that we cannot discuss the occult and spiritual warfare without addressing the condition of our own hearts?

It will be the same for our Muslim friends. The occult is a very tender subject. How can we encourage the fear of the Lord in our Muslim friends' hearts?

Most essential is that we ourselves model for our Muslim friends a true delight in the fear of the Lord. (See Isaiah 11.) We can effectively model living in faith, not fear, at the junctures in our own life cycles. In the Indah setting, how we face spiritual danger and deal with feelings of vulnerability during pregnancy and childbirth is very relevant.

Another way to encourage fear of the Lord in the hearts of the fearful is to magnify the Lord, to praise his works aloud, to make known that God is good news.

This is high-profile faith. By example, it exposes unbelief and can engender courage. This is one of the greatest blessings of our regional Women's Forum: one woman's testimony empowers the others to take steps forward in the ministry themselves. But testimony is also something that God uses to encourage the hearts of those who do not yet follow Jesus.

Changing Worldview through Chronological Bible Storying

Another very effective way to influence worldview and bring theological change is to use chronological Bible storying. We try to choose a series of stories based on our discernment of the way Satan's counterfeits have bound our people group. This can tear down demonic strongholds and build a true perspective that can lead Muslim women toward Jesus Christ and into his freedom.

1. Give a biblical "beginning." Start with what happened before creation. As you tell the story of the first chapters of Genesis, lay a strong foundation for the hope of Messiah who comes to destroy the works of the devil (1 Jn. 3:8).

2. Give a biblical "ending." Remember to emphasize not only the death of Christ but also his resurrection and ascension! Teaching on the ascension is very important for the identity of the believer as victor in Christ and for the vision of all creation bowing to him at the end.

A clear challenge for language and culture-learners is to know your people group's creation myth and pray about what they do not know about their Creator/Father. Then choose a series of Bible stories that will meet their need.

Another key for ministry to Muslim women in the occult is this: As you think about your gospel presentation and an appropriate chronology of stories for your folk Muslim hearers, don't forget one of the most important proclamations of scripture: Don't be afraid! Fear not, I am with you! Fear not—I bring you good news of great joy! Is this not the truth we preach? "Fear not" is one of the keys that will set Muslim women free.

One Last Story

In closing, I'd like to share how the fear of the Lord has released me from my own fearfulness.

Here's an example from my little daughter. She asks, "Mama, can I watch *Sleeping Beauty* again?"

I answer, "I thought you were afraid to watch that movie!"

"Not anymore, Mama."

What made the difference? She knows the end from the beginning! This shapes her interpretation of everything that happens between now and then. Perspective chases fear away!

This issue of fear of the occult came close to home just two years ago when my own terror was exposed. A friend was telling me the story of how her Southeast Asian friends were delivered from demons. As I heard the story, fear overwhelmed me, making me feel so nauseated that she had to drive me home and put me to bed. I felt like a tiny child who was watching *Sleeping Beauty* for the first time. Do you remember the wicked Maleficent? What a frightening image she is. And how terrifying her boast: "You stupid fools—thinking you could defeat *me*, the mistress of all *evil*!"

Of course, at the end of the story, the good prince's sword of truth cuts through the briers, and he slays the evil serpent. But we are conditioned to believe Malificent's words. They make an imprint, don't they? Then later, we must un-do the lie we had believed.

Now that we know the beginning and the end, we have the big picture. We are not easily fooled, because we know the truth and can recognize the counterfeit power and resist a false fear.

So in the end, who is the fool? The one who fears Maleficent. Who is the wise? The one who keeps hold of the truth and fears only God. It is still so.

Here's the sequel to my little story: Just two months ago, the same woman friend walked me through a jungle to show me the ruins of an ancient pagan temple, including the grave of a powerful sorcerer, and I felt no fear at all. In fact, we stood tall in faith together and waged warfare, praying for the kingdom of God to come with power to the people who live in the area. What a difference I felt.

What made the difference for me? The same thing that makes the difference for my little girl and my missionary colleagues and my Muslim friends: knowing the end from the beginning! —and knowing him who is from *before* the beginnings of heaven and earth! The fear of the Lord makes us fearless in the face of our enemies. Having eyes to see how great he is makes all the difference in the world.

> The fear of the Lord transforms
> fearful women into fearless warriors,
> that the Kingdom of God might come to the women of Islam!

Part 3

Applications

A Challenge for Women Planting Churches in Volatile Climates

In 2 Corinthians 9:6-8, we find our challenge for serving Muslim women during a season of great darkness in many areas of the world. If "harmony" is the basis of well-being for the Indah, then they must be feeling tremendous inner turmoil. The whole nation is in disharmony. A spirit of fear shrouds the land.

Our role is to give light—to give it generously, trusting that God will make grace abound to us for every good work. We must be ready to give light to those who live in the gray of fear! Are we prepared to give light? Or do we live in the gray ourselves, not believing God for a decisive victory over the powers of the occult?

Here is a challenge for us all: Wherever you serve, and whatever the lie Satan has used against the Muslim people you love, you have a choice to make. Will you be fearful in the face of the occult, or fearless? God wants to use you to set Muslim women free from fear.

Steps toward Victory in Your Spiritual Warfare among Muslim Women

Begin with delight in the fear of the Lord yourself. Ask these questions: Do I delight in the fear of the Lord? Is he my only fear? Is my obedience current? Am I obedient to God's call to freedom from all fears? Am I obedient to the truth that I serve in the authority of Christ himself? What do I hope for? Do I anticipate that the kingdom is coming with power to my Muslim community?

Identify hunger for spiritual power in the women of your people group. How is it expressed?

Minister to them as to a power-oriented society. Seek to discern whom they believe to have superior power. Watch for counterfeits. (Know the truth very well, and the counterfeits will be exposed.)

Do you need to be prayed over for spiritual gifts to minister in power to your people group? My testimony is that special anointed prayers have launched me into new phases of ministry to the hearts of Muslim women.

Understand blessings and curses from a biblical perspective.

Take your cultural observations to intercession, identifying the lie that women are believing and acting on. Recruit friends and intercessors for special assignment praying.

Act in faith on what God reveals to you. Remember that when you are walking in Jesus' authority, you will draw in the seeking hearts around you!

Live in the reality of Christ crucified. Stay healthy by leaving prayer burdens at the cross each day. Conduct your warfare praying carefully, following the Holy Spirit's lead. Then patiently watch for signs of him in the lives of the Muslim friends for whom you have stood in the gap.

Share your heart with your husband/male teammates. Share any insights that could benefit Muslim men as well. Hope together for the coming of the Kingdom!

Women's Forum: A Model for Women Partnering for the Sake of Muslim Women

We want to encourage women in other countries to form their own Women's Forums, similar to our Women's Forum on the Indah people. Simple guidelines are listed here for your benefit.

What is our purpose? We meet in order to encourage and equip one another for the tasks of research and intercession, to see the Kingdom come to Muslim women of our unreached people group.

Who is involved? Women who are called to love the people group to whom they minister. Women who are called to any one of the various supporting tasks that help us as a group move toward reaching Muslim women.

What are our tasks and how do we do them? (1) Intercession. We use our own observations and research as fuel for intercession. Through intercession we recognize the lies by which Satan deceives women, and we pray for deliverance in Jesus' name. (2) Observation. We ask women to attend life-cycle events in their neighborhoods (e.g., celebrations surrounding birth, circumcision, marriage, death) to discern hidden meanings of these rites and rituals. (3) Cultural Research. Anthropology books such as James Spradley's works and language learning manuals such as the Brewster's LAMP book suggest cultural themes to research [see References Cited]. We examine local parables, myths, wisdom sayings and legends for clues that might reveal worldview. (4) Analyze data. We analyze what others have written about the people group and culture along with our own observations and research. Then we write about what we learn. (5) Share data and observations. It is important to encourage all women to share everything, no matter how small, about what they are learning. This data needs to be compiled and recorded, usually by the leader of the forum.

What Have We Learned about This Model of Women in Partnership?

(1) Generally we meet every 6-8 weeks, but we have found that during special times (such as Ramadan or times of social crisis) we may meet more often since we have more questions. We are also more aware of our need for one another during times of increased spiritual warfare. (2) We found we needed to invite women to participate in this forum. Our objective was to be inclusive of the various agencies working among the people group of our region, even inviting women outside our city limits. We explained the different ways women could be involved, we affirmed them in their self-chosen assignments, and then we equipped them to go as deep as they wanted. (3) We learned we needed to focus. There is much we can study, many directions we can go. For example, after meeting for nine months and discussing our observations of the cultural values of friendship and perceptions of well-being of the women in our people group, we were compelled to shift focus to fear and the occult, specifically how bondage to dark powers is perpetuated through the life cycle events. (4) We learned to interchange our meetings between an equipping session and an encouragement session. In this way the personal needs of the missionary women are also being addressed. (5) We learned to release leadership to women who have a vision for the women's forum. We also recognized our need for facilitators who can help with administrative details

such as organizing the meetings, planning hospitality, and distributing communiques and invitations. It is important that women with different gifts are involved in the planning and carrying out of the forum meetings.

Conclusion. While this simple research effort is valuable, we put our trust not in any method but in the Lord himself. We ask him to move us to the core issues of the worldview of our people group. We wait on him in prayer to expose the power centers where we are to wage strategic spiritual warfare.

Participants' Discussion

From the Arabian Gulf—I have to admit that I fear the women in my country will never come to faith. Or if they do, that Christ will not be enough to carry them through the persecution they will face. What I realized today is that I have allowed myself to be misled. It has also been difficult for me to believe, considering their circumstances, that if they come to Christ they will be able to live their lives for him. It's been difficult to believe that the Lord will be enough for them in their extremely bad situations.

From the Philippines—I am afraid of my own personal failure. I'm afraid of making mistakes and failing in the eyes of the people we work with.

The author—What effects can fear have?

From a US mission leader—Fear can immobilize me and keep me from taking steps of faith.

A mobilizer from Canada—Fear causes me to be self-centered. My fear is of being ineffective.

From France—For me, the fear is of being rejected. If I really talk to these Muslim women about the issues that need to be talked about, I fear they won't want me to visit again. Recently, I was in the home of a new believer who is experiencing many problems. I noticed that she had an amulet around her neck that I had never seen before. I sat through the entire meeting thinking, "What am I going to do about this?" Yet I was afraid to talk to her about it, because I was afraid of the answer she was going to give. It would mean I had failed because I hadn't discipled her enough and she had reverted to trusting this thing to help her. But God wouldn't let me leave her home without asking about it. She explained that it was a gift from her father. She was afraid not to wear it because he had given it to her. We studied Ephesians 6 and the next time I saw her, she wasn't wearing it.

Honestly, I was also afraid of what would happen if we went through the study, she took off the charm, and then something coincidentally happened to her. What would that do to our relationship? She is still such a baby in Christ. It was a major struggle for me, all related to fear. I wasn't afraid of the amulet, but I was afraid that our relationship would be damaged.

From the Arabian Gulf— I have been afraid to share the gospel boldly. I've been fearful that Muslim women would reject me, and they wouldn't want to be my friend anymore because of my faith.

I also had a question. In my country, Muslims use a type of amulet to ward off the evil eye. A friend of mine gave one to me when we bought a new car. How do you reject a gift such as this without offending or breaking the relationship?

From France—When I receive such a gift, I say, "I appreciate your gift, but let me make sure—what is this is for? If I wear it, do you think it will protect me from evil?" After they explain what it is for, I reiterate that I appreciate their kindness, and say, "I'm sorry, but I can't wear it. Will you let me tell you why?" Then I explain where my protection comes from. My friends have accepted that and the relationships are not broken.

Thinking through the Issues

1. *What occult activities have you observed or learned about in your culture? Which of these are practiced most often or seem to hold the most power over the women?*

2. *In what way do these occult activities provide insights into the predominant fears of the women? What needs do they represent? Try to group them under the different categories of needs suggested in this article or Musk's or Kraft's books.*

3. *Can you relate to or empathize with these women's fears and needs? Their occult activities give them a greater sense of control, power, or protection. What feeling do their occult activities inspire in you?*

4. *Some Islamic cultures do not have ancestor worship, or underlying Hindu views of God. However, they have other widespread practices not mentioned here, such as veneration of Muslim saints' tombs. Different saints provide different kinds of help, such as fertility or health. What institutionalized or formal forms of occult activity do*

you see in your communities? Who is responsible for conducting occult procedures in your neighborhood?

5. The author quotes a researcher as identifying seven components of folk Islam among the Indah: powers, power, power person(s), power object(s), power time(s), power place(s), and power ritual(s). How many of these power categories can you observe in your culture? Which of these categories exist also in orthodox Islam? Which (if any) are consistent with a biblical worldview?

6. If we lay our biblical view of "power(s)" over the categories of folk Islam (see previous question), we can see that some of their understandings are fairly accurate. However, others are demonic counterfeit-power or lies, which, in biblical understanding, have no real power. We must be careful not to subtly accept their view of the different powers and the fears and constraints (bondages) that go with them. Which of these categories are, in fact, demonic hoaxes—like the carved idols of the Old Testament, which God repeatedly states have no power either to help or to harm, whose only power is the fears/hopes Satan encourages people to attach to them?

7. The author calls the "fear/hope" combination people have in these counterfeit powers "reverent love-fear." The hope for help or protection causes people to love their idols or amulets and to worship them. (If they saw idols/objects as curses, having solely evil power but no ability to help or protect, they would be repulsed by them and experience "terror-fear.") It is a double bondage—beginning in "terror-fear" of a counterfeit (nonexistent) power and moving toward "love-fear" when Satan persuades them they can control, appease, or obtain the help of these "powers" (hence, hope) through rituals, sacrifices, rules, or certain behaviors. What does the author claim will set them (and us) free from both unwarranted fear of and unwarranted hope in these counterfeit powers? What is the only power we should fear or put our hope in?

8. The author states: "God is showing us that the weapons of warfare are in our prayer closet," i.e., we pull down strongholds (true spiritual powers and principalities, Satan and his deceptions) through listening, discerning prayer. Has your team, or have you personally, been able to believe and implement private prayer as the primary weapon of spiritual warfare in your neighborhood? Under what conditions would you use public "power encounter" prayers?

9. How can we avoid prolonged shadowboxing with counterfeit powers

and tear down true strongholds? What do you believe are the true spiritual strongholds underlying the occult practices you see?

10. How does the author demonstrate that understanding the "ending" and the "beginning" are a crucial part of spiritual warfare? Do you agree or disagree?

For Further Study and Reflection

*   *The author encourages us to evaluate ourselves, in order to better understand and help Muslim women. What, for example, do we fear or put our hopes in? (Perhaps we fear poverty and, therefore, put our hope in secure finances. Or is money a "counterfeit power" that can deliver neither health nor happiness? Is education a "counterfeit power" unable to ensure success or godliness for our children? Is it possible that we tie it around their necks like a heavy, expensive amulet?) Don't we secretly believe that our fears are reasonable, whereas Muslim women's are not?*

*   *What false powers would you say women in your home culture put their faith in or fear the most? What new fears have you experienced on the field? How can we deal with our own anxieties and fears, thereby learning how to help them deal with theirs? What are the true spiritual strongholds underlying our own attractions to counterfeit saviors? How can we fear the Lord our God only (Deut. 6:13)?*

*   *The example of Tracy shows the power of identifying, confessing, and praying for deliverance from strongholds in our own lives. It is too easy to rationalize our own hurts, fears, or grievances and succumb to them on the field instead of finding freedom, peace, and spiritual power. Do you employ "long-held mechanisms which are like an amulet" to protect yourself or your loved ones? What is in your "bag of tears" that the Lord may want to use as a "bag of seed"? Follow the steps the author recommends for freedom and fearlessness as the Lord answers the above questions for you.*

*   *The author has found that getting together with women from other agencies working in her area has provided a powerful context for information gathering, insight, and intercession. Would it be possible for you to encourage the formation of such a group in your situation? Who could team with you to organize it?*

*   *Create a series of Bible stories that lay proper foundations for the fear of the Lord and fearlessness toward the occult. Determine what biblical characters can be our best reference as we encourage MBB women to be set free.*

Islamic Reformation and Fundamentalism's Impact on Muslim Women

Diana Colby

The women under the sway of Islamic fundamentalism are often out of our reach. We pass them, covered from head to foot, on the street in Cairo or Detroit or Jakarta, but we do not know them. Or maybe they are women we know well, who have turned to fundamentalism because they have felt the tug of the gospel and shrunk back, fearing the capacity to change that they have glimpsed within themselves.

Islamic reformation and fundamentalism represent the antithesis of the gospel. It is a growing force not only in the traditionally Islamic world but also in the world in general. Indeed, the most strident fundamentalists are at this moment working tirelessly to spread Islam to the ends of the earth.

Here I will not attempt to delve deeply into the details of Islamic fundamentalism and reformation as movements. I want to approach them broadly defined—as forces that pull Muslims further into Islam—and leave aside the evangelistic elements that seek to draw in non-Muslims. Because our particular focus is on women, I will approach the issue differently than I would if we were including both men and women. By nature, such movements are driven by men in the public/political, macro sphere and women in the private, micro sphere. Given this, I want to pay particular attention to how they affect women's lives at the personal level.

Diana Colby describes herself as a researcher in the social sciences with experience among Muslims—some brief and some more extended—in four Middle Eastern countries and two Southeast Asian ones.

By visiting a variety of locales and peoples, I have discovered firsthand the diversity of the world of Muslim women. Although for the purposes of this discussion group we must make some generalizations about Muslim women and fundamentalism, I hope we do so only with the awareness of the tremendous diversity of lived experience found among Muslims. I expect that our group discussion will shed light on some of the specifics of this diversity.

Further disclaimers: I have spent time in Muslim cultures as a researcher, not as a missionary. Although I have engaged in evangelism, my stance has been different from that of a person who is primarily focused on church planting. In addition, my schooling in social science has occurred largely in secular settings—so when I consider missiological issues, it is without the benefit of formal training. Here I will focus on social points and not so much on spiritual ones, although I believe there to be a major overlap between the social and the spiritual. I intend for us as a group to see how we can apply some of these points to church planting realities.

Islamic Prayer and Embodiment

Islam is an *embodied* religion. As people seeking to reach Muslim women with the gospel, we must contend with this embodiment. What do I mean? Embodiment is a term used frequently now in the social sciences, and I believe it to be very useful for our understanding of Islamic renewal movements. Islam resides at the very core of a Muslim woman's self. It is this self that is in contention: will she remain trapped in Islam, or will she break away into freedom and newness in Christ?

Consider for a moment the contrasting ideas of belief and practice. Evangelical Christianity is very belief-oriented. In fact, if we were to draw this schematically in a continuum, evangelicalism would probably be at the very end of the belief pole, with nearly all other religious forms worldwide leaning more toward the practice pole. In contrast, I think most of us would agree that the average Muslim is concerned less with belief than with practice. If we take a look at Islamic renewal movements, it is interesting to note that the first thing they appeal to is the practice of religion. We do not see the Taliban filling stadiums with people and asking them to profess faith (belief) in Allah as the one God and Muhammad as his messenger. No, we see them enforcing certain practices—penalizing men for shaving their facial hair, penalizing women for failing to cover themselves. This is not to say that the Taliban and other fundamentalists are not concerned with belief—they are! But that is not their starting point, because as we have said, Islam as an embodied religion has as its point of departure the practices that are lived out in the body. Whether belief follows from there is of secondary importance.

Islamic Prayer and Its Role in Women's Lives

Muslim women who become involved in Islamic renewal movements tend to start by applying tremendous pressure on other women to be more religious. The starting point for this is almost always the five daily prayers.

Social theorist Michel Foucault (1977) has written that Islamic prayer is "inscribed" on the body of a Muslim. How many of us have watched our Muslim friends pray day in and day out, like clockwork? In my own experience, a Muslim woman's faithfulness in keeping the prayers is by far the most important gauge by which her religiosity is judged by the ever-watching community of relatives, neighbors, and friends. I want to bring in an idea from "embodiment" theory to illustrate why this is such an important thing for us to consider in the process of reaching Muslim women with the gospel. Sociologist Pierre Bourdieu (1977) has introduced the term *habitus*, which Brubaker (1985:758), in an article summarizing Bourdieu's theory, defines concisely as "the system of internalized dispositions that mediates between social structures and practical activity, being shaped by the former and regulating the latter." As Young, who applied Bourdieu's ideas to Arab society, put it,

> People learn a culture-specific habitus unreflectively, without explicitly asking questions about it ... The process of learning a *habitus* has a lasting, constraining influence on thought, feeling, and behavior ... Any *habitus* is a collection of countless associations and abstract images that is held together only by the common reference points of the human body (1996:73).

Young goes on to describe the act of Islamic prayer in detail and to comment,

> Learning how to pray is an aspect of becoming an adult. At first they find it difficult, because each of the five daily prayers varies in some details from the others; one must concentrate in order to keep track of the number of prostrations that have been completed. As time passes, however, the prayer becomes a part of them. The posture that is required becomes habitual (74).

Social theorists Fiske and Haslam (1997) have made the suggestion that many regimented religious rituals found in non-Western cultures seem to share behavioral characteristics with activities that psychologists label "obsessive-compulsive" in the West. While to my knowledge they don't apply their comparison to Islamic prayer, I think the application can be easily made. Obsessive-compulsive behavior grips a person behaviorally and bodily with the same type of power as an addiction. Fiske and Haslam's point is not that people who engage in rituals are abnormal; on the contrary they are suggesting that something powerful and innately human is present in both types of behaviors.

So when we watch our Muslim friends pray, we are watching them engage in something that is incredibly powerful and appeals to some of their deepest human needs. I remember well the first time a Muslim friend said to me, "When I miss a prayer time, or even if I am a little bit late, I don't feel right. I feel uneasy, unsettled. But after I complete the prayer I feel like everything is okay again—that my day is back on track and my life in order." I have since heard other women say similar things.

We excitedly tell Muslim women that they can "talk to God" in an unregimented fashion like we do. And when they come to Christ they, too, are excited. But those who remain in Islam may well do so because they cannot break away from the compulsion of Islamic prayer, which is "inscribed" on their very bodies. We need to ask the Lord of the harvest to give us insight into how best to break through this formidable barrier.

Gender, Sexuality and Polarities of East and West

In the 1960s the "sexual revolution" took place in the West. Among other things, this served to link the idea of women's equality to men (something Western feminists had been seeking for decades) with sexual permissiveness. On campuses across the country, young men and women absorbed the new idea that if men and women were equals, then they were equally entitled to sexual freedom. Earlier feminists had not made this link and were simply working to increase women's rights, such as that of the vote.

When we as Western women enter into the world of Muslim women, we unfortunately carry the legacy of the sexual revolution with us. I am sure all of us could tell stories of how, especially when we first arrived and were strangers, we were misjudged as sexually loose. I know I can! Muslim men often assume that a woman who has freedom of movement will use her freedom to seek sexual relations. Thankfully, I have found that although this first impression is probably unavoidable, by carefully modeling a righteous lifestyle and adopting a reasonable adaptation to local standards of modest dress, we can show our Muslim friends that we do not live the way they expect. Christine Mallouhi's book, *Mini-Skirts, Mothers & Muslims: Modeling Spiritual Values in Muslim Culture*, does an excellent job of helping us work through the practicalities of these issues.

This change in the West has provided endless fodder for Islamic reformation and fundamentalist movements. Muslim leaders such as the Ayatollah Khomeini could point a finger and say, "See? Freedom for women leads to immoral behavior—the West proves this!" The sexual revolution in the West and the rise of fundamentalism in the Islamic world have created a state of polarity that, while already salient, seems to be on the rise.

By "polarities" I am referring to the same force in human nature that keeps enemies in opposite camps, that keeps the U.S. Congress deadlocked, and that keeps ethnic boundaries alive around the world. It boils down to the need that humans have to distinguish between "us" and "them." As long as we know who "they" are, we are able to define who "we" are. As Westerners and in particular as American Westerners, we are the ultimate "they" for Islamic fundamentalists.

In one Muslim neighborhood where I lived, my neighbors referred to a woman across the street as a "fundamentalist." (I don't know if this was a label that she herself accepted.) While she wasn't a friend of the host family I lived with, she did seem to be overly concerned about their activities, especially whether or not they were praying enough. During Ramadan, she invited the women of the family to a women's group at the mosque, pleading vigorously with them to come with her. However, the matriarch of the house flatly refused. "I can pray at home just as well as with other people," she insisted. "Besides, it's too far to walk to the mosque, and it's dark and cold outside ...." The woman came frequently during Ramadan but was unable to change their minds. However, I noticed that she did have an impact, even though she may not have known it. Largely because of her, my host family became vigilant about praying and keeping the fast, and this lasted long after Ramadan. They obviously felt the need to prove to her that they were religious enough already, without making any major changes.

In that case, fundamentalists were at one pole and my host family at another. This kept them from turning to a more radical Islam. But what about their form of moderate Islam and its relationship to another pole, Christianity? In the same city, I watched Muslim background believers endure endless accusations that they had become Westernized. To a large extent this was true. Many of the MBB women adopted less conservative forms of dress. While quite a few other women in the city were also modifying their dress, this change in the MBB women sent a message to others. They tried hard to learn English, and some succeeded. Ultimately, a large number of them emigrated to the West, and of those only a few are today following Christ. Meanwhile, the fundamentalists are busy back in that city reinforcing the stereotype of a "Christian West" which encompasses the television show "Baywatch," Calvin Klein, consumerism and Christianity. These images are keeping countless Muslim women away from the gospel. So while they don't embrace fundamentalism, they yield to the pressure to show that they are good Muslims—not too influenced by the Western "other," but not too fanatical either. They sit comfortably between the poles of following Christ and intensifying their practice of Islam.

What kind of implications does this have for evangelism? Again, Christine Mallouhi offers excellent guidelines in her book for our behavior as Westerners living among and modeling the way of Christ to Muslims. In the long run, we need to think carefully about what MBB women are modeling to their watching communities, so that they can preach a gospel undistorted by nonrelevant Western baggage.

Honor and Shame

Most of us are familiar with the quintessential Arab gender system. In it, the honor of a household and patrilineage (an extended family based on descent through males) is borne by its females, who must maintain their virginity until marriage and faithfulness to their husband after marriage. If they do not, at minimum they risk bringing shame on their families, and at worst they risk their lives. (In *The Arab Mind*, Raphael Patai does a good job of summarizing how this system works.) Islamic renewal and fundamentalism almost always reinforces these values if they are already present, or introduces them if they are not. (Such has been the case in Southeast Asia, which has a distinct history of kinship patterns.)

Practically speaking, the system of honor and shame poses a great challenge in church planting. Personally, I believe it to be the single most important reason why we see such an unbalanced ratio of females to males in MBB fellowships, with more males coming to Christ than females in many settings. I don't want to suggest ways around this system so much as to urge that we always consider its importance in each particular location.

In many Middle Eastern countries, a female of child-bearing age (between adolescence and menopause) cannot be seen alone anywhere or at any time, because she would be leaving herself open to accusations that she had been engaging in sex or in activities that would lead to sex. In one host family I lived with, the mother didn't let her adolescent daughter go on the roof alone, for fear that it would appear as though she was trying to communicate with males on the street. Maybe she would be seen as trying to set up a rendezvous, or maybe she just wanted them to notice her. The mother never thought that her daughter actually wanted to do these things. Her concern was that the community would *perceive* that she wanted to, which was just as bad. I have observed countless other examples of this kind of thing, and you probably have too.

I believe that in places where the honor/shame system prevails, many families and Islamic renewal leaders actually care more about a woman's proper behavior than about whether she chooses to follow Christ. In each ministry setting, it is imperative that we find creative ways for seekers and believers to meet together without asking them to compromise the sexual reputation of their household and extended family. This can be logistically challenging, but I believe that we must give careful thought to it, or we will attract only women from exceptionally permissive families, the educated, and those from the upper classes. Do we wish to rule out all the others who deserve just as much to hear the gospel?

Women in the Quran and the Bible

The Quran refers respectfully to Christians and Jews as "people of the Book." In other passages it is less respectful, but in most Muslim countries, this passage is famous and taken as an admonition to treat Christians as a type of religious cousins. Muslims who promote Islamic renewal or fundamentalism, however, tend to emphasize the authority of the whole Quran and the Hadith, including those passages which foster enmity between Muslims and Christians. At first glance, this may seem to be a great disadvantage to the advance of the gospel. However, I believe it is something that God is going to use to bring Muslim women to Christ. Why? Because both the Quran and the Hadith are full of passages that denigrate women. Here are some samples:

> Those (women) on whose part you fear desertion, admonish them, and leave them alone in the sleeping-places and beat them (Quran 4:34, M.H. Shakir translation).

> When a woman comes she comes in the form of the devil (Salih Musim, English Translation, Hadith No. 3240).

> The Prophet said, "I have not left any calamity after me more detrimental to men than women" (Salih Bukhari, Arabic-English translation, vol. vii, Hadith No. 33).

Nawal El Sadawi, a Muslim woman and writer who has challenged the treatment of women in Islam, writes that in Islam

> it is probably not accurate to use the term "rights of the woman" since a woman under the Islamic system of marriage has no human rights unless we consider that a slave has rights under a slave system. Marriage, in so far as women are concerned, is just like slavery to the slave, or the chains of serfdom to the serf (1980:139-140).

What a joy to be able to bring to Muslim women the message of the Bible! Jesus, whose cultural setting bore many similarities to the Middle East today, treated women as people—and this was revolutionary. Many Muslim women feel they must strike a balance between fundamentalist Islam on one hand and global trends of consumerism, sexual freedom and secularism on the other. But Jesus offers a third and refreshing option—one not without its costs, but unparalleled in its rewards. This is good news not only to Muslim women, but also to us, women called by God to bring the message of Jesus to our Muslim sisters.

Recommended Reading

See the Reference List for publication information on the following resources.

The Arab Mind, by Raphael Patai, and *Honor and Shame: the Values of Mediterranean Society*, edited by J. G. Peristiany. While these two books address particular ethnic and geographical settings, much of their content is applicable to Muslim societies anywhere.

And while written by men, they both offer excellent insight into the social forces that shape Muslim women.

Postmodernism and Islam: Predicament and Promise, by Ahmed S. Akbar, while written by a liberal Muslim scholar, grapples with many of the issues confronting a globalizing, modernizing Islam. It is especially recommended for those working in an urban or plural settings.

Accommodating Protest: Working Women, the New Veiling, and Change in Cairo, by Arlene Elowe Macleod, written by a political scientist, examines political Islam from the inside out. The author lived among women in Cairo as they began to adopt Islamic dress and to become seemingly more conservative. She found that despite the appearance of yielding to a male-imposed system, the women took change only as far as they wanted and maintained essentially the same level of autonomy as before. The book deals with many issues that bear on ministry among urban Muslim women.

Islamic Resurgence in Malaysia, by Chandra Muzaffar, offers useful insight into an Islamic resurgence movement in Southeast Asia.

Islam in Practice: Religious Beliefs in a Persian Village, by Reinhold Loeffler. While Islamic renewal movements call Muslims to a "pure" Islam, in most settings, Islam is practiced loosely and the Quran is not followed in a literal fashion. This book is useful for understanding many of the issues on which fundamentalists call for clarification.

Participants' Discussion

The author—What attracts the Muslim women you know to fundamentalism? Do you feel they are farther away from Christ than moderate or folk Muslims?

From the Caucacus Region—Most of the women I know are fundamentalists simply because of their husbands and family. But one I know is the most searching religious woman I've probably ever met in my life. She is doing what she thinks is right in her search for God.

From Morocco—I felt as though more women than men in Morocco were becoming fundamentalist for several reasons. First, it gave them a sense of solidarity with a larger community. They felt a sort of power in their international connection. Second, it gave them much more specific guidelines on how to be accepted by God. They felt a greater sense of being received and honored by God than if they were more moderate. Finally, they were proud to be religiously pure.

Some of them definitely projected a self-righteous attitude, looking down on others as more marginal Muslims.

From Turkey—A group of women I knew went to classes with a female Islamic teacher to recite passages of the Quran. That in itself was redemptive from a ritual viewpoint, for they started feeling very important. I once attended this meeting with a friend, and afterwards, when they served refreshments, some of the women declined to eat because they were fasting. They fasted not just at Ramadan but for three months. Everyone was impressed that they were so religious and said, "May God accept your sacrifice." It gives these women status, importance, and security. We should not underestimate the attraction.

The author—Do you believe the compulsive nature of habitual Muslim prayers reflects an innately human need for ritual behavior? Can this need be incorporated into true Christian worship? Or do you believe the compulsiveness stems from a spirit of fear and is a form of addiction or bondage that requires deliverance?

From the Caucasus Region—One aspect of my spiritual life that has been most attractive to my Muslim friends has been when we prayed together. When I prayed with a group of friends before a meal, most of them responded, "Oh, I love that prayer. Can I have a copy of it?" I replied, "Sorry, no copies. It just came from inside. That is the way I pray. I simply talk to God." To them, it was inconceivable that something from inside just came out. It was attractive, but they didn't think it could be part of their lives. Over time, I continued to pray with them; it became something that bonded us together. When they did come to the Lord, they wanted to be able to talk to God right out of their hearts, yet they didn't know how. I suggested they write down something in a form that would be familiar to them but as much from their heart as they could. I understood how hard it was for them to verbalize what they wanted to say to God.

From the Middle East—Our team asked lots of questions about this ritual need. After all, the more liturgical church provides ritual prayers that are full of scriptural content and can actually provide instruction for new converts. Plus, I think we all need and desire familiar words. As evangelicals, I wonder if we haven't lost sight of the value of written prayers and well thought out words. We think everything needs to be spur-of-the-moment. But written prayers can help new believers.

Unknown—The danger lies in the expectation that the prayer itself is the thing that matters. We always have to consider to whom we pray and avoid turning prayer into a magical activity.

From the Caucasus Region—We need to help them understand that what is in our hearts matters more than what passes our lips. A woman once told me, "I cannot pray because I only cry. Every time I start to say anything, I cry." I assured her that the crying in itself was a form of prayer; God was understanding all the things that came into the crying. So we cried together for a long time before she became a Christian. I think God was hearing the cries of her heart even when she couldn't put them into any kind of words. She did her formal Islamic prayers all through the day, but it was her heart that needed to connect to God.

The author—In my opinion, this question comes back to belief and practice tugging at each other again. We are coming from a belief-oriented perspective, so we are concerned about what comes from their hearts. I want us to consider their emphasis on the doing of the thing. We don't want to leave new converts' *practice* impoverished. We want to give them something to do. Does anyone have any experience at seeing new converts adapt something more liturgical?

Working among Kurds in USA—Our team has been discussing what would happen if a church forms. One of the questions we addressed was hand washing. Our Muslim friends told us that one can pray without having done the washing, but if you do the washing beforehand, God will hear your prayers more clearly. So the issue we are discussing with them now is whether God hears your prayers because of the washing or because the time spent washing is a time of preparation, when you focus on God and prepare your mind and heart for prayer. I think that preparation for prayer is something we are missing in our Western culture.

The author—I think fundamentalists would agree. That is why they start with practice but their end goal is belief. They understand the value inherent in doing something.

From Morocco—My concern is that we must always keep the Bible's teachings in view. The Jews were taught to perform a number of ritual practices; however, scripture contains some fairly severe passages in which God says, "You're caught up in the practice but you've lost the meaning." I know missionaries who have taken on the practice of using Muslim prayer beads. After a time, from my perspective, they appear to be addicted to the practice. I grew up as an MK among a Catholic population where people were addicted to rosaries, so this experience was a flashback for me. I struggled, wondering whether this is simply expressing a human need. If so, is it a human need that leads toward godliness or does it lead to a form of bondage? To what extent should we promote it, accommodate it or accept it? How can we ensure that they don't go off the track in some of the ways that the Jews and the Catholics did by carrying over practices into the church that end up not containing the meaning that God would prefer?

My very religious Muslim friends would comment that I didn't wash before I prayed like they did. Of course, they thought that made them better. But I would ask, "Is the cup clean if you wash the outside and not the inside? When I pray, I make sure I wash my heart." Then they asked, "How would you do that?" This gave me the opportunity to speak of Jesus Christ, who washes our hearts.

In some ways, the ritual practices prescribed in the Old Testament were a foreshadowing of a meaning. If we can use the forms to create biblical meaning, I can see it being more beneficial in the long run than if we simply use the forms for fulfilling a human need for ritual. I think that will lead to a loss of meaning again.

From the author—In what ways do you think an MBB woman should change her behavior? Should she observe the same regulations to protect her honor as before? Should she, for example, leave her house and walk from point A to point B alone? She could be saying to the world, "I am not under this system for the same reasons anymore. I am free in Christ and am living righteously because of that." What do you think of that?

From Morocco—We must realize that for many Muslim women, to walk in public without a head covering would be akin to walking down the street in a bathing suit. Even in our promiscuous culture, there are certain lines we do not cross.

From the Caucasus Region—In my area, Russian influence has produced more freedom than in the Middle East or other Islamic countries. Still, she wouldn't prove anything by saying, "I'm a Christian; I'm stepping out of this culture." In our church, the male leadership has taken on the protector role for women who don't have husbands, because it is an important part of life.

From Turkey—One way we prove that we are decent on the inside is by the way we dress ourselves on the outside.

Unknown—The Islamic world has such diversity! I am living in a culture that is obsessed with the West. I adopted the local dress except covering my head, since many of the women there don't cover their heads. Because I was adopting their ways, several women told me they were willing to discuss their deep dissatisfaction with the system. "We have to do this here, but if we were in another setting we would not follow these kinds of rules at all." I do think there is a very strong desire to see the whole society change. I didn't meet many women who wanted to be the one to change it, but they hoped someone would. I'd love to see some sort of moderate alternative on the part of the new believers.

Thinking through the Issues

1. *The author states: "Islamic reformation and fundamentalism represent the antithesis of the gospel." In what ways do you agree or disagree? How is Islamic fundamentalism similar to the Pharisaic movement of Jesus' time (in comparison to more moderate Islam or Judaism)? What can we learn from Jesus' answers to the Pharisees' questions that could apply to relating to radical Muslims?*

2. *From your experience with Muslim fundamentalist women, what is the attraction for them in becoming fundamentalists? What needs do they have that are better met than in moderate Islam? Or folk Islam? What have you sensed their motivations to be in seeking more converts? Do you feel they are farther away from Christ than moderate Muslim women or folk Islamic women you meet? Why or why not?*

3. *Fear and a need for control often fuel occult practices. However, these two attitudes also are foundational in highly legalistic practices or religions, such as fundamentalist Islam. What fears (or desire for more control) could be fueling the Islamic renewal movement's emphasis on practices over belief? What can we learn from their emphasis on practices such as penalizing men when they shave facial hair or women when they are immodest? What can we learn from the things they choose to denounce Western "Christians" for? How can we use these fears or concerns as a bridge for reaching them with the gospel message?*

4. *Do you believe the compulsive nature of habitual Muslim prayers is a reflection of our innately human need for ritual behavior? Can this need be incorporated into true Christian worship? Or do you*

believe the compulsiveness stems more from a spirit of fear and is a form of addiction or bondage that requires deliverance?

5. *The author describes in detail the polarization radical Islam is promoting. Just as communism denounced capitalism as a means of consolidating its control and spreading its influence, so radical Muslims denounce Western Christianity, purposely making it an unthinkable alternative ever to a moderate Muslim. Instead of engaging in their polarizing debates by defensiveness or counterattack, how can we sidestep the debate and communicate the true meaning of the gospel: grace? What can we learn from Jesus about sidestepping legalistic debates and getting to the heart issues?*

6. *Much of their critique of the West we would agree with. How can we use this to convey God's love and truth?*

7. *The author states, "In places where the honor/shame system prevails, many families and Islamic renewal leaders actually care more about a woman's proper behavior than about whether she chooses to follow Christ." How does this emphasis on outward appearances intensify guilt, shame, or self-righteousness? How can we use it to the advantage of the spread of the gospel?*

8. *The author points out that dressing and acting modestly by Muslim standards is important to not give the appearance of evil, especially among fundamentalist Muslims. Have you noticed any difference in people's (especially fundamentalists') attitudes toward you if you dress very modestly? List some biblical passages that speak about this type of accommodation of another's conscience.*

9. *How can we convey to Muslim women the freedom and dignity we have in Christ, and distinguish between our adoption of dress and our acceptance of the shame-based Islamic view of women?*

For Further Study and Reflection

- *The Islamic oppression of women is primarily based on fear and partially a result of the sexual obsession and immorality widespread among the men. The author quotes sections of the Quran and Hadith that refer to fear of desertion and of temptress powers of women, for example. How can we train believing Muslim women to identify these underlying fears in themselves and the men in their lives and fight these fears as they would occult fears—with spiritual weapons, not human ones? For example, can we help them see the males' anger and control as an expression of fear? Or can we help them recognize their own dependence on lying and duplicity as an unbiblical form of self-protection?*

- *Do we really believe Jesus can give them new self-respect and honor and deliver them from the bitterness and hurt they feel from having to put up with unfaithful husbands or cruel treatment by men, even if the men never change?*

- *Are we ourselves ready to fight this spiritual stronghold of Islam with spiritual weapons and not promote a rebellious attitude that has not worked well in our own countries?*

Understanding the Spiritual Hunger
of Muslim Women

Lea Ruth

O how we each long to be able to climb into the heart and mind of
our Muslim sister. We desire to grasp what is beneath her often-
wearied and burdened countenance, and to design ways in which
the touch of the Savior will truly be felt as healing and hope.

This paper is not intended to give answers to this longing or to
speak from some position of expertise on the subject, but is a simple offering from the musings of a fellow traveler on this road of
witness and ministry. I will draw from events that we have actually witnessed and will hang some of my thoughts on the structure of two helpful books I have studied: *Gods of Power: A Study of
the Beliefs and Practices of Animists* by Philip M. Steyne, and *The
Unseen Face of Islam* by Bill Musk.

I have never lived or worked in the heart of formal Islam, the
Middle East. However, for the last 14 years, my teammate and I
have had the privilege of being a part of a traditional Muslim clan
in a small Southeast Asian village. We have worked as health care
providers and teachers among these friends and have found
incredible opportunities to teach the Word. Here we have witnessed many of the day-to-day issues of living under Islam. Thus,
we have sought to feel the pulse of the Muslim woman's heart and
have seen Jesus touch some of those hearts with his love. The best
way to feel that pulse together here is to hear their stories as they
live them, themselves:

Lea Ruth has worked as a health care provider and teacher for 14 years in a Muslim
village in rural Southeast Asia.

It was about 3 a.m. when we were awakened by a flashlight coming through our bedroom window and a cautious but insistent voice calling our names. I came to the window blurry eyed and called out, "What's up?" I was answered by a simple "It's me." No name could be uttered. It was Arsad. He called out, "My knee hurts," which was a cue—subtly expressed to avoid drawing the attention of the spirits to the fact that his young wife was in labor.

It was Sittie's first baby. She was a frightened teenager. There are no Lamaze classes in this village. She only knew the stories of older women, stories of hardship, death, and fear surrounding the birth of a baby. As we sat down to calm her and help prepare her for the hard hours of labor still ahead, others around us had a different idea. All they knew was that they want to get babies out as fast as possible, and so let this dangerous time pass by quickly. Soon someone woke the seemingly ancient Grandfather Sami. He brought a glass of water to his chin, cupped his hand over his mouth and the glass, and softly uttered: bismillah (in the name of God). Then, he then gave it to Arsad and told him to have her drink it. Sami then gave instructions for Arsad to get some of the guava leaves that were hanging on the woven bamboo walls at the four corners of the house outside, an attempt of camouflage against the spirits. He also gave Arsad some oil with words spoken over it that he was to rub on Sittie's stomach. Near dawn, the pains grew stronger. So began the ubiquitous barrage of coaxing, threatening, and accusations: "If you wouldn't walk/sit/move this way/face this direction then the baby would come." "I just knew you were always lying down in the afternoons these last months—and now the placenta is stuck firm on the inside!" "I told you that you shouldn't have eaten mangoes last week." "Don't close your eyes and rest, the baby won't come!" "You're not working hard enough!" And the constant "Push! Push!" long before it was time.

Another middle-aged man appeared and spoke with stern authority, scolding the family that Sittie had no belt around her waist to keep the baby from sliding back up, so an old head scarf was found to serve the purpose. More oil was rubbed on her belly, people ran around nervously, and some cried out "Slippery eel!" After another half hour or so, a baby girl gave a lusty cry. She was left there on the hard cold floor until her "sibling," the placenta, was successfully delivered. During that time—which seemed to be the peak period of dread for all present—old Grandpa Sami whispered words over her belly.

During the excitement of the delivery, Mother of Makmud— the tiny shriveled grandmother and traditional midwife—had quietly slipped in. As we took care of the baby and mother, she set about to her role of caring for the placenta. She ordered the men to fetch for her a clean piece of cloth, a coin, some banana tree shaft, and hot water in a basin. She gently bathed the placenta, wrapped it neatly in the cloth with a small coin inside, and tied it with a strip of the banana stalk fiber. Then she placed her hand on the bundle, said some words under her breath, and moved her hand to the baby. She gave the bundle to Arsad, instructing him to bury it in the East-West orientation. Only when this twin spirit was properly honored could the household breathe a sigh of relief and enjoy the new life that had come into their home.

If one word could characterize the heart of a Muslim woman, I believe *fear* would be that word. Our friends do not live in a secure environment by any definition. They have never found it safe to trust anyone, unseen or seen, in their life. Perhaps these fear issues can be helpfully categorized into three types.

- the fear of shame, always being the recipient of blame for the fallen condition of their world
- the fear of powerlessness, living in a world of fickle spirits and vengeful ancestors
- the fear of rejection by a male-ego-focused community

Let me illustrate and discuss each of these separately:

The Fear of Shame

From an early age, all children in our community are socialized by the fear of being shamed. But women, especially, relive this fear from birth to the grave. It appears that Islam is set up to cause a woman to fail. One simple case in point is the thirty-day Ramadan fast, which must encompass at least one period of ceremonial uncleanness in all normal women with a normal 28-day menstrual cycle. In addition, both the Quran and the Hadith seem to give license for men to blame all of their sexual misconduct on the woman's lure. Bill Musk describes it in this way: "Islamic theology would appear to blame [women's] sexuality, and inconsistency, for producing a situation in which men's innate weaknesses are easily exploited; menstruation places the category of ceremonial uncleanness regularly upon women" (1989:118).

Let's look at a few small yet painful examples:

Sarai stood unyielding as the religious elders gathered around her. After all, she had just returned from Saudi where she had given herself as a slave—a domestic worker—for four years. She had faithfully sent home much of her meager earnings to her eight children for food, clothing, and schooling. While she was gone, her sister had cared for her children, as her husband was too busy to be bothered. During those four years, two of her children had died because her sister had been unable to fully care for them or keep Sarai's hard-earned money from her own alcoholic husband.

Upon her return, Sarai's husband had begged her to give him all of her savings that he might use it to pay the recruiters to find him a job in Saudi. He would be taking his turn at slave labor. But word had just arrived from the city that he had used the money as a dowry to marry another wife! Now the elders were insisting that somehow Sarai had been an inadequate wife, that it was her fault that he had needed to seek another woman, and that she had just better give in to the idea. After all, she must consider what further shame she would bring on his family if she insisted on a divorce.

Further shaming comes across the radio waves:

We had just finished a quick prenatal exam of our young friend. As we all sipped native coffee on the mat on the floor, a variety of family members began to discuss the latest announcement on the Islamic radio. The program had actually reported that a young woman, on her trip home from her pilgrimage to the holy city of Mecca, had shamefully stopped at a beauty parlor to get a cut and perm. Afterwards, she again donned her new white hajja head covering. Upon her arrival back in the country, she had removed her white turban to find that her hair had turned into a mass of crawling vipers, which struck her dead on the spot. As an older woman relayed the story, heads of both sexes began to nod in agreement with Allah's judgment on this worldly woman. Some of the young women turned to us with poorly hidden panic on their faces, asking if something like this could really happen.

> *The conversation turned to further teaching they had heard about women. Again, the general consensus among the older ones was that women are by nature deeply full of sin and unclean; they are the cause of men falling into lust because of the way they dress or carry themselves. The younger women, being socialized into this concept before our very eyes, appeared to me as though the knife of death was sinking deep into their hearts.*

Blame throwing is a common means for the men to release responsibility, particularly in the feuding culture in which we live:

> *The feud between our two villages had produced a deadly sit-uation for many months. This morning, two of the young men in our neighbors' house had stealthily attacked some fishermen of the enemy village. They had not succeeded in hitting anyone directly related to the our village's previous offenders. Worse than that, they had acted unilaterally—without the Sultan's knowledge or approval. So what reason unanimously rose from the neighbors' usual bench gathering? Of course, the morning's foolish blood-letting was not the result of the young men's impet-uosity. No, their actions were the responsibility of their sister, who had loudly spoken out of her anger and served as the cat-alyst for their deed. Didn't she know to keep her mouth closed and not risk her brothers' lives unnecessarily?*

As we have turned to the Word to see Jesus' offer of hope to shame-ridden womanhood, we have seen the story of his encounter with the woman caught in adultery come alive to our friends (John 8). Also, they hungrily listen to stories of a Lord who takes time to turn and speak gently to the woman who dared touch him for healing from her long uncleanness (Mark 5).

I believe as we move among our friends, we need to incarnate this gentleness and acceptance of the person. We cannot accomplish this from a distance; it requires intimate day-to-day involvement in a lifestyle similar enough to theirs to be identified as touching the same painful issues of life. Through our medical care, my teammate and I have the natural privilege of living in such a manner. Particularly as we deliver babies in the community, we are involved in one of the most intimate events in the lives of families. It took many years before the average village woman trusted us to join this event, especially since there are some taboos about a single woman such as myself observing a laboring mother. Sadly, this honor came to us only after one of the traditional midwives overstepped her knowledge base and experienced some obstetrical disasters. Often, women marvel that we ourselves are willing to become rather unclean to help bring a new life into the world. During a delivery, we commit the mother to the Lord's care from the beginning, and we gently counter the blaming and threats with gentle affirmation that she is doing well and honest explanations about what is happening. We always speak to the whole crowd after the baby is born of the wonder and miracle of the Lord's creative work in the whole birth process, and we pray, committing the baby to the care of a sovereign Lord who has victory over the unseen evil world. Not everyone needs to be an obstetrician to point a blame-ridden woman to the Savior. But I would challenge each of us to find creative ways to identify with their weariness and uncleanness. We must point them to a Christ who hates and deals with sin in our lives yet sees beyond our sin to our need.

As we teach seekers and new believers, we need to emphasize the Christian's identity in Christ, our position of wholeness, cleanness, and total acceptance by the Lord of Lords. Some of the key concepts of scripture, brought out in books such as *Victory Over the Darkness* by Neil T. Anderson, would be worthy reminders for us as we prepare teaching materials in this area.

The Fear of Powerlessness

The unseen spirit world is very real to our Muslim friends. Perhaps it is even more so to women, who are at best unnecessary in the more formal expressions of Islam, yet who have to act as primary caretakers of others in a fallen world that is neither fair nor safe. We must carefully listen to the stories of their pain so that we might extend the very real victory available in Christ in a way they can hear, through the din of spiritual clamor.

> One-year-old Akmad had meningitis and a huge abscess on his leg. The baby was very near death, but during the first 48 hours, through much prayer and intensive care, he began to show slight signs of improvement. This family was fearful and not used to trusting us. So during our care, the family also asked Aunt Isar, the spirit healer, to visit. She entered in a flurry of authority and announced the cause of the problem: the lad's angels had been scared away because the mother had clumsily dropped the baby three months earlier when she had fetched him from his hammock. She declared that she had come to do Muslim

medicine but added that she alone knew how to do this. It was something Allah could not do.

First of all, Aunt Isar picked up an egg and turned it over in her hand in the smoke of incense burning in a coconut shell. Then, she held it up to her mouth so that she could whisper words over it. She did this twice, then took the egg and placed it in a saucer with oil, on its larger end, and tried to make it stand up by itself. A few times it fell over, and she seemed to note carefully in which direction it fell. But after a few times, the egg actually stood up on its own. After a few seconds, Grandma grabbed the egg and waved it above the baby's head, across his face, down the right side of his body and then down the left.

Aunt Isar repeated the whole procedure three times. The second time, it took her a long time to make the egg stand up, and the tension seemed to mount among the observers, but at last it did stand. During the ceremony, she kept a close watch on the direction in which the smoke rose from the coconut shell. She seemed not to be pleased with the direction, as though it was not a good omen. When someone asked of the outcome from the signs, she said, "Only Allah can tell. It would be sin for me to say." She said the angels had indeed fled, but she was able to call them back. Shortly after this, she took her leave.

The next day, as we were returning to the house, Aunt Isar was walking along the road also. Clicking her tongue and protruding her lip, she confided in us that she knew the baby would not live. To our knowledge, she never returned to see the patient. After several more days, much prayer, and an obvious spiritual battle within our hearts and in the peculiar progression of the sickness, the baby did recover and went on to lead a normal childhood.

As we interacted in the lives of this little child and his family, we keenly sensed the spiritual battle raging for his life. Aunt Isar nervously knew her powers were somehow hampered by our presence, and we knew that this was not merely an infectious process, as we watched the antibiotics strangely working in one area but not another. In addition, during this episode, my partner was awakened in the middle of the night sensing an urgency to pray. Although this was no widely publicized Mt. Carmel experience, Christ did get the victory.

We must all heed the rebuke of Dr. Musk as we step into the lives of Muslim women. He writes,

Perhaps it is partly due to the idolatrous, rationalistic spirit from the kingdom of darkness at work among Western believers that many missionaries to Muslims are blind to the real issues at stake. Mission to Muslims is not necessarily so much a matter of trying to convey primarily intellectual information, against most of which the Muslim is already "inoculated." It is a question, rather, of preaching the gospel with power, with the Holy Spirit, and with deep conviction, as well as with words (1989:250).

It was another steamy hot afternoon as we sipped an equally steamy cup of powerful native coffee. We ladies were lethargically draped across the big bed in Elizabeth's room, discussing the latest development in the strange behavior of cousin Lillian. She had been having severe panic attacks, hearing voices that were telling her that her sons would be killed. The family had followed the advice of a spirit healer and completed an expensive ten-day ceremony that involved constructing a little yellow spirit house, replete with pillows, combs, and fresh betel nut to chew. Now another spirit healer had snapped instructions to destroy the spirit house and instead chant prayers from the Quran. Lillian's family was not extremely confident in this new treatment plan, so they begged Elizabeth to let them just hide the spirit house in her basement. There it lay, directly beneath some very nervous cousins, none of whom were too sure of the potential power of these banished—thus probably offended—spirits. But they had no choice in this community decision. It has been made in the best interest of the patient.

The conversation meandered to another time when community pressure had led them into a fearful ordeal. It was about two years before our arrival in the village. Tamara, one of the most mysterious and powerful of the midwife-healers of the community, announced that a spirit boat would be landing along the coastline of the village. The spirits were coming to take away all the young men and women of the village. She made an urgent call for each household to send a representative to her home on a given evening. They were to bring one water jug filled with fresh water from the spring, and one hard-cooked egg for each member of the household. She ominously noted that if even one household failed to attend, Tamara's work of protecting the village from this disaster would fail. As Elizabeth had been chosen to represent the family, she took her jug and eggs and joined the procession to the big dark house at the end of the village. Someone was playing the pot-gong xylophone and drum, and as they entered, Elizabeth felt deadly fear gripping her. The music stopped, and as they all obediently opened their water container and cut each egg in half, she felt a distinct cold wind blow into the room and over the mouth of each jug. She wanted to scream and run but was frozen with fear. Tamara spoke some words to an unseen visitor then demanded that each leave one half of each egg. She instructed everyone to take the jugs home so that each household member could drink from the now-treated water. Then all would be well in the village. And all was well. No spirit boat came, and no young people were lost.

What was happening in these two brief vignettes? Obviously evil spirit power was considered to be operating each time. They feared the power and knew it to be beyond the control of the average citizen. So how should we, as ambassadors of Christ, respond to these crisis events: shall we make an immediate call for power encounter and release, or reassure them that these superstitious beliefs will merely fade away once they trust Christ as their Savior? I believe that although both teaching and living the power and the truth of our Lord are imperative, neither of these approaches provides a complete answer. I believe we also need to look deeper, at the underlying social and emotional issues involved.

A closer look reveals that each encounter with the dark world seems to be, at least in part, an instrument of social control in the community, offering a means to maintain community solidarity. Musk, in his discussion of the evil eye, a dark world concept ubiquitous in the Muslim world, writes: "The evil eye concept brings direction and sanction to a community that operates within the bounds of the 'limited good.' It helps maintain the tension between potential for growth at others' expense, and accepting a [self-limiting] norm" (1989:266).

He goes on to ask the challenging question,

> In Christian witness to people for whom the evil eye is not only a surface belief, but also an expression of deeper assumptions or processes, the question must be asked: what are the ramifications for the whole worldview, as the surface phenomenon is confronted? Can a peasant society survive without the sanction of the evil eye belief? ... Is there an alternative sanction, in Christ, which will effectively regulate interpersonal behaviour? (1989:267).

One afternoon, we were startled out of a relaxed merienda by a call from Mariam's brother that she was delivering her second child. We arrived just in time for the last push and to literally catch her healthy son! The old midwife, Mother of Makmud, came in later, and the details of postpartum care went as usual.

A week later, when we had also delivered Sittie's first baby, Mariam mentioned to us that we must have some amulet with barakat (spiritual power) to make our patients deliver easily! I answered that we trust only in the power of the Lord in our lives.

Some time later, Mariam came to our house one morning to invite us to come to the naming ceremony for her son. We arrived to find several pots cooking goat and chicken and a bustle of activity. Earlier, the Imam had come to slaughter the goat and had done so under an umbrella while holding the baby in his arms. He said that at his death, the child would ride to heaven on this goat. He also cut off a bit of the baby's hair and gave the baby his name. A bit later, the holy men, including the Imam who had named the baby, returned and were served the meal in an outer room. During this visit, they prayed for the baby to have long life and chanted some Arabic prayers.

As Mother of Makmud arrived, the men were taking their leave, each being handed bags of the food and an envelope of money. One lady nervously said that what Mother of Makmud does is really not good, not "Muslim." But we noticed no looks or words of rebuke from the holy men to her when they left. Mother of Makmud immediately took over with authority, and people began to scurry as she barked out instructions, often shaking her head and clicking her tongue, disapproving that things were not already prepared as she would like them. Items of the ceremony began to be gathered.

First there was a bowl with several live fish. The children had fetched them from the spring earlier that morning. We were told that Mother of Makmud would take them back to the spring and ceremonially release them later that day. If they took off swimming to the east, it was a good omen for healthy long life for the baby. If to the west, the omen was not good. Mariam was told to fetch three types of leaves. These were bunched together to use to sprinkle water from the fish bowl.

There was a large tray, with a banana leaf covering, piled high with a generous amount of cooked rice. Mother of Makmud ordered one person to arrange the parts of one whole cooked chicken as if it were lying still together across the rice. They were embarrassed that one of the wings could not be found, so they replaced it with a leg bone, hoping that Mother of Makmud—

being old and with poor vision—might not notice or rebuke them. It seemed to work. But it did seem very important that the chicken's tongue was found and placed correctly in its head. Also on the rice, they placed four small bundles of rice wrapped in banana leaves with some chicken inside. Then someone brought a coconut shell with a strong, sweet incense.

Mother of Makmud gruffly asked where the boat was, and the intestines of the goat. There was then much flurry, each one scolding the other for not preparing these things. Quickly, someone located a piece of the banana shaft, and someone else crafted a small boat. Unfortunately, the intestines had not been saved, so some of the chicken feathers were substituted as boat sails and decorations. We were told that these were to keep the spirits away so that the child would have smooth sailing and a prosperous life. Someone also constructed a small woven bamboo frame, covered with a banana leaf, as a stand for the fish bowl.

Then Mother of Makmud called for a red piece of cloth. None could be found, so the little daughter of Mariam was forced to donate her red shirt for the cause. Her shirt became a flag, which was hung out the window on the southwest side of the house, and the boat was placed below the window. The food tray and fish bowl were placed on a mat on the bed where Mariam had given birth, and a pillow was placed at the head of the bed, with two cigarettes on it. Mariam, her husband holding his new son, and their daughter sat on the west side of the tray. Mother of Makmud took the leaves, dipped them in the fish water, and walked behind the family, sprinkling the water on them all. Then she took the shell of incense and circled around each of the items including the pillow, and three times around the head of each of the family members as she muttered softly to herself.

Abruptly, the old midwife cried out, "Pick it all up!" The family and those standing nearby started grabbing the chicken and rice and eating it eagerly. We were told beforehand that it was bad for the family to call out to invite anyone to come and help eat the food (a normal part of hospitality in other circumstances), but everyone joined in without invitation, and soon the plate was cleared.

This event fascinated us as we noted the blatant and peaceful side-by-side coexistence of formal Islam and animism, and the clear division of roles between the sexes in these two realms of reality for the average Muslim. I see this now succinctly expressed by Dr. Musk:

> The common stereotype of an Islamic community relegates women to *purdah* (seclusion), childbearing and menial tasks. In reality, though often from within the walls of their husbands' homes, women extend a strong influence over their families' lives. Such influence frequently derives from an association with the occult world. Besides a general power in activities involving the supernatural world, individual women hold specific positions in Muslim communities which give them authority in matters pertaining to folk religion. ... Female Muslims may be given a somewhat secondary place in the practices of formal Islam: Islamic theology would appear to blame their sexuality, and inconsistency, for producing a situation in which men's innate weaknesses are easily exploited; menstruation places the category of ceremonial uncleanness regularly upon women. Within the home, however, and in certain aspects of crisis and cyclical rites, women shine as power possessors. Men and women alike seek their help (1989:118-119).

What can we conclude from this issue of the fear of powerlessness, about keys to the spiritual hunger of our Muslim sisters? Our friends typically find themselves exposed and vulnerable in a cruel and fickle world of seen and unseen enemies. What do we, through Christ, offer them as release? How can we introduce them to the One who "has rescued us from the dominion of darkness, and brought us into the kingdom of the Son he loves" (Col. 1:13)? We need to give tangible evidence that we live in personal relationship with a God who is all-powerful. This is my daily challenge, as my Western mindset heads me first toward the pharmacy shelf for our patients' needs, and only afterward to prayer.

Digging deeper, I believe our friends do understand strong power—perhaps much better than I. They firmly grasp the fact that Allah is more powerful than all. But I believe our sisters' question to us is: Can he be trusted any more than all the other powers they know? I believe that even before we emphasize the power and victory of our Lord, we first need to introduce them to this God who is totally trustworthy. We can teach from Scripture, showing examples of God's faithfulness. We have found that a series on the life of Moses, particularly the wilderness wanderings, speaks well to their desire for Someone stable and trustworthy. Along with this, we must live lives of visible dependence on a trustworthy God. I sometimes find this a convicting challenge, as we bring attitudes of our Western no-risk lifestyle to the field. And obviously, with our foreign passports and elaborate contingency planning, we do not share the same vulnerability of our sisters. These issues need some honest self-examination, so that we can transparently present a God who can be trusted by any people in any circumstances.

A third issue arises from these vignettes. If it is indeed true that women in traditional Muslim settings have a prominent role in the animistic issues of life—as healers, midwives, and diviners—then what are the roles of redeemed women to be in the new believing community? If the church is structured along the patterns of conservative Western Christianity, where male leadership is dominant, might we unwittingly project the message that the woman is not valuable in this new replacement higher religion, thus opening the door for her to retreat into syncretism with animism, only this time with a "Christian" flavor?

The Fear of Rejection

The measles epidemics had become less frequent over the years, but certain clan pockets had resisted immunizations at the advice of their local patriarch or shaman. Martha happened to be in one of those pockets. A woman in her forties, Martha was one of a series of wives of a more than 90-year-old man. Her daughter, six-year-old Torry, was one of our favorites—a tender listener to the gospel message in our kids' classes. Her four-year-old brother, Basir, was the typical naughty only-boy, highly indulged by his mom since he would be the only one Martha could count to carry the traditional responsibility for her care in her old age. Both children were among the dozen who contracted the dreaded high fevers, red eyes, and deep cough, and it soon became clear that both needed hospital care.

The next morning's scene at the hospital broke our hearts, as limited financial and emotional resources forced Martha to sit on Basir's bed sponging his fever and coaxing his medicines down him, while little Torry gasped for both breath and love, alone on her cot against the other wall, and quietly slipped into eternity.

Our Muslim sisters are under incredible pressure merely for survival in a hostile, uncaring world. Social security is not a political issue here, but it often involves heart-wrenching decisions and actions. Their community is the only source of security that they know, but it is filled with landmines of potential failure.

As light-bearers, we need to learn to empathize with our sisters as they feel the darkness and fear of being rejected from community. Steyne, in his book, *Gods of Power*, explains that because of the general fear of consequences in the spirit realm, the worst wrong in an animistic society is innovation. He writes, "Diversity or nonconformity is costly and may signal the activity of evil spirits" (1989:61). The pressure is incredible for our friends to stay within the confines—and thus the tenuous security—of the community. After a profession of faith in Christ, the pressure intensifies further:

> *Fatima was another middle-aged mother who suffered severely under an abusive, senile octogenarian husband. She was granted a divorce by community decree, but the terms stated that if she returned to her own tribe and people, she must leave her four children behind in the care of her in-laws and would lose all rights of parenthood or inheritance. When she came to know Jesus Christ personally, the messages of rejection intensified. Didn't she know now that if she died, she would surely go to hell, as no one would be able to say the prayers, or even wash her body for burial, because she was no longer one of them? Although she had been taught the truth of being absent from the body and present with the Lord, fear gripped her as she pictured her decaying body potentially lying in the streets one day.*
>
> *Then came the end of Ramadan. Most of our neighbors were making their way down to the spring near the mosque to bathe, a sign of being clean after the month-long ordeal of fasting. This ritual, apparently not found among their Middle Eastern brethren, is sometimes explained to outsiders by equating it to the Catholic baptism they see among their neighboring tribes. We have found it to be a time of expressing good cheer and affection to one another, a characteristic uncommon to the other animistic rituals we have observed. Today, there was quite a festive atmosphere when we left the house to go drink coffee with Fatima. As we arrived at her house, we encountered a flurry of activity among her children and several of the neighbor children. "Did you bathe? Were you baptized?" were the questions we heard from the kids and from several neighbors who were popping in the doorway and then out again. The children were in and out and then finally back in, when someone arrived with a jug of water. The young bearer of the water announced that Uncle Ali was the one who had said the special words over this particular water jug. Each child scrambled for the jug to fill their hands*

with a little water so that they could then splash it on the top of their heads and face.

I asked, "What are you doing?" And the child said, "I'm baptizing myself." When I asked what it meant, she impatiently repeated, "It's baptizing! It's baptizing!" into my apparently deaf ears. Shortly after this, our friend and sister in the Lord appeared at the door a bit sheepishly. She had obviously also been down to the spring. She nervously commented, "This is all just for nothing, just so that it's done." The idea was that she needed to keep the peace with the neighbors.

It seemed as though the fear of rejection from the community drove Fatima to join a ceremony that obviously made her spirit feel uncomfortable. The pressures are great!

I believe the gospel can and will touch these women—living under the imminent cloud of rejection—in their longing for the security of real community. But they will only be able to grasp this insofar as we, the image-bearers of the body of Christ, live out real community with them. Such a community must shed its Western style, and we must resist the temptation to whisk the new believer out of her own culture. This need of Muslim women calls us each to a radical personal and team inspection and a willingness to change our own image of community to a transcultural biblical one.

A final story illustrates some extreme results of the pressures of the fear of rejection:

Shrieks and screams and women running past our house to the Sultan's home nearby intruded on the peacefulness of our afternoon snacktime. As we came out to our front porch to investigate, one neighbor broke her stride long enough to explain. The Sultan, our powerful clan leader and village headman, had just announced to his wife, Amina, his desire to marry a second wife. And Amina had gone wild. Our neighbor shook her head disapprovingly, "Doesn't she know that if she agrees, she'll be guaranteed entrance into Paradise one day?" Over the next several months, Amina went from being a competent and articulate schoolteacher to a catatonically depressed nonfunctional being, requiring numerous and expensive "treatments" by spirit healers from far and wide. Within a few months, also, the Sultan secretly married the young girl he had wanted to marry, who was probably already carrying his child at the time of his original announcement to his first wife.

This dramatic episode brings up the common occurrence we observe of acute mental and spiritual decompensation among Muslim women, often as a result of cumulative pressures. In times of intensely felt rejection, blame, or powerlessness, it is common for women to be vulnerable to the acute control of demonic forces. From my observation, I do not believe these episodes are merely consciously planned theatrics to elicit pity; nor are they plain clinical acute psychoses. Although they do appear to involve real demonic power, there also seem to be underlying social and psychological purposes at work. (1) An acute episode of loss of mental and spiritual control could give the woman a way to transfer the heavy weight of blame either to the spirit world or to another in the community, whose careless insult to a spirit has been unveiled by the shaman's diagnostic acumen. (2) It would also cause people of power to gather around her, to alleviate her sense of powerlessness, or (3) it could potentially reverse the sense of rejection, as the community resources are mustered to come to her aid.

Dr. Musk addresses this issue, as he writes of the zar ritual of group demonic possession common in some Middle Eastern cultures:

> Exorcism of the spirits possessing Muslim women in their zar rituals by a Christian missionary bent solely on power encounter would thus leave a large gap in the social and psychological makeup of the women's world. As much attention would need to be paid to the discovery of alternative Christian customs that fulfill women, as to the spiritual confrontation involved in the power encounter itself. Sensitivity to the unspoken needs beneath the surface of the zar ritual will assist the Christian missionary both in addressing the demonic in the Muslim woman's world, and also in providing meaningful alternative expressions for her social, psychological and spiritual longings (1989:269).

Conclusion

We have looked at three of the many spiritual hungers of the Muslim women we love and long to reach. The fear of shame and blame can be met with love and acceptance, as well as an emphasis on the new believer's identity in Christ. The sense of powerlessness needs to be addressed by the tangible reality of a trustworthy and almighty heavenly Father. Finally, we must address the reality of their potential rejection as we build true community among those "living stones" who reflect him who himself was "rejected by men but chosen by God and precious to him" (1 Peter 2:4).

May we be found faithful.

Participants' Discussion

From North Africa—The women I know go directly to God for help. If the situation doesn't change after they have prayed, they will seek help from the spirit world. Then when something happens—and often something dramatic does happen—they give glory to God. They don't look at the answer as having come from a woman's visit to the shrine per se, but it is God's help behind those things.

Arab MBB working in USA—The Arab Muslims I work among think that if they make any mistake, then they are going to "get it" from God. They feel, "How can I trust this monster God? He is all-powerful, but I don't know if he is going to be for me or against me." It is not a safe power; it is a strong power.

From Central Asia—I think that is true. Though they offer him prayers, God can still, at his whim, take it one way or the other. So the person is rendered powerless by God's awesome power. This fatalistic view pushes people toward the occult.

From North Africa—I agree. It's ironic that Islam officially denies any intermediary between God and man; it has such trouble with Christ because of that. Yet they go to *sheikhs* or saints and shrines because they perceive them as being close to God and having power.

From Morocco—One highly educated MBB said that all women have demons because of their greater involvement with folk and occult Islam. A male MBB once told me that many men sincerely believe women have evil spirit powers.

From North Africa—I would say that statement represents their fear of women. They fear the power of women. That's why they try to keep them suppressed. In North Africa, some of this comes from the tales of the past. In the tales of "A Thousand and One Nights," which came out of Persia, what happens? It is the women who caused all the problems for the men, conspired against them and led them into sexual depravity.

Personally, I think that women are powerful. Morocco is a country where magic and the occult run very deep. The men don't know what goes on in that realm. They see their mothers or their sisters doing certain things, and men are afraid that the women are constantly doing magic against them. And often, the women are. When we lived in Morocco, my women friends were always telling me to do this or that to protect myself or make magic.

The author—If a woman has been involved in the occult, what steps should she go through as she becomes a believer? As disciplers of such a woman, what should we do to break those bondages to the demonic world?

From Indonesia—I think the main thing we need to do is to help them understand the love of God. An MBB I'm discipling has taught me that she so yearns for God's love. When I read just a short passage of scripture with her, she will sit and look at it and meditate on it, soaking in the love of God. I see that the love she has for God overcomes a lot of her fear. It is wonderful to see how she experiences the love of God. I myself don't experience the love of God in the way that she does.

From North Africa—There is a time-honored tradition in the Christian church that deals with spiritual bondage among new converts. In the baptismal vows of the early church, converts said, "I renounce Satan and all his ways." However, we never deal with all of these things in a moment's time. In my own life, I have discovered that God gradually released my bondages through a process that kept me going deeper and deeper.

I think, too, we need to discern the difference between true occult activities and superstitions. One requires a power encounter, the other a change of thinking.

The author—How have you been able to teach women to come out from under the cloud of shame?

From Kenya—When I was discipling one believer, I taught her the names that God gave himself when he dealt with the women in the Old Testament. As Easterners, they can identify with the women of the Bible. These stories are rich with images of God's love, forgiveness, trustworthiness and power.

Thinking through the Issues

1. *The author points out that women in Islam are often forced to accept the blame for everything from male promiscuity and irresponsibility to mishaps beyond anyone's control. Have you seen this blame/ shame cycle in women's lives in your own culture? How do the women respond? Does this make them more spiritually hungry or make it more difficult for them to believe? How can they understand the grace of God with this upbringing? What principles or spiritual warfare skills do you believe are most important to teach and model, to deal with the shaming and blaming women experience?*

2. *One highly educated young MBB in Morocco said, "All women have demons." Because of their greater involvement with folk (occult) Islam, many men sincerely believe the women have evil spiritual powers. Can you think of any statement, saying or proverb that reflects this belief in your culture? Do you believe women in Islam tend to seek occult power because of their relative powerlessness in Islam or because of powerlessness against deeper problems such as life, health, and fertility?*

3. *How do women in your area perceive God's power: as one of many powers, as all-powerful but unavailable, or something else? How do they respond if you suggest going straight to God for help?*

4. *The author admonishes us to "live lives of visible dependence on a trustworthy God"—yet often we feel more comfortable depending on scientific medicine, finances, etc. How can you become more actually and visibly dependent on God?*

5. *The author points out that women have powerful roles as healers, midwives, and diviners in folk Islam, then asks, "What are the redeemed roles of women to be in the new believing community?" What is your experience in this? Have you seen believers "retreating into syncretistic animism," only this time with a "Christian flavor?" What do you recommend? What spiritual hunger could be causing this slide back into animism?*

6. *Islam is full of polarization, judgmentalism, and rejection all the way from the international level, through ethnic groups, down to splintered infighting communities or families. In Muslim communities, rejection is a common form of punishment or revenge between families and relatives. The author speaks poignantly of the deep anguish women face when their husbands divorce them or take new wives. Have you seen any significant progress made in dealing with the deep-seated relationship patterns of rejection, or fear of rejection, that can cripple even the believers? What are some keys to victory over rejection?*

For Further Study and Reflection

• *Most animistic or saint-venerating cultures understand the concept of a mediator between the spirit world and us. This is also true in folk Islam. Before they even understand the full mission of Christ (salvation), which may not speak to a current felt need, how can you teach them that Jesus can give them direct access to the Supreme God? In what ways could Jesus replace the local spirit healers or*

Islamic saints? How can we avoid becoming ourselves the replacement for spirit healers in the lives of MBBs?

- *In centuries past, the Catholic Church exchanged a number of pagan rituals for Christian ones, such as exchanging Christmas for Saturnalia (winter solstice), honoring the resurrection of Christ instead of celebrating spring fertility rites, and even building their churches over ancient shrines to interfere with continued pagan practices. The author quotes Dr. Musk as saying we need to not merely exorcise demonic rituals but also fill the gap left by the "discovery of alternative Christian customs." However, some Christians denounce even wearing Hawaiian leis because in centuries past they were used to ward off evil spirits. What biblical passages speak to these issues? Have you seen successful implementation of Dr. Musk's ideas in a Muslim or folk Islamic setting? Who would decide what is irredeemably evil, what can be cleansed and used for God's purposes, and what needs to be replaced with completely new rituals? Who would develop these new alternative Christian customs? How can we help keep these new traditions from taking on largely non-Christian meanings or roles?*

SECTION 2

Muslim Background Believers

Why Muslim Women Come to Christ

Miriam Adeney

There are all sorts of reasons why Muslim women come to the Lord Jesus Christ. Some come when they read the gospel story. Others come because in visions or dreams they see Jesus. Others, during a struggle with demons or spirits, find that the name of Jesus brings liberation and help. Some have been abused in dysfunctional relationships. Others have been schooled in the ideals of righteousness, and long for justice in their society. They find the power for this in the Lord Jesus. Some come because of Christ's affirmation of women. Some who have lived promiscuously cry out for a moral foundation for their own lives. Others fear death, and long for assurance of paradise. Two women whom I have interviewed hungered almost single-mindedly for God from their earliest childhood. Many come because their family has decided jointly to follow the Lord Jesus Christ.

Who are Muslim women? Clearly they differ according to their national or ethnic identity. Beyond national ties, a woman's concerns also are shaped by her role in the life cycle, her economic situation, her ideological community and her personality.

At different points in the life cycle, women dream different dreams and feel different needs. Consider ...

- A daughter in her father's house
- A single professional woman sharing an apartment with other young women
- A married mother

Miriam Adeney, Ph.D., is an Associate Professor of Missions and Cross Cultural Communications at Seattle Pacific University. This article is excerpted from her forthcoming book, *Hagar's Daughters: Ministries with Muslim Women.*

- A childless married woman
- A divorced mother, head of household
- A widowed grandmother living in her son's household

Sometimes knowing a woman's role in the life cycle may be even more important than knowing her nationality.

Economically, four of the ten richest countries in the world are Arab. Yet in other Arab communities, poverty may be cruel. Certainly among the Muslims of South Asia are many malnourished women, side by side with millionaires. Some Muslim women have Ph.D.s and big stock portfolios. Others are illiterate. Some rich women move regularly between homes in Arabia, France, London, and the U.S. These are not necessarily "liberated" women. Some of the very rich may not be allowed to drive cars or to go out without a male companion or a veil.

As for religion, many Muslim women know little about Islamic doctrines and theology. They resort to folk religion, shrines, sacrifices, amulets, divination, and spirit possession as often as they turn to Muslim institutions. Others are well grounded in the teachings of the faith. Some belong to radical fundamentalist sisterhoods. For others, political activism in solidarity with other Muslims or co-nationals is what counts, rather than religious activism.

Even in a simple village, some women may specialize as herbalists, others as textile weavers, others as food dryers, others as cheese makers, others as perfumists, others as Quranic reciters, others as musicians, others as occult women, and others as land speculators.

Finally, each woman has a distinct personality, and distinct life experiences and opportunities.

Why do such women come to Christ? Muslim women are human beings, and their motives are complex. Several milestones recur on these journeys, however. We will consider five ...

- Scripture
- Power encounters
- The love of Christians
- Sex and beauty issues
- Social justice issues

No disrespect for Islam is intended when we write about Muslim women coming to Christ. Spending time with Muslims, I have been blessed by their high concept of the nature of God. Their prayerful life. Their emphasis on community, their insistence that faith must be expressed in the public sector. Their concern for ethics in society. Islam reminds us of our Creator.

And yet, in the end, if a faith doesn't lead to God in Christ, it misses something right at the core. In Christ, God visited this planet in human form. In Christ's death, God entered into human pain. In Christ's resurrection, God generated the power for new beginnings. God, whom the Muslims call "the merciful and compassionate," demonstrates those qualities of mercy and compassion most of all in Christ. This is why Muslim women come to Christ. Through Christ, the God whom they knew incompletely and from afar becomes their personal Father.

Scripture Brings Muslim Women to the Lord Jesus

Latifa's Story

Latifa's family were ordinary Arab Muslims. But she was not. Large, quick-thinking, managerial, Latifa was anything but ordinary. She aimed for excellence. As a child, she had longed to fast like her parents. Proudly she had abstained from food, even if just for a few hours. As she had grown older and had imbibed modern French culture, her ideas of excellence had broadened considerably. By the time she was a self-supporting schoolteacher, she considered herself a freethinker within Islam. She was not ashamed to sit in cafés drinking with men. She had an apartment of her own. Although both nominally and by deep conviction a Muslim, she welcomed new ideas.

Among Latifa's fellow teachers were two foreigners. Zach was American and Daphne was British. Passionately anti-Christian, Daphne warned Latifa, "Watch out for Zach! He's a missionary in disguise."

"How could that be? Why, what does he hope to accomplish?" Latifa wondered.

"He wants to change your minds. Your culture," Daphne snorted.

That made Latifa mad. She was sick of colonization. First it was political. Then it was economic. Now it was religious. Who do these people think they are? she fumed. What right do they have to overrun us?

To combat the enemy, Latifa invited herself to a Bible discussion at Zach's place. There she met his family, Maria, Susan, and David, and was charmed. Summer vacation arrived, and Latifa found herself going to parks with the foreign family. They played sports and games. They helped her practice speaking English. The children's antics amused her. Over the course of the summer, as Zach and Maria had to make various decisions, they were transparent. So Latifa got an inside view of the way they operated. It seemed to her that something extra was present in everything they did.

When they prayed in the name of Jesus, though, Latifa hated that. "It was against my identity," she says. "It reminded me that I was there to attack them—whereas really I was having fun!"

In the fall they started a Bible study on Christian ethics. This intrigued Latifa. "What do Christians actually think about anger, forgiveness, or holding a grudge?" she wondered. "I accepted a Bible, because I wasn't going to be stupid and not know what was in that book," she admits.

At first she just looked up the references recommended for each topic of study. Then she got hooked and began to read the Bible from cover to cover.

Consistency was what she found, both in Jesus and in Zach and Maria. "That is rare in my world," she comments. "That started my problem. This guy Jesus was saying things I admired. The teaching was beautiful. But you couldn't have that and throw out the teacher."

Soon her conscience began to nag: "If this is true, you ought to try it."

"I felt sick," she says. "Before I was even awake, Christ was in my mind. The Bible attracted me so much. At the same time, I loved the Quran. The chanting of the Quran was so beautiful. Sometimes I'd hear it on the radio and my whole being would go into turmoil."

Every day when she prayed as a Muslim, she would recite the Quranic words:

Show me the way.

Don't let me be among those who are lost

because of the blindness of their hearts.

One day she gritted her teeth and added, "Okay. Show me. If Jesus Christ is the true way, show me."

Not long after that, Latifa came home one afternoon to find a note under her door:

Come to the beach with us tomorrow. We're going to have a Christian communion service. This is something you will want to see. We'll stop by at 10:00.
—Zach and Maria

But she already had an invitation to go to the beach with some Arab friends. What to do?

She was tempted to break the first date and go with Zach and Maria. They and their Christian fellowship had become very important in her life. Should she go with them? Or should she go with her other friends? She couldn't decide.

"I'm tired," she shrugged. "I'm going to bed. Whoever comes first I'll go with. Anyway, one way or the other, I'll get to the beach."

The next morning both parties arrived at her door at exactly the same time.

"God didn't make it easy," she comments. "God was saying, 'Don't let circumstances decide for you. Always follow me.'"

Latifa decided to go with the Christians. "Do you mind?" She asked her Arab friends. They acquiesced amiably and went on their way. She turned to Zach and Maria and Susan and David, and experienced a rush of great joy. But why? A beach is just a beach, after all.

Once at the sea, they swam. They played ball. Finally they began their communion service. Latifa was asked to read aloud the traditional verses from 1 Corinthians 11:

The Lord Jesus, on the night he was betrayed, took bread, and when he had given thanks, he broke it and said, "This is my body, which is for you; do this in remembrance of me." In the same way, after supper he took the cup, saying, "This cup is the new covenant in my blood; do this, whenever you drink it, in remembrance of me." For whenever you eat this bread and drink this cup, you proclaim the Lord's death until he comes.

"As I was reading," Latifa recalls, "I was in the Spirit. I was transferred to the upper room. I could see Christ. I could hear Christ. I could sense him saying, 'This is my body, broken for you.'

"I don't know how I looked. Everybody disappeared. Time stopped. I was there with Christ, with the awesome presence of his holiness.

"I started looking at my life with his eyes. Suddenly my life, with which I'd been content, looked terribly dirty. I wanted to run away. Then I heard him say, 'Eat. I came not for you to run away, but on the contrary for you to come close to me.'"

Latifa began to cry, a deep, cleansing cry. "Joy replaced everything I felt was wrong," she says. "At that time I knew all my questions about the Trinity had no meaning because I had met Jesus personally."

All that happened nearly twenty years ago. Today Latifa is the busy mother of several children. As well as being a public schoolteacher, she actively disciples others in the small Christian fellowship.

"I am a teacher," she says, "so I teach new believers how to read the Bible." She also visits people in her country who respond to Christian radio broadcasts beamed from overseas.

Scripture brings Muslim women to the Lord Jesus. On a beach two decades ago, scripture spoke to Latifa. And she discovered that the ocean of God's grace in Jesus Christ can touch any of us—even a Muslim woman—at any point on earth.

Power Encounters Bring Muslim Women to the Lord Jesus

Suna's Story

Suna and Ali, husband and wife, came to Christ together. They were students from Turkey studying in the U.S. Competent and cosmopolitan, Ali and Suna made friends easily. But when Suna's mother died, she fell into a pit of grief. "Why did I have to be so far away?" she cried.

As the weeks passed, Ali wondered what to do.

Suna continued to mope. "If only I could have been there. If only I could talk to her even now. Oh my mother—"

One day, browsing through the Seattle public library, Ali stumbled upon a book, *How to Contact Dead Souls*. Aha! Was there any possibility that Suna could communicate with her mother, even though her mother had passed on? Ali settled into a chair by a window, and began to read.

"Get a ouija board ... " was one of the first pieces of advice.

"Right. That I understand," Ali nodded. When he left the library, he had embarked on a hunt for that occult tool.

No doubt about it, the ouija board made a difference. They asked questions, and they got answers. A spirit guide became their personal consultant. On the other hand, as time passed, the answers and the experience became more unsettling. In fact, they weren't sleeping well. They didn't have anymore appetite. And Suna began to get strange messages, like one telling her to hit Ali over the head with a tennis racket.

Time to draw the line, Ali decided. But how? Now that they had opened Pandora's box, how could they close it? Ali was not trained in research for nothing. He located the author of the volume, called him up, and described their experience. "We bought your book, followed your advice, and now look what's happened. So what do we do?"

"Contact your religious leader," the author yawned, and hung up.

"Much help that was," Ali fumed, as he put down the receiver. "Our religious leader is twelve thousand miles away."

Still, something had to be done. A religious leader. Hmm. Wait. Suna attended a TM group occasionally, as kind of an exercise experience. In a pinch, maybe the TM leader could function as a religious leader?

But when asked, the TM leader demurred. "Sounds to me like a demon has entered Suna's body. And when that happens, frankly, there's nothing you can do."

"That's not true!" Ali retorted. "I've seen The Exorcist movie, and I know that Christians can get demons out of bodies!"

Nettled, the TM leader agreed to try. He took the pair to the Unity church downtown. Here they were directed to a local Hindu temple where they paid their money and received mantras and ritual instructions. Back home, as they recited the mantras and performed the rituals, they experienced some relief. They were able to sleep and eat more normally, and the weird messages decreased.

"Still, this is no way for civilized, god-fearing people to live," Ali grimaced. "As a one-time crisis solution, okay. As a continuing lifestyle, it's bondage." Periodically they had to return to the Hindu temple to get recharged. "This can't go on," Ali finally decided. "Enough is enough. We've got to go to the Christians. We've tried everything else. There's no other alternative."

For years Ali and Suna had known Christians as friends, students and international ministry workers at the university. They had heard the gospel. They had never felt any need for it, however. Now, when they approached their Christian friends with their dilemma, they knew what they were getting into. They were prepared.

"Well, if you want us to pray for deliverance from this demonic oppression, you must open yourselves first to the lordship of Jesus." That was what Ali heard. Whether the international ministers were in fact this stark in their presentation, Ali was desperate for action and set to act decisively.

"Right. We're ready," he nodded.

So the couple prayed to receive Christ as personal Lord and Savior.

Raising his head, Ali said briskly, "Right. Now what about the exorcism?"

Confused glances darted around the room. These international student ministers didn't know much about exorcisms. Still, they believed in the Holy Spirit. So they pulled themselves together and timidly began to pray. It took some months, and help from some Pentecostals, but Ali and Suna were delivered completely. They learned to rebuke in each other any openness to powers other than the Lord Jesus. Today, Ali is a seminary-trained ordained pastor in a Presbyterian church. And although up to this point, during seven years of marriage, they had had no children, within the next five years God gave them three lovely babies.

"Suna, what were you thinking while all this was going on?" I asked her one day.

"I prayed to receive Christ because my husband told me to," this elegant, college-educated woman replied. Then she added, "But after that, I decided I should study what we had gotten ourselves into. So I began to read the Bible seriously. Actually, I had read part of it back in Turkey in an English literature class. Now I began to study the Bible. I had the time. I wasn't enrolled in classes. So for several hours every day, I read the Bible and meditated on it."

"What happened then?"

"One night I had a dream," Suna remembered. "I was in a fast-flowing sewer. I scrambled to get out. But the more I clawed for a handhold, the more I was sucked down. Suddenly a great strong hand came out of nowhere and lifted me up, and set me on solid ground. I stood in front of a glorious high throne. The Lord Jesus sat on the throne."

"I've taken you out of a filthy place. What are you going to do now?" the Lord Jesus said to Suna.

"I'm going to read the Bible, and teach the Bible," Suna answered.

In mothers' groups, in church classes, with international students, and with her own children, that is what Suna has done.

Through a power encounter, she has been freed to live for the Lord.

Loving Christians Bring Muslim Women to the Lord Jesus

Esmat's Story

Looking up at the stars, Esmat lay on the board sleeping platform that her family always placed over the garden pond on the hottest nights of the year. Three year old Naqi snuggled close. For how much longer? Thumb in mouth, he lay content and secure. How would he sleep when his father took Naqi to his new wife's home? Would Naqi revert to wetting the mattress again? What would his stepmother do? Legally his father had the right to take Naqi. But oh, it was intolerable!

Esmat fled her country, slipping Naqi out with her. They made their way to the U.S. with little more than the clothes on their backs. No family, no networks, no money. New Iranian acquaintances snubbed her when they learned of her divorce. So did old friends.

It was in a Presbyterian church in San Mateo that Esmat stumbled upon people who cared for her alone. Although she was proud of being a Muslim, and insisted on it for a long time, there came a day when she said, "I don't care about doctrines, about God, Christ, heaven or hell. Just give me what is in these people. They care about me and they care about God. I want to be like them." Today Esmat radiates competence and peace. Far from looking lost or lonely, Esmat looks like a woman who knows where she is going, and who knows that she is loved.

A retired man was the first to reach out to Esmat. They met in a park a few months after she arrived in the U.S.

Irving was 82. He played with Naqi, and tried to talk with Esmat. He invited her to church. She didn't understand him.

Six months later Esmat happened to be walking down the street past Irving's church. For some reason, in the middle of the service Irving got up and came out onto the front steps. He saw Esmat, remembered her, and called out.

"Esmat!"

She was startled. Who was this who knew her name? She had forgotten him. When he reminded her of their time in the park, she stepped into the church out of politeness, and stayed for about ten minutes. That was an appropriate amount of time to spend in the worship service, she thought.

Somewhat to her surprise, however, she found herself back at the church the next Sunday. Well, she told herself, she was lonely. The church seemed to be a clean, well-lighted, warm and happy place. She enjoyed being with all the nice people there.

She drew clear boundaries, though. "I'm a Muslim," she smiled as she shook the pastor's hand. "I come to church only to learn English."

"Excellent!" he exclaimed. "This is a fine place to improve your English. Let us know how we can help."

Orville and Margaret, retired missionaries in their 70s, took her under their wing. When Naqi got chickenpox, Margaret stayed with him for a whole week while Esmat worked. Frequently Orville would sit with Esmat while she read the Bible aloud. He critiqued her pronunciation, and explained the things that she did not understand.

One sentence she understood clearly from a Sunday sermon was, "God is love." That shook her up. Yes, God is Creator and Judge, omnipotent and holy—but loving?

Some things the church people did puzzled Esmat. Single women like herself asked for prayer and counsel about their dates and romances. To her, they seemed to view themselves as sex objects. Other church people drank alcohol. Didn't they have respect for their physical bodies? Still, Esmat loved the church and the Bible readings more than she would admit.

"Don't forget that I'm a Muslim," she would remind her fellow parishioners.

Nobody objected. Nobody criticized her. During Bible studies and fellowship meetings, she would offer her perspective: "The Quran says this——" or "Islam teaches that——."

"That provides some helpful insights, doesn't it?" her fellow discussants would respond.

Margaret invited Esmat to everything going on at church, and always volunteered to take care of Naqi. Esmat felt so at home. Yet as she increasingly glimpsed Jesus Christ as Lord of the Universe, she became increasingly uncomfortable. She compares her pilgrimage to going through the birth canal. The more Esmat learned, the more squeezed she felt. "It is hell," she says now, looking back, "from the time when a person starts to believe until the time of their decision." For effective outreach, then, we need to respect people's beliefs and give them time and space, she counsels.

One night Esmat had a dream. Earlier that day, a brother had prayed for her, with beautiful words and kind eyes. "Why can't the mullahs' eyes back home look like that?" she asked herself as she went home. Why couldn't they convey that kind of love? That night she dreamt she was in Iran, going down the street dressed in her chador (head covering). She had to go through a narrow passage lined by rows of armed guards on both sides. They were like walls hemming her in. "I want to be free!" she cried to the Lord. At once the walls fell down, and the face of the man who had prayed for her that day showed through the broken wall.

During this period Esmat attended a communion service.

"This table is for people who want to be healed," the pastor said. "Jesus came for the healing of the brokenhearted. He died for the healing of the nations. He burst out of the category of death, rising to life again, in order to bring us to health. Our wholeness is in him."

Esmat knew she was a walking wounded case. She knew she hurt. She wanted to be healed. She began to cry. Then she felt something special in that room. She went forward to the table, and knelt down.

When she touched the table, the warmth of God filled her. The pastor prayed for her.

Later she would trace a new integration and sense of wholeness and well-being to that therapeutic incident.

But the God she had known so far in her life was a lawgiver and judge. Who was this God who healed?

Some time later, she was attending a prayer meeting. Suddenly she opened her eyes, and looked around. "What am I doing here?" she asked herself. "These aren't my people. This isn't my religion."

"Someone here is not trusting God," said a man suddenly.

Esmat was pierced. God had spoken to her. She felt a weight and began to cry. As she did, it seemed that a man came and touched her and fell down alongside her.

"I'm so tired. I'm in hell," Esmat said to God. "Who am I? Where should I go?"

A verse flashed into her memory: "Jesus said … 'I am the way, the truth, and the life; No one comes to the father except by me.'"

Esmat fought it. She didn't want to admit that something was changing her. It took her a year to make a decision for Christ. When she found herself following Christ and experiencing his transforming presence, it took some time before she could acknowledge this, even to herself. She didn't want to be a Christian. But she found that the only peace she experienced came through the church and nowhere else.

When Esmat was a Muslim, God seemed very strict, always watching what she did wrong. When she met God through Christ, he changed from a strict master to a loving, constant Father. Esmat still gets lonely and tired, weighed down with all the decisions facing a single mother in a strange land. But, she says, when she feels most like a leper, when no one wants to get close, God comes and touches her sores. This gives her the confidence that she radiates today. Because Christians loved her, Esmat has come to the Lord Jesus.

Sex and Beauty Bring Muslim Women to the Lord Jesus

Zaide's Story

Zaide was a Muslim who heard God through a story about sex—one of the strangest in scripture.

Women in traditional Arab families seem to talk about sex quite a lot. After all, attracting and keeping a man's attention is the major road to success. Throughout the Muslim world, breeding and birthing are frequent and focal activities. So, whether the focus is attractive appearance or the ability to bear sons, sex matters.

Surprisingly, sex leads to many bridges for talking about the Lord Jesus. Take beauty, for example. What is true beauty? Maidenly beauty? Matronly beauty? Beauty if you are infertile? The theme of beauty is rich in scripture. Many texts may be a basis for meditation and discussion.

Sex leads to children, and children are a big bridge. How do we raise these children to be moral and godly people in the modern world? This is the heart cry of many sincere Muslim families. Child discipline, child moral training, child health, family planning, and even prayer versus distribution of condoms in schools may be points of contact.

God's attitude to a woman's body is another bridge. In Islam, women are polluted and polluting. All bodily processes which secrete substances are unclean. Men must wash ceremonially after urinating, defecating, ejaculating semen, or touching something ritually unclean. Women do more: We menstruate, give birth, suckle infants, and clean up children's messes. Menstruating women cannot pray. God will not hear them. Pregnant and nursing women do not fast. Given a high birth rate, a woman may miss fasts for years. But every missed prayer and fast adds to a person's spiritual indebtedness. All in all, then, women are always "behind" spiritually. And "this required abstention from worship is a proof of their deficiency in faith," according to a saying attributed to the prophet Muhammad. Even though women may try to "make up" days of prayer and days of fasting, they never really catch up with what God requires.

Furthermore, women are passionate, not reasonable. Thus women ensnare men, incite men to lust, and distract men from reason and righteousness. For this reason, women in Morocco often are called a "rope of Satan" (*hbel shitan*). Naturally, then, a woman's testimony is worth only half a man's. And a woman's relationship with God is shaky.

But Jesus reached out his hand to a woman who had been bleeding steadily for twelve years (Luke 8). What a breath of fresh air it is for a wounded Muslim woman to hear this. How many need this good news.

Consider Zaide. Graduating with honors from the university, Zaide went on to get a job in national radio. From there she went on to do TV and advertising, and eventually became national marketing director for some large companies. She made a great deal of money. Also, in her early years, when she was at the university and soon after, she was popular as a singer and performer. She got caught up in music, clothes, dancing, dating, and entertainment.

A young man returned from the U.S. with an M.A. in theater.

Soon he was head of a major theater group. Jorum was handsome, he was a good dancer, he knew all about music. He strutted around, he flirted outrageously, he was radical, he tasted everything. Zaide was a person hungry for knowledge and hungry for experience. They began to date.

"Why won't you go all the way with me?" he pressed her.

"Let's wait for marriage," she said.

"Ha! You put on a façade that you're so sophisticated, but really you're not," he taunted her.

So they had sex. Then he began to abuse her. Then she got pregnant. He sent her to a doctor to get an abortion. The doctor was incompetent: he gave her injection after injection, but nothing happened. Eventually, because of personal pressure and even political pressure, Jorum married her. The baby was born prematurely, weighing four and a half pounds.

Zaide tried to be a good wife, but Jorum would bring friends home to gamble and if things weren't just right he would swear at her: "You bloody——, why don't we have more rice?"

At night he would dress up and go out to night clubs.

"Can't we spend some time together, Jorum?" she would ask.

"I'm going out, and you're not coming with me," he would strut. "If you want to go out and find your own fun, do it. But not with me."

One night she went into the backyard, and looked at the stars, and clenched her fists, and said, "I will have my way. I will avenge myself."

Right after that she got a better job, and was sent to London to do a course in TV production. There many men wanted to sleep with her. She had her pick. With nothing to look forward to in marriage, she lived loosely. Once back home, loveless or not, the marriage produced another child.

Then she fell in love with one of her husband's chief rivals, one of the leading poets in the Muslim world. She abandoned her husband and her children, and moved in with Sharif. They had a daughter.

Zaide loved Sharif, and thought he loved her. Still, he had a wife and they continued to have children. After a time she noticed that although she networked Sharif with important international business contacts, he didn't return the favor.

Zaide had lived with Sharif for eight years when an hour-long TV documentary on his life was produced. Everybody who figured importantly in his story was interviewed—even their daughter. But she was omitted. "It would not look good for him," the producer told her.

She was heartbroken. "Where is the woman who gave birth to your daughter? Where is the woman who was interrogated by the police because of a printing of your poems? Where is the woman who paid for the printing?" Zaide felt she had given Sharif everything, even her good name. Yet she was just a small part of his life, not even important enough to be interviewed. If not for her little girl, the last shred of reason for living seemed to be gone.

At one point during this period, Zaide became quite religious. She started wearing the veil, praying five times a day, fasting, and participating with an activist Muslim women's group. This did not give her a sense of meaning, however. She went through the motions hollowly.

"I just went through my day making money, writing film scripts, but I was a shell."

One day she ran into a fellow journalist she had known years earlier, when they were both starting out. As they talked, his peace impressed her. "Bob, what's happening in your life these days?" she asked. "You look so relaxed."

"Well, to be honest, I'm involved in a Bible study group. And on the weekends I go to prisons. I talk to the drug addicts and other prisoners there. I get a lot of fulfillment out of that," he answered.

"A Bible study!" she exclaimed. "I haven't seen a Bible in thirty years."

"I'll find you one," he said.

A few days later, she came into her office. There were all her secretaries, looking at her strangely. "Ma'am, Mr. Yu put something on your desk," one said.

There was a Bible. Of course the secretaries were thinking, "What's this Muslim doing with a Bible?"

"How kind of him to bring me this book," she thought. "It's time for prayers, but I think I'll take this time to just read the Bible." She picked up the Bible, which she hadn't handled for thirty years, and opened it up at random to the book of Hosea, where she read:

> Rebuke your mother, rebuke her, for she is not my wife and I am not her husband. Let her remove the adulterous look from her face and the unfaithfulness from between her breasts. Otherwise I will strip her naked and make her as bare as on the day she was born; I will make her like a desert, turn her into a parched land, and slay her with thirst. I will not show my love to her children, because they are the children of adultery. Their mother has been unfaithful and has conceived them in disgrace.

She said, "I will go after my lovers, who give me my food and my water, my wool and my linen, my oil and my drink" (Hos. 2:2-5).

Zaide looked up from her reading. "This is for me," she said, amazed. "My children were conceived this way. I abandoned my children. I chased after men. And I am a desert."

Hosea is the strange story of a godly man whose wife becomes a prostitute. He goes after her, at God's direction, and loves her back. They live a metaphor of God and his people. God's people were faithless, but God went after them, and loved them back. That is what Zaide discovered when she read on. So many promises—

> I will heal their waywardness and love them freely. I will be like the dew to Israel; she will blossom like a lily. Like a tree of cedar she will send down her roots; her shoots will grow. Her splendor will be like an olive tree, her fragrance like a cedar. Men will dwell again in her shade. She will flourish like the grain. She will blossom like a vine, and her fame will be like the wine from heaven (Hos. 14:4-7).

Zaide looked up. "In all my relationships with men, no man ever gave me an oath like this," she said. And she came to the Lord Jesus Christ.

That was ten years ago. Since then, all her children have chosen to live with her. One has come to the Lord. Zaide has taken formal Bible training, and is using her media experience to witness to people of several cultures.

Social Justice Brings Muslim Women to the Lord Jesus

Irin's Story

For some women, it is not gender but justice that is the issue. If we care for communities, for equality of opportunity, for freedom from poverty and oppression, we can affirm these women's struggles. Swallowing our pride, sometimes we may need to apologize for the Crusades, for Western colonial domination of their country, or for porno videos exported from the West today—all unwarranted intrusions from so-called Christian nations.

Muslim women aflame for social justice constitute an unreached people. No Christians have focused on them, to my knowledge. Yet we share a common longing that "justice may flow down like a river, and righteousness like an ever flowing stream" (Amos 5:24).

Consider Irin, for example.

Stepping across the bathroom threshold, Irin murmured a prayer as she always did when entering a polluted area. She poured out water and picked up her washcloth. Morning mist scarved the hills. Roosters competed in a crowing contest. Hens toddled out to scratch the ground. Then, as Irin wiped her face, lines from the secular poetry in yesterday's Indonesian Literature class drifted unbidden into her mind.

Disgusted, Irin threw down her face cloth. "Why do my countrymen fail to keep themselves close to God? Allahu Akbar, God is most great," she muttered.

"Irin!"

"Coming, Mother—"

"Take your grandfather his morning tea."

Not only her grandfather but two of his former students lounged on the front porch surrounded by red hibiscus. He at least kept the true faith in this forest of ignorance that was Indonesia. Through all his years of Quranic teaching, he had protected the Divine Law against the pagan crudities of traditional custom. He had earned the respect that surrounded him now.

Irin was determined to follow in his steps. Playful though she might look in her tight wraparound sarong skirt and colorful headscarf framing a pretty face, Irin was serious and focused. She intended to serve God and her country through some position of leadership. Southeast Asian women always have taken a lot of community responsibility. Irin determined to use all her powers to increase the honor of Allah in Indonesia.

As a high school senior, Irin was chosen regional secretary of the Muslim Students Movement. Following graduation, she entered law school. One term she had a course in Islamic law.

"What other kinds of ethical bases for law are there?" she wondered aloud.

"Christian law. Marxist law—," her friend Sita suggested.

"It would be fun to compare them, to prove what a superior ethical code for modern people Islam is," Irin mused. "Remember our speaker at the prayer meeting last week? Remember how he said the Quran contains the core of all modern thought?"

"Right. Hygiene, medicine, chemistry, physics, astronomy—all the necessary rules are in the Quran."

"So, without the Quran, how can Christian or Marxist law work?" Irin wondered.

"Well, if you want to compare them, I have a Bible, as it happens, " Sita shrugged.

"Can I borrow it?" Irin asked.

With a Bible on loan, Irin began a formidable task. Struggling through the complexities of Leviticus and Romans, she noted down comparisons between Muslim and Christian law.

This was not her first brush with Christianity. In high school she had had a friend named Mary.

"Why don't you fast?" Irin had asked with great surprise when she found that Mary was eating right through Ramadan.

"My family's Catholic," Mary explained.

What was Catholic? Not the true faith, Irin soon learned. But Mary remained a friend. One week Irin asked, "Your day of worship is what—Sunday? Could I, do you think, go to worship with you once?"

They did go to church together. But, already a budding lawyer, Irin's aim was not reverence. She determined to find weaknesses in Christianity so she could prove how false it was, and could poke holes in it.

Now, with the Bible in her lap, her aim was the same. Imagine her surprise, then, as the chapters unrolled. "Abraham is a great man of faith and our spiritual father," she read. "Yes. Ishmael is the 'seed of Abraham' in which the world is to be blessed, and the forerunner of the prophets Jacob, Joseph, David, Jesus—Wait. What's this? Isaac? Isaac is the ancestor of all our Quranic prophets? No. It couldn't be." And yet, with Irin's honest respect for evidence, she couldn't alter the record to suit her preferences ...

How about the genealogy of the Prophet Muhammad? He was descended from Ishmael, she had been taught. Sadly, her Bible study didn't show this. Ishmael's descendents simply didn't count for much in the prophetic line ...

As she continued reading, she was struck by the prayers. Miriam's prayer. Hannah's prayer. David's prayers. Daniel's. Paul's. Irin was a woman of prayer, five times a day. But how different these biblical conversations with God were from hers.

"Our Muslim prayer words are all the same," she mused. "But human needs and problems vary from time to time and from person to person ..."

"And why—," she cried out in her heart,— "why must I pray in Arabic, which I don't really understand, which I've learned by rote?—and which most Indonesians comprehend even less? Why can't we pour out our hearts fully, like these holy people in the Bible?"

"Never mind," she told herself. She returned the Bible and shelved her interest in comparative law. "Even though Christianity may be more attractive than you'd expected, it would be impossible for you to leave your Islamic faith," she muttered.

Idul Fitri burst upon Irin's community, that great festival at the end of the Ramadan fast, a holiday as crucial as Christmas in the West. There were colorful new sarongs for everybody in the family. Coconut-and-rice candies. Six kinds of curry. Mass prayers at dawn in the town square. Gifts handed out to the poor. Parties. Visits from long-absent relatives.

At the heart of the activities, everybody asks forgiveness from his superiors. The worker begs pardon from his boss, going to the boss' home and being received with tea and snacks. The student begs pardon from his former teacher, the cured patient from the traditional healer. The child begs pardon from his parents.

Bowing to her parents and grandparents, Irin thought wretchedly, "You received the faith of Islam from your ancestors. There is no one among your folks who is not Muslim. You can never leave."

Four years passed. Irin was striding toward graduation and a job with the government. Then she met Subadjo, a fellow student who loved Jesus.

Subadjo could argue apologetics. Sometimes mystically inclined students criticized Irin's conservative Islam. "Pilgrimage to Mecca! How misguided! What a waste!" one of them mocked. "The real holy place is within a person, in his inner spirit. I make my pilgrimage to that."

Subadjo cut the foundations from that argument. "How can inner mysticism provide a demonstrable basis for social ethics? If people just do what feels good—if they believe whatever feels harmonious—with reason thrown out the window, we're a prey to clever manipulators—"

Subadjo's realism and care for society attracted Irin. But Subadjo did more than talk. His denomination had an arm that pioneered economic self-help in poor communities. They had small outreaches to the handicapped and even to prostitutes. Quite a remarkable percentage of Indonesia's government and professional people had been Christians, Irin mused. Christian doctors and nurses had lived compassionate lives throughout the islands. So had Christian teachers. Christians edited newspapers, wrote poetry, painted. Christian lawyers had helped shape the Constitution. Among other things, these fledgling politicians had deleted seven words in an early Constitutional draft which would have made Islam the state religion. Irin didn't know about that. But she did see Christians serving society. Subadjo was one of these socially concerned citizens. He didn't see people merely as projects, however. In his everyday encounters, love bubbled out.

For quite a while, Irin watched Subadjo's life. Finally she went out and bought a Bible for herself, and started to read once more.

Jesus' teachings, so full of love, drew her.

Often Irin had prayed the Quranic verse, "Oh God, show me your straight and true way."

One afternoon she read the words of Jesus in John 14:6, "I am the way, the truth, and the life."

That was it.

Grandfather, heritage—all were superseded. When God points the way, you go: Irin became a Christian. She entered government service in 1966, where she worked until 1974, when she left for full-time Christian work as an administrator and editor for a large and lively church denomination. As a young girl and as a law student, Irin had hoped to serve her society, to work for a set of values that would revitalize her culture. Today, through her writing, speaking, and directing, she does just that. The virtues of thrift, hard work, efficient use of time, individual effort, and sound business methods which Irin learned in her serious Muslim family now are put to use in the service of the Lord Jesus Christ.

Unfortunately Irin isn't as typical as she should be. A leading Indonesian churchman confesses, "The Church is more regressed than the rest of the society when it comes to women's leadership. We haven't thought about how Christian women can be used fully to the glory of God."

But Irin, in the tradition of Indonesian women leaders through the centuries, serves God and her country from a position of strength.

Words and Ways to Bless

Scripture, power encounters, and loving friendships: These are probably the three main ways that Muslim women are drawn to the Lord Jesus. Beauty/sex and social justice issues are the paths for some women. But there are many more ways to build bridges:

- visiting
- prayer
- song
- rituals
- thanksgiving services
- books, videos, cassettes, storytelling, proverbs
- health care, ESL, micro enterprise development
- sewing or craft groups
- classes—aerobics, parenting, beauty, fashion, history and culture, gardening, conflict resolution

More specifically, many topics can be springboards for talking about the Lord Jesus. For example:

- Jesus' story
- earthy biblical symbols—bread, water
- women in scripture
- Psalms, Proverbs, parables, Bible narrative
- God's names, Jesus' names
- women of history and today
- charms
- veil
- fasting
- creed
- submission
- dreams
- sacrifice feasts, especially Abraham's
- fulfilled singleness
- pornographic videos: what Christians think about sex
- child-raising
- family planning
- solving family conflicts
- community social ethics

- God's creation, ecology
- cultures: God-given creativity and sinful exploitation
- repentance for Western sins
- Christ versus Christians
- forgiveness
- confidence
- love
- release from anger
- power to do right

A question remains: Can women be evangelized and discipled just like men? Should women's evangelism be subsumed under men's? The answer is: sometimes. How beautiful it is when a household follows Jesus together. This is natural and appropriate in cultures where nearly all important decisions are made corporately.

Unfortunately, Islam so resists the Lordship of Jesus that even if a kin group initially hears the gospel together, members usually tend to hold each other back from moving toward conversion. Individual seekers then must continue to pursue truth privately.

Sometimes the opportunities to go to women, or the personnel to serve them, appear before there are resources to reach men. And sometimes the abuses women have suffered, or alternatively the richness of women's worlds, call for a more gender-sensitive approach.

The Sword of Christ: Muslim Women Make a Costly Commitment

B. Linda Smith

I have lived in a Muslim land for twelve years and women here have become some of my dearest friends. As sisters in Christ, we've talked and prayed into the night, cooked together, laughed together and shared our common suffering.

But women who have come out of Islam have been pierced by the sword of Christ. Jesus warned, "Do not suppose that I have come to bring peace to the earth. I did not come to bring peace, but a sword. For I have come to turn a man against his father, a daughter against her mother, a daughter-in-law against her mother-in-law—a man's enemies will be the members of his own household" (Matt. 10:34-36).

Twice Abused

Nehad is one of my friends who has experienced the sword of Christ. Tall and darkly beautiful, she became a believer through a friend at work. Growing up with an abusive father, she escaped into an arranged marriage, only to find her husband even worse. After she had a child, the marriage broke up, and she was once again with her parents, desperate for saving grace. It didn't take long for her to set aside Islam, where she had only known falseness and hypocrisy, and embrace the message of the cross. But when she made her new faith known to her family, the attacks

B. Linda Smith was born and raised in a Hindu country, then worked for two years in a Buddhist country. For the past 12 years, she has lived in a Muslim country. Her ministry includes friendship evangelism among national women and discipling, counseling and teaching MMB women. Prayer is also a large part of her ministry.

came immediately! She was regularly locked in her room, and beaten by her father and verbally abused.

Her parents accused her of immoral behavior. "You're a prostitute, just as we always thought! You're sleeping with men at those Christian meetings! You're a disgrace to our family!" they shouted. "You're too dumb even to understand the difference between our religion and theirs."

Day after day the heart-wrenching accusations rang out. "You're not worthy of Islam! You're dung! We don't want you in this home anymore."

The haranguing to leave the house continued until one night Nehad fled into the dark. Her heart ached, for she had to leave her young daughter behind. For months, Nehad has not seen her daughter nor even been permitted to talk with her on the phone.

Weeks after she left home, she ran into an uncle on the street who asked her where she was staying. He accused her of sleeping with men at the church. "That's how you're managing," he mocked.

After several months, she ventured a phone call to her married sister to try to reestablish contact with her family. But to no avail. Her sister denounced her for bringing disgrace on the family. "Father is too ashamed to go to the teahouse anymore. Mother won't even go out on the balcony, she is so afraid of the neighborhood gossip. You have ruined your family, Nehad." And so the pressure continues.

Believers' Responsibilities

Nehad now lives with me. She is not the only woman who has been thrown out of her home because of her faith. The body of believers has to be ready to care for and shelter these "widows and orphans." James instructs, "Religion that God our Father accepts as pure and faultless is this: to look after orphans and widows in their distress and to keep oneself from being polluted by the world" (James 1:27). Not only our homes, but our time must be available to them, to sit with them, listen to their distress, and comfort them.

We must encourage them with the promise of scripture, "… no one who has left home or brothers or sisters or mother or father or children or fields for me and the gospel will fail to receive a hundred times as much in this present age (homes, brothers, sisters, mothers, children and fields—and with them, persecutions) and in the age to come, eternal life" (Mark 10:29-30). We must become that promised family for them.

I am always pleased when I see the little son of a couple in our weekly home fellowship crawl into Nehad's lap, sitting contentedly during the meeting. This attention helps soothe her grief for the daughter from whom she has been torn. Legally, she has rights to be with her daughter, but what court will defend her, one who has done such a heinous thing? In their eyes, she is not fit to be a mother. So we wait with Nehad, praying for the day that her daughter will be restored to her.

Marriage Is a Matter of Honor

Muslim parents are eager to see their daughters enter a marriage that will reflect well on the family. But believing girls often find it difficult to meet a Christian man. Nabila and Mysoun became believers in their late teens. As beautiful young women, they had many offers of marriage from men in the community. As they turned down the offers, their parents felt embarrassed and ashamed that their daughters were not married, and rumors were spreading about them. Their father had already threatened to kill them and had beaten Nabila once because of her faith. But they were firm in their resolve not to marry a Muslim.

The parents finally went to a medium who told them that a curse to prevent their daughters' marriages had been put on them. For a price, they brought home "blessed" water and sugar, as well as incense to burn. Now the parents began harassing the girls in earnest. "Drink this water! Use this sugar! Jump over the burning incense!" they urged. Day after day, the demands grew more threatening. Tension mounted in the home. Still the girls refused to comply.

Their father grew increasingly angry."You'll never get married if you oppose the spirits! Why are you being so stubborn?" he yelled.

Nerves raw and exhausted from the daily battle, the girls retreated to my home for help. Gathering believers together, we prayed and ministered to them, calming, comforting and encouraging with God's word. And one day, the bottle of "blessed" water fell off the table and shattered.

Nabila has since married a believer, but after five years, Mysoun is still at home, still facing the almost daily taunts of her father: "What have you gotten out of that religion? It can't even give you a husband! Why do you bother to keep going?"

Often she comes to our Friday night home fellowship meeting distraught and tense, close to tears. Before doing anything else, we sit down, hand over each of the "daggers" thrown by her father to the loving, capable hands of Jesus. We renounce the lies and wash away the effect of the evil with the cleansing words of Christ. Only then is she released from their effect and able to join in our time of worship and fellowship.

Spiritual Warfare

Over the years, Nabila and Mysoun have had to deal with the occult practices of their parents. This is common in many Muslim countries, where almost everyone makes regular use of mediums and their wares. Since believers need to know how to resist the powers that will be used against them, we need to teach and regularly demonstrate to believers how to take part in spiritual warfare. They have no trouble believing in the reality of the power of darkness since they have grown up surrounded with it. But they need to be confident in the truth of scriptures such as:

> ... the one who is in you is greater than the one who is in the world (1 Jn. 4:4).

> Submit yourselves to God. Resist the devil and he will flee from you (James 4:7).

> The weapons we fight with are not the weapons of the world. On the contrary, they have divine power to demolish strongholds (2 Cor. 10:4).

> ... be strong in the Lord and in his mighty power. Put on the full armor of God so that you can take your stand against the devil's schemes. For our struggle is not against flesh and blood, but against the rulers, against the authorities, against the powers of this dark world and against the spiritual forces of evil in the heavenly realms. Therefore put on the full armor of God, so that when the day of evil comes, you may be able to stand your ground, and after you have done everything, to stand (Eph. 6:10-13).

During the months of pressure to drink the medium's medicine, the strain was sometimes so great that Nabila and Mysoun were tempted to compromise. They'd ask me, "If we take just one sip of the water, just to get them off our backs, will it really matter? God knows we really don't believe in it."

Compromise is a subtle temptation that must be resisted. We need to encourage and support all we can to keep them from compromise, but if they do, they must find our arms open and full of grace, not judgment. We do not walk in their shoes or face the mental and emotional struggle they face. When they fall, we need to be as Christ was with Peter, ready to use failure to strengthen and grow.

The Fear of Discovery

Unbelieving husbands can be a dangerous threat to a new believer. When Julia became a Christian, she was afraid to tell her husband. But one day he came home and found her reading her Bible. His fury was so great that he beat her in front of their two young children, then tried to strangle her, leaving her for dead.

Through her painful recovery, she continued to cling to her faith and prayed daily for her husband. God brought a spirit of repentance to him, not only for his shameful cruelty toward her, but for his sinful, hardened heart. He became a believer.

Fear is a strong detriment to being open about faith. But what Julia and others have found is that openness brings blessing. We encourage openness as much as possible, knowing it brings opportunities for trusting in God and sharing one's faith. It also brings suffering, but we teach Paul's attitude: "… we rejoice in our sufferings, because we know that suffering produces per-severance; perseverance, character; and character, hope" (Rom. 5:3-4). Those who are not open, but hidden believers, often carry a burden of guilt with them.

For years Julia did not tell her neighbors she was a Christian, fearing their rejection. They praised her for the differences they saw in her as she tried to live out her faith. One day I asked her, "But who is getting the praise, Julia—you, or Jesus?" The praise felt good, but it wasn't bringing Jesus any glory, or turning peo-ples' eyes to him. Finally, she took the step and confessed her faith. Yes, there was some rejection, but there was also a flow of questions from neighbors amazed and curious to know how she could dare to do such a thing.

When finally word spread that Julia and her family were Christians, the downstairs neighbors in her apartment building began to rain curses on them, screaming foul insults and slanders that came clearly through the thin walls into Julia's home. For months this continued, sometimes leaving her shaking and afraid of the effect of the wrathful curses. Daily she covered her home and children with prayer.

One day she specifically and prayerfully anointed her door for protection. The following day the neighbor, in an uncontrollable rage, charged up the steps, screaming curses. Though she intended to barge into the house, where the children were alone, the neighbor found she couldn't. An invisible barrier held her at the door. Julia returned from visiting another neighbor to find the woman in a heap on the floor in front of her open door, her ashen-faced children watching in terror.

To help Julia and her family get through this trying time, we used the weapons of scripture:

> Blessed are you when people insult you, persecute you and falsely say all kinds of evil against you because of me. Rejoice and be glad, because great is your reward in heaven (Matt. 5:11-12).

> Rejoice that you participate in the sufferings of Christ, so that you may be overjoyed when his glory is revealed. If you are insulted because of the name of Christ, you are blessed, for the Spirit of glory and of God rests on you... . If you suffer as a Christian, do not be ashamed, but praise God that you bear that name (1 Peter 4:13-14, 16).

> Bless those who persecute you, bless and do not curse (Rom. 12:14).

Rather then being afraid of her neighbor, Julia learned to pray for her and bless her. The other neighbors marveled at Julia's patience and long-suffering. And so another biblical principle came into focus for her: God will always bring good out of evil. We see this throughout scripture, in the story of Joseph, in Jonah's rebellion, but most of all, in the cross of Christ.

Julia was able to demonstrate the "peace that passes under-standing." She was able to demonstrate forgiveness, not taking revenge. She learned what it meant to "heap burning coals"on her enemy's head (Rom. 12:20). And she learned the effectiveness of obedience to the scripture's command, "Do not be overcome by evil, but overcome evil with good" (Rom. 12:21). Gradually her neighbor, seeing her curses were not producing the desired result, gave up. Julia has since shared her experience with many new believers, encouraging them in their faith and suffering.

When Julia moved out of the neighborhood a year later, she invited all her neighbors for a farewell tea, and gave each a Bible. If she had not been open, she could never have planted these seeds.

Humiliation

Women often suffer from the humiliating ridicule of their families. Their intelligence and character are belittled. They are scoffed and mocked, put down and shamed. In a culture where they are already considered "second class," this attitude can be hard to bear. We need often to confirm and teach their value and worth in the eyes of the Lord, as well as their value and worth in the eyes of their new spiritual family.

Amaal is a young wife and mother who experienced humiliation from all sides. She became a believer a number of years ago. I encouraged her to be open with her husband, to do nothing in secret or hidden from him. She spoke bravely, sharing with him her love of scripture, speaking with him often about this new faith she was learning about. At first he listened patiently, but soon grew irritated, turning cold and harsh, refusing to listen or to allow her to pursue it anymore. He demanded that she get rid of her Bible and Christian books. For four years she has persevered, gently asking him for permission to join in Bible studies, to go to church, to be with believers. His usual response is an angry "No!" but sometimes he softens and grudgingly permits her to go. When he visits us in our home, he seems to appreciate the warm fellowship, and we wonder if his heart is softening.

Amaal's mother-in-law who lives nearby is a daily visitor. She ridicules her openly. "You've let them brainwash you," she taunts. "You're a lazy good-for-nothing. Don't ask me to watch your children when you go to visit your Christian friends."

Amaal longs for baptism, but she is waiting patiently before the united front of her in-laws and husband for the day when she can be baptized with his knowledge and blessing.

Forgiveness Is Not Part of the Culture

Believers like Amaal need to understand the importance of forgiveness. Christ gives us a perfect example on the cross: "Father, forgive them, for they do not know what they are doing" (Luke 23:34). When Amaal learned to forgive her in-laws for their abusive words, she was released from the effect of those words, able to be confident in herself and the choice she had made, and able to love them.

For women coming out of Islam, forgiveness is a difficult concept. It seems weak—as though they are letting the person get away with sin, and saying it is okay. We must thoroughly instruct believers about understanding our own sin, and God's forgiveness of us. Often, the emphasis on God's love, which is so attractive, is what draws a person towards Christianity. But if they don't have a clear understanding of the depth of their sin and spiritual poverty, obedience in forgiving others will be difficult.

A Daughter Is Forever a Child

Nadia became a believer while studying abroad. When she told her family about her conversion, they wrote back, "That's okay while you're over there, but if you come back here, don't bring that new religion with you!" After several years, she felt the Lord calling her to be with her own people, so leaving a good job, she returned home. As a single woman, she was expected to live at home with her parents, but as time passed and they realized she was as committed as ever to Christianity, the atmosphere grew tense.

She found it difficult to live with the constant questioning: "Where are you going now? Who are you with? Why are you spending so much time with those people?"

If she wanted to pray, her mother always seemed to interrupt. When she sang praises, her mother yelled at her to stop, or she started reading Quranic prayers aloud. One day she complained to Nadia, "When you sing like that, our spirits leave the house and yours come in!" Once, while Nadia was praying in the privacy of her room, her father called out, "I can hear you! Stop right now or I'll come and stop you!" Sometimes she found herself locked out in the dark, unwelcome. At night disturbing sounds often woke her up, and her room would be filled with a dark presence.

Nadia found herself arguing with her parents often. They viciously attacked her faith and her friends. She was disturbed by her own reaction, wanting to respond righteously to the attacks, but instead finding herself using cutting words to fight back. When her mother began to curse her fellow believers, Nadia responded in anger. This only increased her mother's fervor.

One day it reached a dangerous peak, and Nadia came to me for help. After I counseled and prayed with her, she went home, and when her mother began cursing again, she quietly, in prayer, countered each curse with blessing, rejecting the words spoken against her and other believers, covering them with the power of the word of God. Instead of anger, her gentle words had a calming effect on her mother.

Some time later, her ailing grandmother, also living in the home, asked Nadia to pray for her. "When you pray, the demons leave me alone," she confessed. Nadia's mother was furious to learn of this and hindered her whenever she could. But through it all, Nadia tried to be a loving daughter to her parents. It pained her to see the confusion and anger she was causing in her home. Yet she continued to faithfully attend Bible studies and worship services in the tiny local church.

One Sunday morning, the police interrupted the service and arrested the believers, including Nadia, on false premises. Worse than spending the time in prison was the publicity. Her picture appeared on the front page of the newspaper along with other believers. No longer could her family hide from relatives and neighbors what to them was their daughter's traitorous act. After her acquittal and release from prison, she returned home with trepidation. Her father was cold and quiet, her mother weeping and lamenting. But her younger brother, living downstairs with his wife and child, was the one who forced the issue: "If you don't throw her out of here now, I will personally kill her!" he screamed. "She is a traitor to us and to her people! She can no longer be a part of our family!" He insisted that her parents force her to leave the home.

As Nadia packed to leave, her parents' sorrow pierced her heart. Her mother continued to weep inconsolably. "What have I done to deserve this?" She saw Nadia's actions as God's punishment. The loss of her daughter was more than she could bear. It was a fate worse than death.

When Nadia arrived with her suitcase at my home that morning, I folded her into my arms and we wept together. She said sadly, "My choice has hurt my family. I have to make this choice, but I feel guilty. I know I'm doing the right thing, but it hurts me to hurt them. They are suffering because of my decision."

This pain is real. The sword is heavy and it cuts deeper each time she tries to call them and they hang up the phone or turn her away from the house.

I asked Nadia what has helped her the most. Thoughtfully she responded, "Knowing in my head I need to choose what is right. Knowing that God is in charge, and that he'll comfort my family as he comforts me. Knowing that I have to leave them in his merciful hands." Prayer has become her strongest weapon. Nadia has also found great comfort in Jesus' promise that "no one who has left home or brothers or sisters or mother or father or children or fields for me and the gospel will fail to receive a hundred times as much in this present age."

In our home, along with Nehad, she has found a new family. She has also been blessed with love from a young Christian man.

A few months after she left her parents' home, they were married. None of her family came to the wedding, but she was surrounded by her new family, the body of believers, who were delighted by her marriage and rejoiced with her.

Accepting the Fate of Loved Ones

Often, MBBs must face a more subtle kind of suffering. Iqbal, an energetic physical education teacher, came to me a few months after she had decided to believe. Four years earlier, her father had died suddenly in an accident. She still mourned him and was troubled by the implications for her father from scripture. In choosing to believe Christ's words, she faced the realization that her father was eternally lost.

She believed the words of scripture that "salvation is found in no one else, for there is no other name under heaven given to people by which we must be saved" (Acts 4:12). But in doing so, Iqbal had basically chosen to be with Jesus for eternity, rather than to follow the teachings of the father she loved.

MBBs who are the only ones in their families to believe are constantly faced with this reality. In choosing Christ and the eternity he offers, they are acknowledging damnation for their loved ones. In this way, their love for Christ is put to the test.

Some Can't Hold Out

I had experienced delightful fellowship with Samia, a young new believer who was full of enthusiasm and eager to learn. We were together often over three years and she grew to enjoy scripture and our times of prayer.

Then she met and fell in love with Maher, a young artist. She shared her faith with him. For months he listened, saying little. Then one winter morning, she saw cold rage in his eyes. He took her Bible, all the Christian books she had been reading, and her notes, and in front of her threw them into the coal stove yelling, "It's either me or this Jesus! Choose which one you want! I want nothing to do with him!" In tears, she came to me and told me what her choice was. The sword was too heavy for her to bear, and she has not looked back since. We still see each other, but she refuses to talk about Christ, and her heart has grown cold.

When I asked an MBB woman how she would sum up their suffering, she responded, "The men in our families are offended by our choice. They feel we don't respect them as we should, for they are our leaders and they feel we are rebelling. Our close friends also reject us. We lose our relationships with them and become separated from them. We've changed too much. We are constantly being misunderstood and faced with prejudice. We are seen as traitors to our people. They ask us, 'Why did you choose the Western way?' We seem to have taken sides with those who traditionally have been looked on as enemies. Not only are we going against all that our fathers and forefathers believed religiously, but against our country as well. We have become political traitors. We're looked down upon; we're seen as narrow-minded and boring by our peers. In their eyes we've made a very stupid, bad choice."

Suffering Must Be Expected

Our attitude towards suffering is a key to perseverance. There is no room in scripture for self-pity or rebellion. I have often told my sisters that I can't find any allowance for pity anywhere. Instead, we read such passages as:

> ... everyone who wants to live a godly life in Christ Jesus will be persecuted (2 Tim. 3:12).

> For it has been granted to you on behalf of Christ not only to believe on him, but also to suffer for him (Phil. 1:29).

> But if you suffer for doing good and you endure it, this is commendable before God. To this you were called, because Christ suffered for you, leaving you an example, that you should follow in his steps (1 Peter 2:20-21).

We must arm ourselves with the same attitude Christ had towards suffering. Having the right attitude is the best way to resist the bondage of self-pity and rebellion. We must teach and model this attitude continually before MBBs.

Though I will never suffer in the same way as an MBB, as one who has come to live among them, I also encounter some suffering. I am sometimes misunderstood, rejected, mocked, looked down upon, ridiculed. I am a stranger in a sometimes very strange land. I have been threatened with deportation, I have been imprisoned. I am now a fingerprinted alien with all the possible repercussions that could bring.

But what I have found essential is to "walk my talk." Over the years, I have discipled many women who are crushed, who have been abused, who have come out of awful home situations. As they become Christians, I talk with them about the biblical way to face suffering.

As I share this with the ladies and talk about forgiveness and about how to handle deep sorrow, I can sometimes see in their eyes—"it's easy for you to say"—because I have never suffered as they have. I had a wonderful background. I had godly parents. I was never abused. I had a dear husband and healthy children.

But two years ago my husband died of cancer, and I lost not only my lover but my best friend. Now I have the opportunity to put into practice what I had been teaching over the years. I can say to them, this is the way the Bible tells us to suffer and to walk through sorrow. I understand it because now I'm doing it. And you can do it too.

I remind them of Peter's words: "These have come so that your faith, of greater worth than gold, which perishes, even though refined by fire may be proved genuine and may result in praise, glory and honor when Jesus Christ is revealed" (1 Peter 1:6-7).

Or I share the words of James, "Consider it pure joy, my brothers and sisters, whenever you face trials of many kinds, because you know that the testing of your faith develops perseverance. Perseverance must finish its work so that you may be mature and complete, not lacking anything" (James 1:2-4).

A View from the Other Side

To fully understand suffering we must realize how our Muslim friends suffer when one of their family members converts to Christianity. Lydia is a dear friend of mine, not an MBB. We have been neighbors for many years, and through our friendship our husbands became friends. Eventually her husband came to the Lord. To Lydia, this was the worst thing he could do. Though she saw positive changes in him, she was angry and grieved over his decision. And the only one she could share her burden with was me. No one else must know her dark secret. She was ashamed and scared of the consequences if her family and neighbors were to find out about her husband's conversion.

While the four of us were sitting together one evening, she cried out to her husband, "I wish you had committed adultery, or thievery, or even murder! Those I could handle. If only you had done anything but this! You will never be forgiven, you will burn in hell for ever. You have done the worst thing you could possibly do by changing your religion!"

Lydia has often threatened to leave her husband, but she knows there's nowhere she can go. She feels betrayed and trapped. When it gets too overwhelming for her, she comes to me, to pour out her heart. I grieve for her suffering, for the hardness of her heart and the fear that binds her. I know she is torn between her love for me and her hatred for what we have brought into her life. I understand her sorrow, but I cannot give her the sympathy she wants. She is alone in her torment. I love her and pray for the day when the sword Christ has brought will no longer be the divider between her and her husband.

Called to Costly Commitment

Sometimes when I share with women the message of Christ, I shudder to think of the consequences for them if they choose to follow him. I know the suffering it may cause them. For all of us in this situation, it is imperative that we are absolutely certain of the truth of our words. There must be no doubt in our minds because we are calling these women to a costly commitment. The words in Hebrews have been a rock to me in times when I feel my perspective slipping away:

> Therefore, since we are surrounded by such a great cloud of witnesses, let us throw off everything that hinders and the sin that so easily entangles, and let us run with perseverance the race marked out for us. Let us fix our eyes on Jesus, the author and perfecter of our faith, who for the joy set before him endured the cross, scorning its shame, and sat down at the right hand of the throne of God. Consider him who endured such opposition from sinful men, so that you will not grow weary and lose heart (Heb. 12:1-3).

Keeping our eyes fixed on Jesus, scorning the shame and suffering that may come our way, and anticipating the joy set before us—these are invaluable tools we must use and pass on to our MBB sisters.

Participants' Discussion

Editor's note: The foregoing article by B. Linda Smith was written for this compendium but was not presented at the Consultation. The discussion recorded here was a general discussion on suffering and was not a follow-up discussion of the article.

Question—What can you or your mission agency do to better prepare missionaries and converts for suffering and persecution?

From Central Asia—There's no way you can fully prepare someone for what will happen on the field. We knew a believer who was hacked to death with a hatchet. There's no way you can prepare someone for that.

I can think of only one thing that will help us prepare for persecution. We hold Easter outreaches every year. During these, we always face threats from the community. It strikes me that the missionary community handles these threats differently. Some people, when they come to the field, are prepared to die; others are not. You have to settle this matter in your heart before you leave: you may never come back home. This commitment gives us courage and faith to go on in times of persecution.

From the Maldives—The girls and women who came to believe in Jesus through our ministry were not practicing Muslims. They were searching for God but not really living Islam. So when they came to believe in Jesus, the workers discussed how to train and disciple them. It didn't seem reasonable, since they had not practiced Islam before, to teach them to pray five times a day in a contextualized Islamic way. So they learned how to pray as we prayed, with their own words. And they did really well. But then they went to prison, where the authorities made them pray five times a day in the Islamic form.

What I would like to do differently next time would be to teach them to pray to Jesus, pray to their Father in heaven, in a way that they could practice in prison. I would want to better prepare them with practical tools that would help them through the persecution and prison.

From North Africa—For me, the most difficult part of these situations is feeling blame. We feel blame because we came with the gospel, and the result of our bringing the gospel to them is that they suffer. And of course, as missionaries, we will never have to pay the price that they pay. I have felt as though their blood was on my hands, so to speak.

One way we can be prepared to help believers through their suffering is to thoroughly prepare ourselves for it. Once we've reckoned with the likelihood of suffering in our own lives, we may be better equipped to prepare believers.

From Turkey—Meeting Richard Wurmbrand and reading his book, *Tortured for Christ*, helped prepare me for suffering. Also, while I was in Bible school, I read books about the missionary martyrs to the Aucas of South America. Many are familiar with *Fox's Book of Martyrs*. From these books, I knew that suffering was a price we would have to pay.

A good friend of mine disappeared in Pakistan. But we need to remember that the church has always grown through suffering. We need to come alongside our sisters, but we have to tell them, right away, that there is a price. Jesus never promised us an easy life. We all should fortify ourselves with thoughts of heaven. No matter how hard it is here, it's only a pilgrimage.

From Pakistan—As we begin to witness to Muslim women, it's wise to say to them, "Not only is it given to you to believe on Christ, but also to suffer for his sake" (Phil. 1:29). Then they will understand that it is part of being a Christian. We've urged our people never to rush to tell their family about their profession of faith in Christ. Instead, we encourage them to live Christ before their family so that their family will have the opportunity to ask why they have changed.

We've seen our young people threatened and beaten. Many of them have been threatened to have their limbs cut off or their arms broken. Some of them have been put out of their homes. Many of our women have been beaten. I don't know of any of our children who have escaped beatings in school. But we've taught them from 1 Peter 2:20: "If you do wrong and suffer for it, what is that to you? But if you do no wrong, but you suffer for Christ's sake, it is glory."

What Helps Muslim Women Grow in Christ

Iliam

When you consider the world of Muslim women, you can easily feel, "Why bother? Who am I among so many? How can anything I say or do ever make a difference?" as you throw up your hands in surrender. However, throughout scripture, God deals with individuals and small groups as a communicator and a listener. It is essential for each of us to examine our own hearts regarding our faith, our vision of who God is, his power and sovereignty, our own perception of his Word and obedience to it, our personal focus on the Lord Jesus, and our confidence in the work of the Holy Spirit.

When I first arrived in Pakistan, I was shocked to realize some of the missionaries there did not really believe that Muslims could be saved and mature in the Lord Jesus. Therefore, only a small handful were actually working among Muslims. The remainder worked among nominal Christians or in institutional service. Repeatedly, my colleagues scoffed at and questioned the validity of our reports about God's work among Muslims.

What about you: Do you really believe that Muslims can be saved and go on to maturity in the Lord Jesus Christ?

As we go forward in ministry to Muslim women, we must carefully and prayerfully consider six basic principles: prayer, open hearts, open homes, the needs of the target group, the best methods and means of teaching scripture to that group, and continuing to model evangelism.

Iliam worked in Pakistan for 38 years as a nurse, teacher, and church planter.

Prayer Helps Them Grow

As we prepare for a new area of ministry, we must think carefully about the methods of contact we should use because to a
large degree it is these methods which will help us grow new
believers. Prayer is one of these "methods." By praying for and
with believers with whom we are working, we boldly declare our
dependence on God, not ourselves. When we pray that the Lord
will open a person's eyes, we help her know that she is to be the
Lord's disciple, not ours. Wisdom and blessing come to her from
the richness of the Lord's storehouse. When we pray that the Lord
will help us in our new relationship to be pleasing to him in all
ways, we allow the believer to know immediately our attitude
toward the relationship. When we pray for ourselves in her presence to be an eager, willing learner of language and culture that
we might effectively share Christ, we clearly set forth our goal.

Believers will grow as they hear us praying God's heart for
them and their community. I think it is also important to share
specifically our ministry plans with the fellowships and churches
in our sending countries. Likewise, we should identify the believers (not by their real names, for security's sake) so that our home
churches can be consistently praying for them. Vague prayer
requests result in vague interest that soon disappears without any
effect in the life of the individual prayed for.

Model Personal Prayer

We must model for her prayer that is deeply personal—even
including the confession of public sin in public prayer. The
believer needs now to pray using "me" and "my," not the corporate "we" and "our" that dilutes individual responsibility.

Often pray, "Lord, set a watch before my lips," as the Psalmist
did (Psa. 141:3). Jokes are rarely understood in other cultures and
can greatly damage relationships and the growth of the believing
community. "Let the words of my mouth and the thoughts of my
heart be acceptable in your sight, O Lord" (Psa. 19:14). This prayer
has been often a help to believers, as it was to the Psalmist.

Your Love Helps Them Grow

Genuine love is so basic to ministry. However, your love—my
love—is not sufficient; God's own love must flow through us. We
simply do not have enough love on our own to get the job done.
The first false profession of faith, false accusation, lie or loss of

precious possessions will cripple you and make you ineffective if you operate in your own love! If we love only with human love, we will react humanly. Do ask God to give to you, as he did to Solomon, a heart of wisdom, understanding and love. Daily, we must remind ourselves of the reason we are where we are. This is especially important in times of loss, danger and illness, because Satan will pour into our hearts fears and doubts in abundance.

Redefine "Love"

Teaching scriptural love will require time, examples, and repeated demonstration. Realize that the new believer must now understand love as giving—rather than taking—time, strength and possessions. In her culture, the word "love" has long been understood as simply a sexual act. Urge the community of believers to memorize 1 Corinthians 13 and speak of it frequently to set the stage for a new understanding to develop. Commenting on the Quran (Sura 30, v. 21), Islamic scholar Sayyed Qotb says that "love" is intercourse and "mercy" is offspring. In the common man's thoughts, "love" often means yielding to what is requested without protest.

Study your people's perception of love. Listen not only for the usage of the word "love" but watch for the reactions of the people when it is used. Learn how they comprehend the concept of it. Remember, we are to be known as his disciples by the way in which we love one another.

Your Open Home Helps Them Grow

An open home is essential to ministry, for it opens doors to hearts. Dedicate your new home, room by room, to the glory and presence of the Lord. Ask the Lord to cleanse it of any satanic presence or evil done there before. The Lord can use every event in your home if you give it to him. If you openly share your celebrations of birthdays, new babies, anniversaries, courses completed, recovery from illnesses, fear, crises, dangers, you will open new doors of opportunity because you are being real with people, not aloof from them. Some of these situations, better than any formal teaching, will allow you to say, "I trust God's goodness and love—even when I don't understand it."

As we share rites of passage in our homes as well as in their homes, we become a part of the community or neighborhood. Funerals or visits to express sympathy to the family after the death of a relative give a culturally perfect opportunity to share our hope of eternal life. Tears and grief are common commodities to be shared.

Pictures, verses, magazines, books around in your home may be good "jumping off" points for witnessing, but make sure they are culturally relevant and acceptable. Privacy is a Western-manufactured item. Anything openly displayed in the home is jointly possessed. It may be handled, picked up for closer examination or use, or even taken home to share with others freely. Locks are for those things not so available in most cultures. Breakage and loss of household items may be especially high as you take up a new residence. Remembering these are only things keeps your attitude right. Using things and valuing people is a principle of great profit.

Food left out in the open is, of course, there to be eaten. So it is wise to check supplies again before a meal! Hospitality opens doors to hearts. Formal entertaining is good and profitable, but just sharing what you have right now is greatly appreciated too.

Build Community

Becoming a part of the community is important to the Christian worker. Muslim teachers—male or female—are usually employed in a secular job at least part time. Christian teachers will be asked, "What do you do to earn your salt?" Don't despair or be frustrated if your friend fails to understand when you reply, "I'm studying or preparing to preach or teach." In confusion, my friends have asked me, "Why? Don't you know your book yet?" Remind yourself that the Bible is a living book that speaks anew to you daily. It's important that you study and allow the Holy Spirit to guide you to new truth. In Islam, the concept of memorizing the passage and repeating it accurately is what is emphasized.

Teaching and medical ministry give workers a ready role in the community. Reach out to become a part of the community by attending local events; this will help you understand and listen better and in turn gives you support and listeners for your message. It also provides a role model for new believers. A high prize to be sought is neighbors saying, "She is one of us now."

It will be difficult to develop community trust among new believers. Yet your community participation will show them the difference between real community and the facade of Muslim brotherhood, which is all about control and power. Being aware of that and even experiencing it with the believer helps to sharpen her awareness of the differences and create in her a hunger for real brotherhood. Self-advancement at the expense of others, self-interest and satisfaction are the Muslim way. This needs to be replaced by charity, love and mutual caring. New believers will be attracted to sharing in a brotherhood based on God's love and with the guideline of JOY—Jesus Others You—instead of the me-my-mine of Islam.

Visits to the ill, the dying, those absent from classes or services, and neighbors are vital. Model this activity, and invite new believers to accompany you. We often hear, "No man or woman dwells alone—he or she is not an island." Surely a loving, giving, caring, and concerned network of believers must be developed in order to fulfill John 13:34: "A new command I give you: Love one another. As I have loved you, so you must love one another."

Build trust for the Christian believer in a Muslim community by being known as a person of your word. It requires a long time and much careful observation to the details of your lifestyle. Mutual trust among believers is essential. It requires that believers realize from the beginning that both the Christian worker and other new believers are sinners saved by grace—not perfect, but growing.

Create in the new believers a hunger for the real community that scripture pictures. To do so, you'll need to understand what they have come out from by participating as much as possible in the old Islamic community without violating Christian principles. This requires a long-term commitment. The new community will need to develop new traditions for caring for each other and for the physical plant (classrooms and church building). As women work together in times of need—such as funerals, weddings, illnesses, danger, or even holiday celebrations, they will bond as a new community. Special days of prayer, visitation ministry, retreats, and special evangelism programs are ways of bonding, too.

While they can surely contribute to it, building the new community is not the domain of short-term workers. Community building develops as a result of long-term commitment. This means we must recruit for long-term workers among Muslims.

For the new believer, loyalty to God must supersede loyalty to personal relationships, which was her old guide in the brotherhood of Islam. Defense of principle, responsibility for one's own actions and acceptance of punishment for those actions will be new concepts for her. In Islam, she would have defended a relative at all costs—even to the point of lying in court for him. Now for the believer, truth must become the rule of life.

As you model honesty, loyalty, punctuality and dependability, you will teach these values to the disciple. Your own concern, care, prayer and follow-up on the development of these values will be her pattern.

Meeting Their Needs Helps Them Grow

Using whatever you have in your hand, as Moses used his staff, leads to great opportunities. A gift, skill, hobby, occupation or casual visit can provide you with the privilege of sharing God's love and his Word. Formal programs—such as trade schools, tutorial programs, ESL, dispensaries/clinics, child care, sports training, exercise programs, gardening, cooking classes—concurrent with a study class on the Bible as the "most important thing in my life to share with others" can be very effective. The power of the Word of God applied by the Holy Spirit is what will bring cleansing through the blood of the Lord Jesus. It's not the activity that completes our task!

Take care that such programs produce real results in skill or education. Programs of this nature should never be a front or an excuse. Always declare that the reason for the programs is so that the student will come to a right relationship with God. If you are teaching in a government- or corporate-supported program, such a declaration may not be allowed. In that case, answer the question of "Why are you here?" with the response: "God directed me to come to help you and others to come to know him, as well as to acquire this skill." Such a response often leads to, "You mean God is interested in me?" and opens opportunity. The concept of a "shelter" ministry, through which a teaching program or dispensary/clinic gives women a reason for coming to a definite place regularly, is legitimate in the eyes of the community and does not make them suspect evildoing. This is important to protect the honor of the males in the family as well as to protect the women from physical harm.

Teaching Them Scriptural Principles Helps Them Grow

Scripture teaching is vital because it is his Word that the Lord promises to bless, not our efforts or words. Systematic teaching of the Word of the Lord—in doctrinal studies and book studies, in small groups or in formal classes, and children's classes, on a regular schedule—is important. When teaching in homes or with individuals, it is often wise not to use the same day or same time or even the same access route to the home, because neighbors or family members may become suspicious of the activity.

Memory work is vital because the student may be cut off from contact quickly without the benefit of the written Word. Topics for such memory verse programs should be salvation assurance, power over sin for moral living, the new lifestyle required by God, fear, death, heaven and hell. Assurance verses concerning God's love, care, presence and forgiveness will provide much comfort should the student be separated from the teachers. Longer passages are possible quite early in discipleship training because of the emphasis on memory work in the school systems of many cultures. Creeds; the beatitudes; the Lord's prayer; John 14; and entire books like Jude, Philippians, Ephesians, and Colossians are some wonderful passages to start with. While formal classes require regular planned lessons, remember that for discipling in home visits, you must carefully plan lessons, too.

You may have to carefully time your visits and change your approach routes to the home, but the teaching must not waver. The eye-gate will help the memory much more than the ear-gate. So use visuals even with adults who are literate. To avoid charges of deceit, send home permission slips for parental signatures if you hold children's classes as a part of another program.

Modeling Evangelism Helps Them Grow

Evangelism is a lifestyle, supplemented by special outreach programs. Who you are will create far greater impact on Muslim women than any program you develop. Videos, movies and magazines have portrayed the Western woman in negative terms that your dress, words and actions must counteract—and even erase. Do not teach Islamics, as that is not your mandate. Do not argue either politics or religion, as it only leads to a strong defense of one or both. Do not break the cultural separation of women and men in witnessing or in discipling. Do not spend time alone in an enclosed place with a man, even when you are witnessing or discipling, because it gives rise to accusations.

Actually do evangelism. Do not just plan it or talk it. Use the open heart/home/shelter ministry concept. Do not blame people for not coming to the meetings or church, saying that they are not serious or brave enough. Provide a culturally acceptable way for them to come regularly to you for teaching. Earn the right to be heard by your own participation in the community.

Visits in homes on a regular basis with planned lessons are more effective if you take other believers with you because you teach, evangelize and disciple at the same time. Children's classes with clearly planned lessons and a memory work program are effective. Involve the believers in these plans and lessons from the beginning. Women's study groups can use a Bible correspondence course or a particular Bible book depending upon the literacy level of the students. Gifts of large print Bibles or New Testaments can be treasured as gifts at rites of passage. If it's appropriate to their level of literacy and if the mail service is trustworthy, some women will benefit from doing correspondence courses alone; however, it is more effective to do them as a small group together.

Discipleship and evangelism should occur together. It is wise to have more than two women in a class to avoid rivalry and attempts at control of the teacher. Doctrinal studies and prayer meetings should take place at least weekly—daily, if possible. Ideally, after the course is completed, each disciple should start afresh with several other women, thereby multiplying the number of women who are being trained in evangelism and discipleship.

This leads to a process of evangelistic multiplication, leadership division, discipleship addition, and Western teacher subtraction. This is the goal of women teaching women in a living, growing church composed of men and women from Muslim ethnic backgrounds. God alone is able for that!

Discipleship of Muslim Background Believers through Chronological Bible Storying

A. H.

I have been asked to address you regarding how I disciple Muslim Background Believer (MBB) women. To do this, I need to talk about orality issues and chronological Bible storying. I learned chronological Bible storying from someone who had worked among animistic peoples of the Philippines. Most of my examples will come from my work among the many different Muslim people groups who live in greater Paris. I am aware that the situation in France is different from that of closed countries. I hope, however, that my examples will stimulate you to find ways to use this method in your workplace, just as the Philippine examples helped me.

Why Do We Need to Teach Orally?

Today, one-half the population of the world (nearly 3 billion people) receives most of its information by oral means. One-half the population of the world prefers oral communication. What is an oral communicator? Jim Slack, of the International Mission Board of the Southern Baptist Convention (IMB, SBC), defines an oral communicator as "a person whose preferred or most effective communication and usual learning format, style or method is in accordance with oral formats as contrasted to literate formats." An oral communicator is someone who receives and uses information by oral means rather than by literate means. Many

A. H. has spent 25 years working with Muslims in the Middle East and Western Europe. In the past five years, she has focused on Chronological Bible Storying—using it in her outreach to Muslim immigrants and conducting workshops to teach the process to others.

oral communicators can read but can't really comprehend or use the information read. Rather, they need to hear it in an appropriate oral format (i.e., not simply read aloud but in story or poetry or song format) in order to understand and use the information.

An example is my friend Fatima who speaks three languages and has learned to read French. When she reads aloud, she sounds like a first grader. After reading several verses from the Bible, she will ask me what it means. I can repeat it nearly as written and she understands. While her reading comprehension has greatly improved, she still can't read the Bible by herself and understand its teachings. Being an oral communicator has nothing to do with intelligence levels. It is simply the preferred learning style of about half the population of the world.

I was in a meeting earlier this year during which someone said that all early communication was oral and that God was comfortable with that. The implication was that while God is comfortable with oral communication of the gospel today, we missionaries often have a difficult time accepting it. The Bible was transmitted orally before it was written. Even after the Bible stories were written, the majority of the people transmitted them orally. Jesus used oral communication. In his language of Aramaic, his words were poetry that was easily memorized by the masses. Most of the disciples were illiterate and didn't write what Jesus said. Rather they repeated the teachings to others who also memorized them. Only as the disciples began to die did Mark and the others write the Gospels. The gospel continued to be spread by oral means around the world.

Most Muslim women are oral communicators. Some Muslim countries educate girls but do so in schools that teach by rote memory, which doesn't encourage thinking and analysis. Research has shown that people who study in these types of schools and don't continue to read after finishing become functionally illiterate in just a few years. The girls leave school, marry and start their families. Most of them don't continue to read, and after several years of nonreading, they revert to a preferred learning style of oral communication. I saw this in Gaza. All the girls went to school, but I met very few women other than schoolteachers who could read with comprehension. During eleven years in Gaza, I met one female nursing student who read for pleasure, and she did that in English because it was easier than Arabic. The UN used picture charts for all the health teaching done in the clinics.

Most missionaries who come from Western countries are highly literate. They have completed high school, college and/or Bible school, and many have gone on for further training. Literate people lose the ability to receive and process information orally. My friend Fatima has memorized the phone numbers of all her friends. In contrast, I have trouble memorizing my own phone number! Fatima can read a recipe but can't follow the instructions without seeing someone else make the dish. Once she's seen it made, she can make it repeatedly without mistakes. I need to read the recipe every time I make the dish.

Highly literate people are afraid to trust the memory of an oral communicator. The expressed fear is that error will creep in. Because of this fear, highly literate people tend to work only with the literate few of a society. Missionaries look for someone who can read the Bible and then read it with that individual. The theory I've heard is that we can teach them, and they will teach their own people. The problem is that they don't teach their own people. They've become like us. They are so highly literate that they have forgotten how to communicate orally. Plus, they copy the pattern from which they learn. That's what a disciple is—a person who learns from and copies his/her master/teacher. In Paris, we have monthly fellowship meetings of believers and seekers. Usually several people will give testimonies, which are powerful messages in themselves. Then someone will bring "the message." The MBBs plan the program and want this part included. However, the individual who brings the message is highly literate, has been a believer for several years and is an active member of a local French church. The message he brings is highly expository in style. He is copying the style of his French pastor as well as the style of the missionaries with whom he has worked. My friend Yasmine has been coming to these meetings. She is illiterate and has a minimal level of French. She sits quietly during the message but doesn't understand a word of it. She loves the testimonies and the fellowship of the "party" but totally misses the main thrust of the meeting. She isn't the only one there who misses the point of the message. At the last meeting, an elderly man who attended for the first time told the "message bringer" that he had not understood a word of it.

In many countries, missionaries are reaching the 10 percent educated elite of the country. The rest of the people aren't being touched by the gospel. Recently, I heard a report of a study of the church in Morocco. The individual giving the report said that in Morocco, literacy in the cities was listed at 50 percent. However, when considering men and women separately, the literacy level for urban women dropped to 33 percent. In the country, the literacy rate dropped down to 25 percent overall. He had no literacy figures for rural women. Then this individual studied the Moroccan church and found that it was composed of urban, young, educated men. There were very few women and no one from the rural areas. Further study showed that the men were educated to the level of reading and understanding Modern Standard Arabic, which isn't the language spoken in Morocco. In addition, the church was using primarily printed materials in the worship services. The individual doing the study concluded that there is a literacy filter on the gospel. Literate communicators seek literate individuals to receive the gospel. That's our comfort zone.

Another conference I attended recently scrutinized the media being developed for evangelistic efforts. The conclusion was that the vast majority of the media was print media, suitable only for the highly literate of the society. In addition, much of the print media was a translation from the West and didn't use examples from the local culture, which made it difficult to apply what was written to local Christian lives. Videocassettes and oral cassettes were also highly literate—in that they moved fast, presented the material only once and frequently used exposition rather than storytelling. Another problem with the media is that most of it is directed toward the harvest. There are very few media products for preparing the ground, for sowing and for cultivating. In addition, most of the media products are "generic," meaning that they are directed toward a male audience.

With all this information in mind, how can we reach out to Muslim women with a message that they can hear and understand? Most Muslim women are oral communicators. Oral communicators learn from experience and association—not from logic. They organize content by association with events. They learn by interaction with others. Oral communicators can produce beautiful epic poems and ballads. Oral communicators need to hear something several times in order to memorize it. I saw a video of the Good Samaritan produced by a group of oral communicator Christians who live in Central America. The Christians planned the film and did everything but operate the camera. During the short video, they repeated the story three times—once in action, once as the man was telling what had happened to the doctor and once as a review. The video moved too slowly for my preference but was perfect for oral communicators. Films produced by highly literate people reflect their preferred learning style.

Why Do We Need Chronological Bible Storying?

Perhaps you are wondering what all this information has to do with the discipleship of MBB women. Romans 10:14 says, "How, then, can they call on the one they have not believed in? And how can they believe in the one of whom they have not heard? And how can they hear without someone preaching to them?" I believe that many sincere people have been trying to preach the gospel to Muslim women. I was one of them. However, I've come to believe that the message I was preaching, in all sincerity, wasn't being heard. I've learned a new way to share the gospel message with my Muslim women friends. It's called chronological Bible storying. I want to share with you what this method is and how I've found it to work in Paris. My hope is that you will also find it to be a useful tool for sharing the gospel in a way that the women can truly hear it.

During 25 years of Muslim evangelism that has included working in three different countries, I've had the opportunity to evangelize and disciple a number of MBBs. The only available materials were translated discipleship books that had been written for North American believers who were literate and had some basic knowledge of religious terminology. The dilemma I faced was whether to adapt these materials or to create my own. While I worked in the Gaza Strip, I did a combination of both. Since the people I discipled or encouraged others to disciple were literate nursing students, the materials worked reasonably well. Although I knew that their mothers were functionally illiterate, I wasn't directly involved in evangelism/discipleship of these women. Therefore, I never really considered the need for discipleship materials for illiterate or functionally illiterate individuals.

Two events that occurred in the same week of January 1994 radically changed my view towards discipleship of MBB women. The Baptist World Alliance (BWA) Women's Department organized a consultation on the evangelism of Muslim women that was held in Cyprus at the same time as a workshop on chronological Bible storying. I participated in both the consultation and the workshop.

The BWA Women's Department consultation identified a major problem with current discipleship materials: they require an ability to read isolated verses from the Bible and extract the teaching that supports the doctrine being presented. The consultation decided that discipling of MBB women could be enhanced with specially developed materials that met the literacy level of the MBB, recognizing that up to 93 percent of Muslim women in some countries are illiterate and/or prefer receiving information orally.

At the same time that the consultation was making recommendations about evangelism and discipleship of Muslim women, the workshop on chronological Bible storying was teaching that evangelism needed to consider the literacy level, the preferred learning style and the barriers and bridges to the gospel when presenting the gospel to Muslims. Putting the two together helped me to learn to look at the preferred learning style of the Muslim women of Paris. As I began to study these women with new eyes, I realized that very few of my contacts received their information from literate sources. For example, I noticed that there were no books or magazines in any of the homes. I met women at the grocery store who asked for help identifying products, and I visited one home where a woman had mistakenly purchased a pork product. I realized that in Paris, where literacy classes are available, most of the women I meet still have not learned to read well enough to receive information from written sources. Even though I knew the women were illiterate, I had not considered how that fact should govern my presentation of the gospel.

Thus, the conference also changed my approach to evangelism. Although through reading and personal experience, I had realized that I needed to share testimonies about my relationship with God before talking about Jesus, I had not learned to consider worldview and the barriers and bridges to the gospel in planning which experiences to share. Nor had I learned to look at the women's preferred learning style in planning Bible studies and/or testimonies. After the consultation and the workshop, I began to consider worldview and the barriers to the gospel as I chose stories to tell. Before the workshop, I looked for readers with whom to work. After the workshop, I began to consider how to witness effectively to oral communicators.

What Is Chronological Bible Storying?

New Tribes Missions developed the method of chronological Bible teaching while working with illiterate peoples in Southeast Asia. Jim Slack of the Southern Baptists simplified this method, noting that illiterate peoples could be evangelized, saved and discipled into reproducing churches through storying the Bible. Storying the Bible consists of two parts: the story given in chronological order and the dialogue. It differs from chronological Bible teaching and from chronological Bible storytelling (which includes some exposition) in that no exposition or commentary is added to the story. [See the learning grid chart on the following page.]

Storying the Bible gives illiterate people the Bible in a form that they can use. Illiterate peoples can learn all they need to know about the Bible, biblical doctrine and the Christian life through the medium of storying. It is not necessary to wait until someone can read well enough to comprehend the scriptures before encouraging that individual to take responsibility for teaching others the Bible.

Further research and use of this method demonstrates that following the chronology works with all levels of literacy and with all different learning styles. The main point is to look at the individual's preferred learning style and tailor the presentation of the stories to that learning style. Most teachers, missionaries and pastors present the gospel in their own preferred learning style rather than looking at the learning preferences of the recipient. In the past several years, I have followed the chronology of the Bible with women from several different literacy levels and have learned that it works with all levels. I tailor the lesson to the preferred learning style of the woman with whom I'm working. This means that with one woman I story the Bible, while with another, we read it together and discuss the lessons to be learned from the passage.

How to Use Chronological Bible Storying

Jim Slack and J. O. Terry (IMB, SBC) have developed a learning grid that helps explain the amount of expository material that can be included with a story. The grid shows the importance of knowing the preferred learning style of the recipient when planning how to present the gospel message. The grid shows clearly that illiterate, functionally illiterate and semiliterate people are all oral communicators. In addition, the learning grid helps explain which parts of the lesson can have expositional teaching and how much. By following the preferred learning style of the person hearing the story, the teacher can be sure that the story is being heard and understood and that the essential lessons are being received.

	Oral Communicator	Oral Communicator	Oral Communicator	Oral/Literate Communicator	Literate Communicator	
	Illiterate	Functional Illiterate	Semi-Illiterate	Literate	Highly Literate	
Story	No Expostion	No Exposion	Some Exposition	Story with Exposition or Exposition	No Story or Stories with as Much Exposition as needed	Story
Exposition						
Dialogue	No Exposion	Little Exposion	Moderate Exposition	Exposition in Dialogue	as Much Exposition as desired or interest calls for	Dialogue

How People Learn and the Use of Exposition
A Learning Grid

Story sessions are divided into sections. There is the time to tell or read the story and the time to talk about what the story teaches. Thus, with an illiterate individual/group, the storyer would tell the story and then ask questions of discovery but not give explanations of meaning or extensive teaching (no exposition). The listener will be able to extract meaning from the story and apply it to her life. When teaching a story to a highly literate individual/group, the storyer can read the story with the group and give a high level of teaching material both with the story and in the dialogue time (exposition as desired). This grid helps the storyer (evangelist) to determine the preferred learning style of the recipient and to tailor the message accordingly. The message is heard!

Storying the Bible isn't the same as telling Bible stories to children. When storying to adults, we need to be careful not to treat them as children. Treat adults as adults! I recently saw one of my colleagues try to model telling a story during a conference. She was sitting on a chair and her "volunteer listeners" were sitting on the floor. She started the story but quickly stopped and asked them to move to chairs. She said, "This isn't working. I'm treating you like children." Storying is an adult process. When the listeners moved to chairs, the storyer's demeanor changed. Her way of telling the story, her questions, her gestures, all combined to reflect that her group was adult.

When storying the Bible, it is important not only to know how the people tell stories but also how they receive truth. It would be important to study a people's worldview to learn what conveys truth in that society. In West Africa, one storyer learned that true and important stories are told in only one place in the village. Stories told anywhere else in that village don't convey truth and are treated as if they were fables or fairy tales.

Worldview influences how the story is received. Oral communicators will tend to find truths in a story different from those found by literate communicators. For example, with the Joseph story, oral communicators tend to focus on the forgiveness issue or the issue of relationships over justice. They note the importance of family unity and the fact that God interprets dreams. The literate worldview tends to focus on morality issues, the sovereignty of God, rewards for having followed God's will and character issues. Being aware of these differences helps the storyer use the dialogue time to clarify the essential points of the story. The oral communicator's perceptions aren't wrong. However, the oral communicator can discover additional meaning through questioning and guided dialogue.

When evaluating worldview, it's important to decide which barriers are major barriers. Some barriers will need several stories before the message is communicated. One example is folk Islam. Most folk Muslim women will need to hear several stories that demonstrate that God loves, is involved in the lives of, and takes care of women. They will need to hear several examples of Jesus being more powerful than evil spirits. Another example is the idea of a blood sacrifice for sins. Many reject the death of Jesus because to them, Jesus didn't need to die. It is important to evaluate the worldview barrier and to determine the number of stories that will be needed to bridge the barrier so that hearers will understand the biblical truth.

Chronological Bible storying is a win/win approach because it waits until the individual has all the information before asking for a decision. It is biblically sound in that it presents the theological base for the need for a savior before presenting Jesus as the savior. For example, Paul and Stephen presented a chronological overview of the Old Testament in their witness encounters. Jesus himself, as he walked with two disciples on the Emmaus road after his resurrection, started his encounter with the books of Moses and the prophets before he talked about himself as the Messiah. In addition, the process allows God to reveal himself and then Jesus to reveal himself before confronting the hard issue of Jesus' death and resurrection. After all the information has been presented, the person is asked to make a decision. For these reasons, I have found this method ideal for use with Muslim women. In addition, it allows me to teach the Bible to women in groups. By telling the story and talking about what the story teaches us about God, I'm not asking them to believe. I don't get into debates about which story (Quranic or biblical version) is true. I present the truth, help them discover the meaning for their lives during the dialogue time and leave the work of the Holy Spirit to the Holy Spirit (Acts 16:14). I've found that keeping in the win/win mode until decision time keeps the women coming and allows time for the Holy Spirit to use the information to work in their hearts.

After attending a storying workshop in Portugal, one man wrote the following as part of his evaluation of this method:

> It presents the gospel to resistant people (of which we also have many) in such a way that there is prolonged exposure to the Bible in the power of the Spirit, allowing opportunity for barriers to be gradually torn down and penetrated.
>
> Its methodical, chronological approach gives the opportunity to lay the theological groundwork necessary in a confused religious environment such as ours, so that people are better prepared to make a clear, well-founded decision for Christ. (My impression is that people won through storying will be easier to disciple, since much of the religious confusion is dealt with before they come to a commitment.)

The attention it gives to worldview in the crafting of the presentation of the gospel requires a thought process which is missiologically sound and worth the effort for any missionary.

The use of narrative as the primary method of communication is more relevant than ever in today's media-oriented culture.

Our Experience: Storying for Muslim Women in Paris

When I returned to Paris after the workshop and consultation in 1994, I took the information to a colleague who also became convinced that chronological Bible storying was the method we needed to try, and we began to work through the worldview document. Answering these questions directed our thinking toward the Bible stories we needed to use to break through the barriers to the gospel that we were identifying.

We knew that we needed to start at the beginning, at creation, and include enough stories to lay the foundation for the coming of Christ. Many don't want to take the time to start with the Old Testament. However, Rick B. has developed a diagram called "The Unknown: The Whole Counsel of God." Lynne A. has modified this diagram, and the modified version is shown here. The rungs on the ladder represent the books of the Bible. This diagram clearly shows that trying to get to the first rung of the New Testament is an insurmountable leap for anyone other than perhaps Carl Lewis! The Old Testament is needed, but not all the Old Testament is essential in presenting the salvation message. With a clear understanding of the barriers and bridges in a given society, the evangelist can choose a list of stories that provide the base and allow the person to get to the top of the ladder or to full knowledge of God.

From the Known to the Unknown

As my colleague and I began to form a story list, we considered several different things. We worked through the worldview questions and identified the barriers and bridges to the gospel in the Muslim worldview we were encountering. We also had a list of essential Christian doctrines or truths that we needed to communicate. With these two lists in mind, we formed a list of objectives that we wanted to cover in the stories we chose. We were also aware of time and logistics problems for the Paris area. We knew we could only meet with women during school hours and that they would only come once per week. Considering the French school vacation calendar, we calculated that we would have a maximum

The Unknown:
The Whole Counsel of God

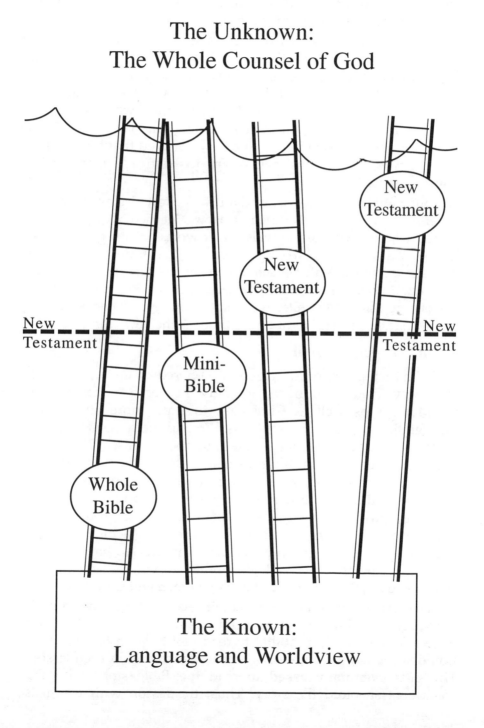

The Known:
Language and Worldview

of 33 story sessions in one year. Thus we had 33 stories to get from the Creation to the resurrection of Jesus with an explanation of what his death and resurrection means for each individual.

We also chose a series of themes that we wanted to carry through the stories. These themes included: the characteristics of God, the sin nature, the separation of men and women from God, the acceptable sacrifice and the promise of a savior. We decided that the major emphasis would be on learning who God is, or learning about God's character. By learning who God really is as he has revealed himself in his Word, we believed that the Muslim woman would have a strong desire to have a personal relationship with him.

Our initial story list was a trial list. We tested it with several different women and modified it as we learned more. My colleague worked with individuals and I worked with groups. We learned that we needed to change some of the stories and learned that some stories, which we had considered unimportant, were very important. We also helped each other in story preparation. On one occasion, my colleague pointed out that I had so many review questions that I didn't have time for the new story.

As an Evangelistic Tool

With each group or individual, we offered an invitation in the same way. They were invited to study the Torah, a sacred book for Muslims as well as Christians, to learn more about God through the stories he has given us. We told them that we would study the story to see what God tells us about himself. We didn't argue or defend the truthfulness of the story. By studying it to learn more about God, we stayed in a win/win position all the time. We used the entire story list with a woman and with a group of teenage girls, and we used a modified list with a group of children. As of this writing, we are in the process of teaching a second group of girls and a group of women. The process has made us stronger believers in chronological Bible storying as an evangelistic method for working with Muslim women and children.

The teenage girls, because of their level of education in middle school, fall into the "oral/print communicator" column on the learning grid. Their ability to read and to learn from exposition determined the amount of teaching included in each lesson. The girls eventually asked to read the Bible story with the teacher as she told the story. Thus, the lesson with the girls

included a combination of telling, reading, exposition and dialogue questions. Using the learning grid helped us plan the lessons for their preferred learning style.

We did not succeed with every effort. I tried to start two different groups without success. I learned that, even in Paris, the group
needs to be a natural group. The women who came from different
people groups, even though they were neighbors who spoke to
each other daily, didn't trust each other well enough to meet
together weekly. The successful group was a group of women
who already spent nearly every afternoon in each other's homes.
With the women and with the teenage girls, some came initially
and then dropped out. Others continued through the entire story
list. I considered each group a "success," in that I learned valuable
lessons for the next effort.

A revised story list for women is included here to illustrate the
sequence of stories we used. Each of the stories on our list teaches
something about God. The repeating themes are:

- the characteristics of God: God keeps His promises. God
  provides. God is just. God doesn't tolerate sin. God is all-
  powerful and all-knowing. God seeks a relationship with
  men/women.

- the acceptable sacrifice

- God provides for and cares for women

- the sin nature

- the promise of a Savior

This is not the original list. This list has developed as a result of
testing the stories. Neither will this be the final list. I believe that
we will continue to revise the list as we teach the stories to groups
and individuals.

Revised Story List for Muslim Women in Paris, 1999
developed by A. H. and colleagues

1. *Introduction: Talk about characteristics of God.*
2. *The creation story. Everything was perfect and good.*
3. *Angels and the fall of Satan: Isa. 14:12-14, Ez 28:11-19. Explains
   the presence of Satan and evil spirits in the world.*
4. *Adam and Eve's sin and the consequences. God knows everything.*
5. *Cain and Abel. God knows everything.*

6. Noah and the flood. God doesn't tolerate sin, and God provides salvation.

7. The tower of Babel. Disobedience to God's command has consequences.

8. Abraham's call and his walk of faith with God. Abraham had faith but he wasn't sinless.

9. Ishmael's birth and life, including the banishment and God's promise for him. The birth of Isaac. God keeps his promises.

10. Sacrifice of Isaac. God provides the acceptable sacrifice.

11. Summary of the lives of Isaac and Jacob, including the birth of Jacob's children. God takes care of us even when we falter.

12. Joseph from birth to his experience with Potiphar's wife. God was with Joseph everywhere. Even though each person has a sin nature, the act of sinning is a choice.

13. Joseph's experiences in prison, the famine and the reconciliation of Joseph with his brothers. God desires that we forgive each other and have reconciliation.

14. Summary of the 400 years, birth of Moses through his call at Mount Sinai. God didn't forget his people.

15. God delivers the people from Egypt, including the story of the Passover. God determined the acceptable act for salvation.

16. God directs the people through the desert and the 10 Commandments. God provides.

17. The Law, the rebellion of the people, a summary of the 40 years.

18. The entry into the promised land, Jericho, with an emphasis on the story of Rahab and her faith, her decision to follow God.

19. Ruth, with an emphasis on her decision to follow God. This story with the story of Rahab shows that women have the power to make their own choice to follow God.

20. Hannah and the birth of Samuel. Hannah demonstrated her faith in an all-powerful God who doesn't need any help to accomplish his purpose.

21. Saul and the Witch of Endor. The storyer needs to review why Saul has lost communication with God. This story deals powerfully with folk Islam.

22. *David and Bathsheba, including enough of David's life to show that he knew the law and chose to disobey. Sin has consequences even when the individual repents.*

23. *Elijah and Elisha, with special emphasis on Naaman and the fact that salvation requires doing exactly what God says and not what the individual wants to do.*

24. *The birth of Jesus, including some of the prophecies for his birth.*

25. *The baptism and temptation of Jesus.*

26. *Jesus is more powerful than nature: miracles of calming the storm, feeding the 5000.*

27. *Jesus is more powerful than evil spirits: Gaderene demoniac.*

28. *Jesus is more powerful than sickness and death: the healing of the woman sick for 12 years and the raising of the daughter of Jairus.*

29. *Jesus has the power to forgive sins. The adulterous woman at the house of Simon and the healing of the man with the four friends.*

30. *Jesus and the Samaritan woman.*

31. *From Palm Sunday to the Last Supper.*

32. *The arrest, crucifixion and resurrection of Jesus.*

33. *The ascension of Jesus and a review of the meaning of the stories told.*

34. *The story of Lazarus and the rich man. The day of judgment.*

35. *Meet with each person individually and ask for a decision.*

I want to explain why we chose some of the stories and offer the points we felt were important to emphasize because of the barriers we found in the worldview of Muslim women in Paris. Some individuals have said that discipleship starts with the first encounter that a nonbeliever has with a Christian. Therefore, the stories, as they are told the first time to a nonbeliever, are influencing her future Christian life.

The two major barriers that we found in Muslim women from several different people groups living in Paris are (1) a belief that God is far away and neither interested nor involved in the daily life of a woman, and (2) a belief that sin is something we do and is punished only if we are caught. One woman used the term "spectator" to describe God. In her view, since God is just a spectator and not involved, he sees an individual's sin only when others draw attention to it. Folk Islam, with its animistic practices, provides another strong barrier to the gospel. Other barriers include these characteristics: Muslim women don't feel valued and loved by God. Women don't have the power to make life decisions for themselves. And the image of the father in most Muslim households does not represent accurately the image of Father God. I frequently see mothers teaching their children to hide things from the father. The mother teaches the child that the father is someone to fear, that secrets can be kept and that if the father learns of the behavior, punishment will be swift and severe. When a woman has that image of a father, it is difficult for her to desire to have a relationship with God as Father.

With these barriers in mind, we selected and told the stories found in Genesis 1-11. These stories laid the foundation for an understanding that God is interested in and involved with us, and he knows everything—even our thoughts. God knew what Adam and Eve had done, even though they denied it. He knew what Cain was intending to do and what he had done even though Cain denied it and there were no witnesses. God knew who the righteous man was at the time of the flood. God knew that the people were being disobedient when they were building the tower of Babel.

We told these stories and then asked questions such as: How did God know what Eve did? Why did God warn Cain? How did he know what was in Cain's heart? The women began to see that God desires a close, personal relationship with each individual, that God knows what is in the heart of each person, and that God cares. They also began to learn about the sin nature and man's disobedience to God's word. Another theme that we emphasized is that God keeps his promises. We did not teach these points, but through dialogue and questions, we helped the women discover the answers for themselves.

With the stories of Abraham, we emphasized the importance of faith, of believing that God will keep his promises. Each time Abraham stumbled, they saw that it is because he didn't have faith that God would keep his promise. They also learned that God didn't abandon Abraham when he was disobedient. The Ishmael story presents risks because of the difference in the accounts between the Bible and the Quran. We told as many stories as possible before the Ishmael story. Then, to help avoid a problem, we told the story of Ishmael in one session and left the chronological sequence for this session. To date, I have told Ishmael's story to children, teenage girls and women in several different settings. Each group has accepted the story and continued meeting with me for more stories. One illiterate woman's response was, "That's a true story." She went on to explain that all the problems between Sarah and Hagar were a result of Abraham's lack of faith that God would keep his promise. She actually said, "If Abraham had waited on God, none of this would have happened." She gleaned that from the story, not from expository teaching!

I have not found a problem with any group or individual when I have told the story of the sacrifice of Isaac. Each group has accepted this and marveled at God's intervention. I have read that others have had a problem and have solved it by keeping the emphasis on God and God's provision of an acceptable sacrifice. When teaching this story, one missionary acknowledged that the accounts in the Quran and the Bible were different, but the important fact in each account was that God provided the acceptable sacrifice and that it was God who decided, not man. Chronological Bible storying, with its emphasis on the character of God, is a win/win method. I don't get into arguments or debates about which account is the true one. I tell the story, keep the emphasis on God and let the Holy Spirit convince them of the truth.

Following the chronology of the Bible also helps to avoid arguments and debates. Recently, a woman came to one of the story groups in Paris. She interrupted the story of Noah to ask a question. She said, "You believe that Jesus is the Son of God, don't you?" I replied by saying, "You know that I'm a Christian and as a Christian I have my beliefs. I know that you are a Muslim and as a Muslim you have your beliefs. We both believe that the Torah is one of God's holy books. Therefore, we can study the Torah and learn more about God as he has revealed himself through the stories. That way we don't have to get into arguments." Her reply was, "Oh!" She dropped the subject and we continued with the story and a discussion on what the story taught us about God. Thus, personal experience has taught me that this method is "win/win."

Because it is important to maintain the chronology, we included a summary of Isaac and Jacob. For oral learners to memorize the stories, they need a context for each story. We wanted to emphasize the life of Joseph, especially his experience with Potiphar's wife.

With this story, we wanted to show that even with our sin nature, breaking one of God's laws is a choice. We also wanted to lay a foundation for the story of David and Bathsheba that we would tell later, with an emphasis on David's behavior. Knowing the law didn't keep David from disobeying God. We used the story of David to talk about the consequences of our actions, even when we repent and God forgives us. However, when we first told the story of Joseph, we were astonished by the reaction of the women and girls to the reconciliation story of Joseph and his brothers. They couldn't believe that Joseph would actually forgive his brothers and rebuild a relationship with them. This opened a door for talking about family problems, God's desire for families to be reconciled, and God's desire that each person forgive the wrongs done to him/her. We decided to modify the story list to include an emphasis on the reconciliation story.

Some stories are essential for teaching biblical truth while others are for keeping the chronology that oral communicators need in order to understand the whole story. The stories of Moses and the law are essential stories for teaching biblical truth. In telling these stories, we laid a foundation for the future. In the New Testament, we wanted to talk about the woman who had been sick for 12 years. Therefore, with the law, we presented some of the laws pertaining to women. When following a chronology, one can refer to what has already happened but not to the future.

We used the stories of Rahab and Ruth to show that a woman has the power to make her own choice regarding her religion. Rahab and Ruth both decided to leave their culture, their people and their religion to follow God. We describe Rahab's faith in putting the red string in her window and then how long she had to wait in faith for God to keep his promise. The teenage girls noted the significance that the string was red. They also learned that God keeps his promises. Some groups might place a political interpretation on these two stories. The storyer will want to be sure that the biblical truth is not overshadowed by political concerns from today's world. (Arab/Israeli conflicts are barriers for some people groups. The storyer doesn't want the people to see Rahab or Ruth as being traitors to the Arab cause.)

We used the story of Hannah and then the story of Saul and the witch of Endor to talk about folk Islam. With the story of Hannah, we emphasized her actions when she couldn't have a baby. During the dialogue section, we referred to God's laws about the use of sorcery and magic and asked questions that helped the women to learn that Hannah prayed what was in her heart. Her prayer wasn't a memorized ritual, and she used nothing else to try to convince God to give her a child. We wanted the women to discover that God is all-powerful; he doesn't need the help of magic or charms—in fact, he forbids their use. With the story of Saul and the witch of Endor, we pointed out how easy it is to make a correct decision, then fall back into the pattern that God has forbidden. The women learned that sin has consequences. They also continued to learn that God doesn't need the help of sorcery or magic or charms. God is all-powerful.

The story of Naaman demonstrates that God expects total obedience to his command. With each story that shows salvation, including the Passover story and Rahab, we emphasized that God decided what needed to be done and that salvation came from following exactly what God said to do. We used other stories from the Old Testament to give further emphasis to God's love for women and his provision for them. The purpose was to help them understand that God considers women to be important, that he loves them and wants a relationship with them. With women, we emphasized the stories about women so long as the story teaches the essential biblical truths. With children, we tried to use stories that appeal to children but also teach the essential truths. We taught the story of Cain and Abel to all groups, including the children.

After laying the Old Testament foundation—including stories that prophesy of a Messiah, we moved to the stories of Jesus. After telling of his birth, baptism and temptation, we departed from the chronology and grouped the stories around themes that allowed Jesus to reveal himself as the Son of God and the promised Messiah: Jesus is more powerful than nature; Jesus is more powerful than sickness and death; Jesus is more powerful than evil spirits; and Jesus has the power to forgive sin. The children and the teenage girls began calling Jesus the Son of God (a term we had avoided using) about halfway through this series of stories. After this series of stories, we move on to the last week—the arrest, the crucifixion, the resurrection and the ascension. The last story was a review lesson with an explanation of why it was necessary for Jesus to come and to die. After that story, we met with the teenage girls individually to ask if each was ready to believe in Jesus. Each girl indicated that she did believe in Jesus as her savior. Many of the women also accepted Christ. The group of women that I have been working with hasn't reached the last lesson yet.

As a Discipleship Tool

When using chronological Bible storying with illiterate or semiliterate people, the discipleship phase involves going back to the beginning and repeating the stories with a changed emphasis. Now the women are Christians. They know about Jesus. Therefore, each time God gives a promise for a Savior, it is possible to talk about Jesus. Other stories can be added as needed to help the new Christian with her new life in Christ. Further worldview issues will appear as the woman begins her life as a Christian. We chose our initial stories to deal with the barriers that kept her from accepting Christ. Now we chose stories and themes to address the barriers that keep her from living and growing as a Christian. With oral communicators, we can add stories as needed, as long as we place the new story chronologically by telling where it falls with the rest of the stories.

Following the chronology of the Bible is a good discipleship tool for those who have come to Christ through another evangelistic method or through dreams or visions. We formed a Bible study group of literate MBBs and followed the chronology with them. One woman was astonished to find that God always reacts in the same way. She said, "I didn't know that God is consistent and that he always reacts in the same way." She learned this through following the chronology of the Old Testament.

Oral communicators need to be discipled orally. This means that the teacher would continue to story the Bible with the MBB while asking inductive questions that would help the MBB discover the biblical truth for her life. By continuing to follow the chronology of the Bible, the MBB is able to insert new stories into the chronology that she has already learned. The discipleship process includes helping the MBB to learn to share her faith by telling the stories to others. Repeating the stories helps cement them into her memory; in addition, of course, it helps her share God's good news with others. By repeating the stories to others, the MBB woman becomes a reproducing Christian.

Discipleship of a new Christian includes several goals: she needs to grow in her faith and to be prepared for the persecution that will come. And she needs to learn how to share her faith with her family and friends. Disciplers need to help her identify and deal with the barriers to her Christian growth so that she can mature in her faith. One of the goals of discipleship would be for her to become a reproducing Christian in a reproducing church. Chronological Bible storying, which allows evangelism in a group, also provides for discipleship in a group. This group can go on to form themselves into a cell or house church or join another existing church. The goal should be reproduction or a church planting movement. With chronological Bible storying, the MBB has all the essential resources. She has a Bible that crosses borders and can't be confiscated.

One of my colleagues discipled MBB women by using stories of women in the Bible. With the teenage girls, we taught the same chronological lessons again but talked about Jesus with each lesson and discussed the biblical truths for believers. Since all the girls are in school, we also decided to use Book One of the Navigators' series of discipleship books and worked through the questions in a group. Thus these girls, who fall between the third and fourth columns on the grid, had a mixture of oral/literate discipleship. However, I've found that each time I've tried to use such a book with Muslim women who can read, they lose interest before we have finished the series of lessons. Even the readers have difficulty understanding the doctrine being taught by proof texts. They are essentially oral communicators.

Because of this problem and others—including many worldview barriers that aren't included in most discipleship literature, I've developed a series of Bible studies on particular worldview issues that seem to be common with MBB women. Most of the studies are based on Bible stories with inductive questions. Depending on the preferred communication style, the MBB can either read or hear the story and then work through the questions to learn the truth that God is teaching in the story. The discipleship lessons cover the following issues: folk Islam, opposition, sin, prayer, church, forgiveness, repentance, witnessing and fasting. Each topic has a series of Bible stories and questions that deal with the subject. The Christian doing the discipleship will need to decide how many of the stories need to be studied to ensure that the issue has been adequately covered. I've learned that I need to do one or two of the lessons with MBB women, then return to the issue later and do more of the lessons.

The MBB needs to meet with other believers for Christian fellowship. One of the best ways to achieve this is to help her form a cell group of believers. This group becomes a church. When chronological Bible storying is done with a group, it is easy to continue with the group as believers who become a church. As the number of believers grows, the group can divide and become part of a church planting movement. We haven't reached this point in Paris yet, but our goal is a church planting movement for each of the people groups living there.

Resources

The following resources on chronological Bible storying can be obtained from the International Mission Board of the Southern Baptist Convention (IMB, SBC); write to Mark Snowden, International Mission Board, Southern Baptist Convention, Box 6767, Richmond, VA 23230.

- *God and Woman*, by J.O. Terry. This set of 90 stories written for women from Muslim or Hindu backgrounds can be used as a model for those who are working with women. (Available on diskette or in print format.)

- *Chronological Bible Storying: A Methodology for Presenting the Gospel to Oral Communicators*, by J. O. Terry and Jim Slack, is available on diskette or in print.

- *Sharing the Message Through Storying: A Bible Teaching Method for Everyone*, by LaNette Thompson has five chapters on how to do chronological Bible storying in an African Islamic setting. The author includes many examples of her actual experiences. Then she gives her story outlines with suggested learning questions for an African Islamic worldview.

New Tribes Mission publishes a catalog with a number of resources for those who want to do chronological Bible teaching, chronological Bible story telling and chronological Bible storying. Contact: New Tribes Mission, 1000 East First Street, Sanford, FL, 32771-1487. Phone: 407-323-3430 or 1-800-321-5375. The following resources are among the resources available from New Tribes Mission:

- *God and Man*, by Del Shultz, is a story set that can be used as a model and help with the initial storying process.

- A picture set that can aid in chronological Bible storying can be purchased in color or black and white, as slides or on a diskette.

Bible Storying: Chronological Bible Storying Newsletter is published quarterly via email. This newsletter has helpful information for anyone who is trying to use this method. To subscribe, contact biblestorying@iname.com

The author of this article, A.H., has developed a set of discipleship Bible studies to use with MBB women called *Producing Mature Fruit*. While they are not presented in the form of chronological Bible storying, they can easily be adapted to storying. Each study uses a story or a scripture passage and provides inductive questions, covering topics such as folk Islam, sin, repentance, forgiveness, fasting and prayer.

Participants' Discussion

The author—Have any of you tried discipling in an oral fashion?

From North Africa—We met a young woman who had completed a set of Bible correspondence courses that were sent to her from outside the country. In fact, she had her Bible course diploma displayed on the wall in her home. A year after we had baptized her, we took her to meet another seeker. I was going to depend on her to lead this new girl to faith. In the course of conversation, the new inquirer said, "Well, how does it work with Muhammad and Christ?" My great believer here, who had finished all these Bible correspondence courses, said, "Well, you have Muhammad and we have Christ. And it is pretty much the same." Then the new inquirer said, "Didn't Christ talk about Muhammad coming afterward?" So I discussed that with her at length. When we left the house, my great helper said, "I didn't understand that. Didn't Christ talk about Muhammad coming after?" Now consider this: for seven years, this woman had taken discipleship and Bible correspondence courses, and she was still so terribly confused. What do we really expect from these new believers? Consider our own lives: how long has it taken us to understand the truths of scripture, and we don't even face all the obstacles they do. We give them information and expect them to accept the package.

Unknown—How do you approach discipleship issues that don't lend themselves to story form? Concepts such as the body of Christ, godly marriage, New Testament exhortations that are not in story form but in letter form?

The author—As Westerners, we've been to church and sat in classes and discussed these issues on the expositional level so much that we feel that's the only way to approach scripture. But if you look at the Old Testament, you will find stories that address raising kids and keeping a marriage together. On the other hand, you can also do a lot of storying of some of the passages of the New Testament. You story the time when Paul was in Corinth, then include some of the letter he wrote. The point is, they can't understand it if you just read the scripture, not if they are totally illiterate. They have to have it in a story form that fits chronologically, so they can anchor it.

Unknown—If they are illiterate, should we use flannel graph or pictures or story cards to help make a visual connection for them?

The author—If you use any kind of visual aid, it must be culturally appropriate and easily reproducible. You want church planting movements—which means you want these women to go tell it to somebody else. If you use an elaborate flannel graph set, are they going to be willing to go tell their neighbors? A woman I know who stories in West Africa finds simple items around the village to use as props. For example, when she storied Isaac and the sacrifice, she used a butcher knife, which every woman in the village has. Then, every time a woman uses her butcher knife at home, she is thinking of that story.

From East Africa—Where I live, much teaching is done through songs. Have you had any experience at putting this kind of thing into musical patterns or some kind of chanting?

The author—Not me. I don't sing! What you need to do is look at how stories are told in the area where you live. What are their normal storytelling patterns? Also, where do they tell things that are important? In a West African Muslim village, a native Christian worker was trying to tell stories from the Bible, but nobody was paying attention. Villagers later revealed to him that a certain place in the village "is where you go if you want to tell something important. If you tell it anywhere else, then it is not important." How do they transmit information that is important? Do they sing? Do they dance? Do they do drama? Do they recite poetry?

From the Middle East—Does everybody know about the cassette tapes that were produced recently about the stories of the prophets and the stories of Christ? They are well done and available in Egyptian and Baghdadi Arabic dialects. The Baghdadi dialect is perfect for the Bedouins we work among. They use Islamic terms, such as *nabi* for prophet. We have found them quite helpful. [1]

Thinking through the Issues

1. *Approximately what percentage of the women you work/worked with could really understand the Bible by reading it? What percentage could understand if it was read aloud and discussed? What percentage understood parables and stories more easily?*

2. *Have you tried discipling in a primarily oral fashion? How has it worked? If you haven't, why not?*

3. *Is literacy of such value that we should try to move all believers in that direction? Why or why not?*

4. *What media have you found to be especially useful with oral communicators?*

5. *What are strengths and weaknesses of oral communication that do not exist in written communication? How can we minimize some of the handicaps of oral communication and maximize its strengths?*

6. *What forms of oral "discipling" communication exist already in your culture of ministry? What oral communications do they memorize? How does this take place? What types of content are covered (genealogies, myths, skill development, etc.)?*

7. *Have you seen other training or indoctrinating forms, such as drama, symbolic dances, poetry or songs? In what contexts are they used? Who leads or initiates them?*

8. *How much knowledge is passed on nonverbally by modeling only? How can we more effectively and systematically model basic teachings of the New Testament, especially to believers?*

9. *How did the author's perspective on evangelism change after she learned about chronological Bible storying? What factors did she now consider important? Which of these factors have you found most useful or have you most overlooked?*

---

[1] Those who have produced the cassettes mentioned here recommend the Baghdadi dialect for use among Muslim background Arabic speakers. The cassettes are available from Domain Communications, Main Place, Carol Stream, IL 60188. Tel: 800-366-2461. Domain is meant to be a wholesale duplicator of spoken Arabic cassettes, preferring to handle orders of 100 or more for resale by local distributors.

10.   *Jesus often told stories with no explanations or exposition. Sometimes he would explain things more clearly to his disciples later. To what group of learners does the author recommend using the "no exposition" style? Do you feel comfortable with this approach? Why or why not? Would you feel more comfortable doing this in your own culture than in a foreign culture?*

11.   *List some problems you are encountering as you disciple Muslim women; for example, do they have trouble understanding the meaning of the scriptural texts or with their worldview of scripture? What Bible stories, parables, personal testimonies, or proverbs could you share that pertain to these issues?*

12.   *Why is it more important to have not merely a needs-based approach but also a systematic chronological approach even with oral communicators?*

13.   *What impresses you most about the chronological Bible storying approach of the author? Have you tried anything similar? With what results?*

14.   *The author lists two major barriers and a number of other hindrances to Muslim women understanding the gospel. Which of these have you found most significant in your area? Are there other key hindrances or needs you would like to add to this list?*

15.   *The author has done a marvelous job of selecting the chronological stories to cover both the heart needs and worldview/doctrine needs of Muslim women. As their faith slowly develops, how can this storytelling time also support modeling of corporate prayer, worship, and intercession including spiritual warfare?*

16.   *If the group wishes to continue meeting after the thirty-three weeks, how could you avoid losing momentum, encourage developing leadership, or cover a transition period when you might be gone?*

17.   *In your culture or community, do you feel it would be important to disciple the older or influential women early on to avoid a backlash? Or have you found that stories repeated by children to adults rarely elicit negative reactions?*

For Further Study or Reflection:

- *In oral cultures, not only teaching, but often wisdom, rebukes, advice, or warnings are communicated in a story, parable, anecdote, or proverb. Have you received any advice in this form (and recognized it)? What can you do to expand your ability to communicate/respond in these forms?*

- *The author mentioned that natural groupings of women worked better than those put together artificially by the leader. Try to list some existing natural groups of women or meeting areas where you could do regular chronological story telling. Try to think laterally. For example, what about doing some introductory stories in a public steam bath at a set time each week until you gather a following, then launch into the chronological flow? An exercise/storytelling combination club for young ladies? A kids' play group/storytelling combination for young mothers? Tell them you are memorizing these stories as language learning exercises and share them each week by the river, public ovens, well, or wherever women are allowed to gather—a sponsor's home is ideal, of course. Try to list as many ideas as possible for different types of women or community subsets. How can you avoid extracting a potentially scary up-front commitment yet ensure that most women will come regularly?*

Evangelism to and through Family Networks

Kay Waters

What do you think of when you hear the words "evangelism to and through family networks"? I think first of my longing to see whole families come to Christ. I really like the first verse of the song "One Shall Tell Another" by Graham Kendrick (1981):

> One shall tell another, and he shall tell his friend.
> Husbands, wives and children shall come following on.
> From house to house in families shall more be gathered in,
> and lights will shine in every street so warm and welcoming.

This is what we would all love to see happen. We long to be able to echo the words of Acts in our prayer letters: "[Fatima] and her whole household believed and were baptized." We know in our hearts that a solid church is not made up of a few struggling individual believers, but that to grow and reproduce, it must be founded on strong families. Some of the organizations we work with have even formalized this definition of a church, specifying how many families/married men must be in the group before we can say it is truly an "indigenous church."

I think next of how unqualified I am to share on this topic. The word "evangelism" intimidates me. I do not consider myself gifted (spiritually or naturally) in this area. This topic also stirs up visions in my mind of legendary stories of whole villages or tribes converting when the chief decides to follow Christ. Maybe this really happens among remote tribal groups somewhere like Papua New Guinea, but can it really occur where we work?

Kay Waters has worked in North Africa for more than seven years, running a health and development project. She is active in church planting among Muslim women.

My team's work in a large city of a Saharan country seems far removed from the steamy jungles of Papua New Guinea in more ways than one. We work in a society that is undergoing rapid, disruptive urbanization. Although tribes and clans are still significant features of the society in rural areas of the country, in the city where we live, social networks and families are breaking down. The only times we've seen the gospel spread along family networks was when several husbands led their wives to the Lord. This sounds wonderful, right? The only problem is that most of these husbands later abandoned their wives and children—and apparently the faith, as well. Most of the wives are still clinging to their faith in the midst of poverty and the challenges of raising and providing for their children alone, but we hardly have anything looking like a "family" in our fragile church! Even among the two believing couples, the husbands and wives spend most of their time geographically separated. The wives live with their families, while the husbands are working elsewhere in the country.

So I am definitely *not* an expert on the topic of evangelizing family networks! But as a part of a team, I can share the lessons we have learned about evangelizing in a way that leads toward the growth of the gospel along networks.

It seems to me there are two aspects of this topic. The first concerns our relationships with and witness to Muslim families. To what extent are we reaching out to families and social networks rather than individuals? The second aspect is the relationship and witness of MBBs to their extended families and social networks after they believe in Christ. To what extent are they able to maintain their ties to community and family and effectively share their faith in Christ with their relatives and friends? We will look at each aspect in turn.

Our Relationships with and Witness to Muslim Family Networks

How can we build relationships that will facilitate families coming to Christ? Most Western evangelistic approaches train us to focus on individuals. Are there different models we can use that are more family-oriented?

With Whom Do We Share?

In developing a family-oriented church-planting strategy, perhaps the first issue to examine is whom we are getting to know and with whom we are sharing the gospel. If the head of household chooses to believe in Jesus, would the whole family follow? Do we understand the culture well enough to understand how decisions are made and which family members might be able to influence many others in the family? A veteran evangelist, himself a Muslim background believer, has said,

> In order to build churches we have to reach families. Sometimes we have a contact, often a single person, and we share our faith with him. If he eventually becomes a believer, he is on his own (in terms of family). We should invest more in getting to know the whole family—and especially the head of the family. This might open up a door to witness to a family as a whole and give them the chance to understand what is going on. As a result they might not feel as though somebody has been stolen from their family and manipulated.

We women, particularly those of us who are single, may need to give this issue careful thought. If a married woman is open to the gospel, perhaps a team couple could invite her and her husband to a meal or a social event as a way to get to know the husband and reach out on a couple-to-couple level. Likewise, if we are working with young unmarried girls, we might look for ways that a man or couple from the team can get to know the father or parents and gain their respect and trust.

Perhaps one of the keys to helping us develop relationships with the extended family is to visit our friends in their homes. We are often schooled in the importance of hospitality in a Muslim context and thus want and need to welcome our friends into our homes. And it may be much easier to hold Bible studies and other forms of ministry in our homes for reasons of privacy. But I am increasingly convinced that alongside our own ministry of hospitality, we must spend time in our friends' homes, accepting their hospitality. Such times allow us to get to know our friends in the context of their families, help us to understand the relationships that are significant in their lives, and may give us a chance to get to know and interact with members of the family who, for cultural reasons, might never be able to visit us in our homes. For these reasons, I am convinced that time spent in our friends' homes will bear fruit in the lives of many in the family. Scanning through the Gospels and Acts, I find at least twelve examples of Jesus or the disciples entering individuals' homes and using them as a basis of ministry. Acts also describes how the disciples in Jerusalem and later the apostle Paul combined public ministry and teaching in the synagogues with a more personal style of ministry from "house to house."

In situations where family ties are not very strong, perhaps we need to look creatively for alternate networks through which the gospel message might spread. Do the women we are eager to reach belong to particular groups or clubs? Groups that are characterized by a high degree of trust and personal commitment among the members (thus providing a kind of surrogate family) might be fertile ground for the gospel. As an example, in the country where I work, many women of a particular ethnic group belong to informal credit societies. Generally, women in these groups form close relationships, and most groups have something akin to a formal covenant that outlines the rights and responsibilities of membership in the group. We've not yet seen the gospel touch such groups, but there is much potential for the church to grow along such lines.

What Do We Share?

Beyond looking at the question of *with whom* we share the gospel, to become effective in reaching families or other social networks, we may also have to reexamine how we share the gospel: What is our message? In doing this, I have had to ask myself, "What is evangelism?" For me, coming from a culture that tends to value black-and-white dichotomous thinking, the witnessing mode I am most comfortable with is one-on-one personal evangelism, sharing directly from scripture with one of my friends. I thus tend to define "witnessing" as a specific list of points about Jesus that I must cover and something that is clearly identifiable and distinct from other activities such as work or social gatherings. Perhaps such a definition allows me to mentally check off a box and pat myself on the back: "Ah, good. I have witnessed to Fatima. Task accomplished. It's up to her to respond. The ball is now in her court. Let's move on to something else."

But apart from the theological problems with such a definition of evangelism, such an approach has practical weaknesses as well. If we think that to evangelize we have to present the "entire gospel" in one sitting, we may not share very often because we think we won't be able to do it "right" or because of time limitations or a feeling that our friend is not yet "ready." Furthermore, such a style of sharing might be threatening to our less educated friends or intimidating to MBB women, causing them to believe they must be well-trained in theology or apologetics before sharing their faith with family and friends.

In fact, it is through my relationships with several MBB women that I feel I am beginning better to grasp what evangelism is all about. As I sit in my friends' homes and drink tea, I am very conscious of my friends' role as light and salt in their homes and neighborhoods. I long to see the gospel spread from their homes to touch the lives of their whole circle of friends. And when I return home, I pray for them that they would be able to begin to share with their family, friends and neighbors what Jesus means to them and how he is answering their prayers. Moreover, I pray that their lives themselves would be a testimony of Jesus' love, faithfulness and the transforming power of his Holy Spirit. If this is how I expect my MBB friends to share the gospel with those around them, then maybe it's how I myself should be sharing! Increasingly, I find myself wanting Paul's words to the Thessalonians to describe my own life and ministry: "We loved you so much that we were delighted to share with you not only the gospel of God but our lives as well, because you had become so dear to us" (1 Thes. 2:8).

Viewing evangelism as a matter of sharing our lives as well as sharing in words may help us become more comfortable in sharing about Christ in a group setting. For years I have felt frustrated in group conversations with local women, feeling linguistically inadequate and discouraged by the seeming superficiality of the discussion. So I have often stayed silent, fearing to introduce serious spiritual themes in such a context. But I am slowly learning that social gatherings can become witnessing opportunities if I am willing to be transparent and share about my life, my struggles, my victories, and my testimony of how God is at work. I think some of my growth in this area, too, is a result of growth in my prayer life. I have had several opportunities in recent months to share on a much deeper level with groups of friends through telling them about a particular work problem we faced and how God intervened, or about how God answered prayer for healing. Because I am interceding more, I am much more conscious of and thankful for God's specific answers to prayer; thus, I am much quicker to look for opportunities to speak about God's faithfulness to others, even to a whole group of women! And prayer itself is a wonderful witnessing "tool." As I have finally grown more confident in praying in the local language, I have grown bolder to pray with friends for healing or other special needs in front of their family members and friends. This is leading to new opportunities to share with and pray for others. Finally, in this context, proverbs, parables and stories also seem well-suited for sharing in a group/family setting because they are generally less threatening and can reach people of many different classes and ages.

How Do We Live?

Later in this paper, we will move from a focus on our relationships and communication strategies to an examination of the MBB's role in sharing the gospel with others in his/her family. Yet we cannot totally dissociate these two topics. They are interwoven. In most cases, we are being watched more closely than we realize, and our lifestyles and reputations often strongly influence how the extended family reacts to a family member's decision to follow Christ and whether they will be open to the gospel. Our efforts to earn trust and respect among members of a seeker's extended family may go a long way in helping to ensure that a new believer is not cast out of the family and can witness from within his or her family network. If the family knows and trusts us and sees our respect and love for their culture, and if they perceive us as holy, God-fearing, hospitable, loving and generous people, they might be much less likely to reject the MBB. This may be particularly crucial for single women reaching out to unmarried daughters in Muslim families. We must be very careful not to be perceived as corrupting or destructive forces within the family. We want Christianity to be perceived as a positive influence.

This is an area of our team's ministry where I see much to be thankful for and encouraged about. As I shared in my introduction, we have not seen much overt success in spreading the gospel along family networks. Yet there is hope that we will see such fruit since it appears that our lifestyle is perceived as holy and has gained the respect of our neighbors, friends, and— perhaps most important—the families of the MBBs we are discipling. Although some have faced intense persecution, all the MBBs we are working with are still accepted within their families.

A story from the life of Pilgrim, one of the "elders-in-training" we are discipling, is an excellent example of how a missionary's reputation and lifestyle can affect the believer's continued acceptance in his/her own family. When Pilgrim's family members found out about his faith, they were furious and wanted to disown him, or worse. His mother, however, made the following observation. She said, "I didn't like it at all when Pilgrim started hanging around those foreigners. Yet he tells us that these foreigners fear God, and they pray. And I see that he is a much better son now than he was before he met them. Before, he was out chasing girls, and he did not help the family. Now he is home every night for dinner, he prays, he has a good job and helps support the family. These foreigners have had a good influence on his life." This incident took place several years ago. Pilgrim has been able to stay in his family and is slowly rebuilding his relationship with his father and the other relatives and friends who were ready to disown him.

In some cultures, we might even hope to be accepted as surrogate members of the family. The author of *Invest Your Heart*, working in Southeast Asia, writes of her experience of being accepted as an "older sister" of a young Muslim girl (Colgate 1997:12-14). Another example I know of personally concerns colleagues ministering among another ethnic group in the country where I work. The team leader was able to gain the respect of the key men in the family of one of the believing women, Lydia, whom they are discipling. When some others in the family were pressuring Lydia to marry a Muslim man against her will, my colleague was able to share his concerns about the matter with the leading men of the family. Eventually he was accepted as a "surrogate uncle," and the other members of the family agreed to let him be responsible to counsel Lydia in this matter.

MBB Relationships and Witness to Their Family Networks

We now turn our focus to the role of our MBB friends in leading their family members and friends to Christ. The words of Graham Kendrick's song make it sound deceptively simple: "One shall tell another and he shall tell his friend ...." Faithfulness in telling others about Jesus is certainly an important beginning, but as in our own ministry, perhaps the *lives* of our MBB friends are even more important than their *words*.

Keeping Believers within Their Family Networks

The obvious starting point to our discussion would seem to be the need to keep MBBs within their family networks after they have come to Christ. One challenge to achieving this is the fact that many MBBs may have first turned to the gospel as a result of disaffection with their culture or with Islam. Dissatisfied with their culture or having experienced much pain and hurt in family relationships, they may be eager to experience Western culture and build relationships with foreigners instead. Jesus' command to the Gerasene demoniac is perhaps one we should repeat to such MBBs: "Go home to your family and tell them how much the Lord has done for you, and how he has had mercy on you" (Mark 5:19). The willingness of a formerly alienated family member to undertake the hard and slow work of rebuilding family relationships can be a powerful testimony to the truth of the gospel and evidence of the sincerity of a believer's faith.

A second challenge to keeping MBBs within their family networks may come from us, the missionaries. Most of us are quick to speak of the dangers of "extraction." Most of us talk of a desire to plant contextualized, indigenous churches, but what does this mean, and how can it facilitate the MBBs' witness to their family networks? I think we most readily tend to think of contextualization as it relates to the efforts and sacrifices we missionaries need to make in order to be respected and gain a hearing for the gospel in the cultures where we work. Certainly, building gospel bridges and minimizing obstacles to the gospel are important goals. Yet perhaps we tend to overlook other aspects of contextualization, particularly the ways in which the structure and style of the emerging church—its worship forms, meeting schedule, respect for cultural values like women's modesty—help new believers maintain the aspects of their cultural identity that don't conflict with scripture. Perhaps we put so much time and energy into sowing that we are not prepared when a group of MBBs comes into being. And if we don't adequately think about what an indigenous MBB church should look like, we might unthinkingly duplicate aspects of our Western church experience. By doing so, we may unintentionally promote conflict between the believers, their families and community so that there are no active networks left along which the gospel can spread.

One possible church model that may help strengthen the MBBs' relationships with their family and friends is that of house churches. The focus in such churches is typically less on the form or structure of the service and more on the relationships and community among the believers. As such, it can be a safe, nonthreatening environment for members to invite nonbelieving friends or family members. Also, to the extent that whole families are involved in a house church, the MBB may be able to observe the process of peacemaking or reconciliation firsthand through watching husbands and wives or parents and children interact, and such lessons may help him or her to rebuild damaged family relationships.

How Can MBBs Share Effectively with Family Members?

Assuming an MBB is able to maintain good relationships with those in her family and community, how can she effectively share her faith with them?

1. Be a shining light. We need to encourage our MBB friends not to fear. I appreciate Jesus' wonderfully practical analogy about oil lamps in this context. "Neither do people light a lamp and put it under a bowl. Instead they put it on its stand, and it gives light to everyone in the house" (Matt. 5:15). We need to remind our MBB friends that they have the light of Christ within them. They are called to freely share the blessing of that light with those in their households instead of hiding their faith. Such a demonstration of their faith doesn't necessarily mean bold verbal preaching. In many cases, such would be unwelcome or inappropriate. Scripture teaches clearly that even without words, our lives can be a powerful witness, even winning over those who look for ways to accuse us:

> Make it your ambition to lead a quiet life, to mind your own business and to work with your hands, just as we told you, so that your daily life may win the respect of outsiders ... (1 Thes. 4:11-12).

> Live such good lives among the pagans that, though they accuse you of doing wrong, they may see your good deeds and glorify God on the day he visits us (1 Peter 2:12).

> Wives, in the same way be submissive to your husbands so that, if any of them do not believe the word, they may be won over without words by the behavior of their wives, when they see the purity and reverence of your lives (1 Peter 3:1-2).

Thus, a holy and pure life is, in itself, an effective and powerful witness to family members and all who are closely watching our MBB friends.

2. Provide practical care for family members' needs. Furthermore, the Bible teaches that practical care for the needs of our family members is an important way of demonstrating the reality of our faith:

> But if a widow has children or grandchildren, these should learn first of all to put their religion into practice by caring for their own family

and so repaying their parents and grandparents, for this is pleasing to God. ... If anyone does not provide for his relatives, and especially for his immediate family, he has denied the faith and is worse than an unbeliever (1 Tim. 5:4, 8).

3. Love others, especially other believers. Although often in the West we are influenced by our culture to have a very individualistic faith that focuses on the importance of our personal relationship with God, the Bible repeatedly stresses the relationship between our love for God and our love for others. Our love for others, reflected in our actions, is the evidence that we know God's love and follow Jesus.

> By this all men will know that you are my disciples, if you love one another (John 13:34-35).

> We know that we have passed from death to life, because we love our brothers. Anyone who does not love remains in death. ... If anyone has material possessions and sees his brother in need but has no pity on him, how can the love of God be in him? Dear children, let us not love with words or tongue but with actions and in truth (1 John 3:14-18).

> Dear friends, let us love one another, for love comes from God. Everyone who loves has been born of God and knows God. Whoever does not love does not know God, because God is love (1 John 4:7-8).

> We love because he first loved us. If anyone says, "I love God," yet hates his brother, he is a liar. For anyone who does not love his brother, whom he has seen, cannot love God, whom he has not seen. And he has given us this command: Whoever loves God must also love his brother (1 John 4:19-21).

The Importance of the Church as a Spiritual Family for MBBs

The verses cited above are some of the most challenging passages in scripture! I've been a believer for nearly 25 years and still I tend to balk at these words in 1 John. How can our MBB friends learn to love others in a way that will demonstrate the truth of the gospel to their family members? Perhaps one of the best and most important means that God uses to accomplish character transformation and teach believers to love others is the church. I find it meaningful that scripture describes the church both as God's family and God's household. This is significant on many levels. The body of believers is a spiritual family, and the church can become a new home for our MBB friends. How important this truth is to those MBBs who are rejected by their families! God gives them a new family in Christ. Also, as discussed earlier, the church can be a place where MBBs see healthy family relationships modeled. But perhaps most important, the church is a family to the extent that it nurtures new believers and allows them to experience the reality of God's love.

Two key phrases from the 1 John passages above bear repeating in this context: "We love because he first loved us," and "Everyone who loves...knows God." Our ability to love others depends on our first knowing and experiencing God's love for us, and God promises that his presence and his love for us will be made real in a special way through the church:

> For where two or three come together in my name, there am I with them (Matt. 18:20).

> My prayer is not for them alone. I pray also for those who will believe in me through their message, that all of them may be one ... May they be brought to complete unity to let the world know that you sent me and have loved them even as you have loved me. ... I have made you known to them, and will continue to make you known *in order that the love you have for me may be in them* and that I myself may be in them (John 17:20-26, emphasis added).

> No one has ever seen God; but if we love one another, God lives in us and his love is made complete in us (1 John 4:12).

In addition to these ways in which God manifests his love for us in and through the church, we as believers can help each other to grow in love as we meet together, encourage one another and exercise the spiritual gifts God has given so that the whole body may be built up in love:

> And let us consider how we may spur one another on toward love and good deeds. Let us not give up meeting together, as some are in the habit of doing, but let us encourage one another... (Heb. 10:24-25).

> From him the whole body, joined and held together by every supporting ligament, grows and builds itself up in love, as each part does its work (Eph. 4:16).

Over the past several months, our team has begun to value the importance of the spiritual family of believers, the church, to the MBB women among whom we work. For several years we'd been working with one or two MBB women individually. Several attempts at organizing regular women's meetings had fizzled out. But then a third woman professed faith in Christ, and we were able to reconnect with a fourth woman believer. Suddenly, we had the makings of a real group! What a treat and joy it has been for each of us on the team to see the growing sense of community among these four women, Mary, Faith, Edith and Jutta, and to realize that these meetings are also strengthening our team relationships! Upon arriving at the meetings, each woman eagerly questions the others: "How are you?" "How is your daughter?" "Have you been able to settle your problems with the purchase of your land?" The growing trust and commitment to one another is perhaps best exemplified by the fact each woman has been quick to learn where others live, and they have begun to visit one another, though most live quite far apart.

Somehow, writing about the women's meetings in this type of article, it is easy to lose the excitement and immediacy of what God is doing. To perhaps convey a better sense of what is happening, I want to excerpt a praise report I wrote immediately following one of our meetings:

> WOW!!! I am filled with great rejoicing! We just had an incredible women's meeting. It far exceeded my hopes or expectations and is far and away the best such meeting I've ever seen here!

> All four women that we'd hoped would attend, came: Mary, Faith, Edith & Jutta. We had a really wonderful time in the Word together, primarily on the subject of prayer. First though, we read Matt. 18:19-20 about Jesus' promise that where two or three gather together in his name, he would be with them. This was by means of introduction: why it is important that we meet together. The fact that the women really understood the truth of this verse was underlined when one shared a local proverb in response: "One hand can't clap!"

> I think what was most exciting, however, was the testimony time that flowed from our reading about how God delights in giving us good gifts. Mary and Edith talked about how God had been working to heal their family members: Mary's daughter Aicha, and Edith's mother, who just a few months ago looked like she would die of tuberculosis, and is now at home and much better. My teammate shared a wonderful testimony of how God has been working in her family life. Faith shared about God's provision for her and her children in recent months, particularly her ability to purchase the right to the land where her house is. Another teammate shared how God has been comforting and encouraging her when she has been fearful. I shared how God has worked to change my attitude toward my work and help make me more peaceful, even when under great pressure, more available for friends and less caught up in my own struggles.

> Finally, before closing the meeting in prayer, we discussed our plans for future meetings. I thought that the women might only want to meet every two weeks, but they all affirmed that they would like to meet weekly even though two of them live far on the other side of

town. Hallelujah! It is clear that these women are not just coming to meetings out of some kind of loyalty to us, but because they want to be together. They all are becoming involved in one another's lives and struggles.

While this small fellowship of MBB women is still relatively new and fragile, it is growing. A fifth woman, Sadie, finally overcame her fear and attended her first group meeting last week. Additionally, there is evidence that the support and encouragement the women are receiving through meeting together is strengthening their witness to family members and friends. Jutta brought her two daughters to see the *Jesus* film. Faith has talked about the Bible with a cousin and hosted a social gathering for our whole group in her home. Edith invited one of her friends, not yet a believer as far as we know, to join the gathering at Faith's house. Mary requested a set of evangelistic cassettes for her relatives in her home village. Edith's mother has testified to the power of prayer in her healing from tuberculosis. Sadie is sharing the gospel with her husband and requested that some of the men believers visit him. Thus, between such active sharing of the gospel and the growth in character and love that is occurring in the lives of the women who are coming most faithfully to the meetings, we hope that soon we will see husbands and children, and then sisters, parents, cousins and friends all "come following in!"

Concluding Thoughts

One final issue related to the spread of the gospel among family networks may be important to discuss: our frequent lack of faith. In the past, seeing one or two Muslims come to Christ was considered wonderful fruit. Do we need to raise our expectations? Do we really believe in our hearts that people movements—or at least the salvation of whole households—can happen among the Muslims to whom we minister? We need to share stories of where it has happened to build our faith.

Although my own team has not yet seen particularly striking growth of the church among family lines and within social networks, our sister team working with another ethnic group in our city has seen exciting things happen. They are discipling about 50 MBBs, virtually all of whom have come to faith within the last two years. Many of them came to the Lord as a result of the witness of their family members. Almost weekly we hear a report of someone else who has decided to follow Christ because they have been watching their family members or friends and seen their changed lives. The team does not need to seek out contacts with whom to share the gospel. The MBBs are continually bringing friends and family members to their homes so that they, too, can hear the good news!

The experience of our sister team shows me clearly that this is not just the stuff of legendary stories from Papua New Guinea! Watching the exciting growth of the church among this nearby Muslim people group, I am encouraged to see that the gospel really can spread through whole families! Often it is not the instantaneous process that we hope for. The book of Acts describes seemingly sudden and dramatic conversions of whole families. Our experience seldom matches that, and the disparity might lead us to become discouraged. We and our MBB friends must persevere.

Recently, I was greatly encouraged to hear Phil Parshall tell how his whole family, once very resistant to the gospel, have become Christians. Yet Phil persevered in prayer for them for 17 years! What a wonderful example of the rewards of patience and persistent prayer. How marvelous to hear Phil share this testimony with our MBB friends! Like them, he could understand what it is like to be the only believer in one's family and to face hostility and ridicule and to endure doubts that his family would ever believe. Yet rather than give up, he prayed. He practiced love and forgiveness toward his family while he was praying. And today, his family believes. Let us pray that we will see the same thing happen over and over again in the families of MBBs with whom we are privileged to share!

Participants' Discussion

The author—What principles have you learned and what struggles have you faced in trying to evangelize family networks?

From Central Asia—We lived in an urban setting for six years, and our efforts to reach a family were frustrating, at best. Then, we moved to a rural setting. What a fabulous change!

One night as my husband and I were praying, we felt burdened to figure out the hierarchical structure of their society. We found out that each little neighborhood was an extended family, because all the cousins and relatives lived around the patriarch, or headman of the neighborhood, who was the grandfather of the whole area. So, we befriended him. Once we got his blessing—after probably a month and a half of drinking tea regularly with him—doors immediately opened for us. He took us around and introduced us to everybody. He told them, "I want you to get to know these people. They are godly people, and their home is open to you. Learn about their book, for their book is a good book."

From North Africa—It is not impossible to find ways into families in an urban setting, either. We met a university student, then her family and had a good relationship with them. She had been baptized, and the family was upset. They told us that they would not accept her following Christ, yet they admitted we had been a good influence in her life. So, though they refused to allow her to meet with other believers, they let us continue to visit with her.

In another family, the parents asked us to recommend a husband for their daughter, who was a believer. By this time, several members of the family had become believers. But the gospel had not taken root in the whole family. In fact, after many years none of the men have yet shared Christ with their wives. I think they are scared of their wives.

From Turkey—I have had a similar experience. A Christian man I know had taken a hands-off policy with his Muslim wife because he didn't want to force her to become a Christian. He said he was taking an "Eastern" way with her. In our conversation, we were talking about how Christians believe that Jesus is the only way. She glibly said, "Oh, don't worry about me in heaven. You serve God. I serve God. We are all just fine." I replied, "There is a problem here—the problem of Jesus. He said, 'I am the way, the truth and the life, and no one comes to the father but by me.'" Her face just dropped. She said, "Do all Christians believe this?" And I told her, "Yes." Immediately, the conversation turned abruptly onto a different course. I thought I had badly offended her. Later I told her husband, "I'm sorry, but I think I have badly offended your wife, and I don't know what to do about it. I hope I have not caused you problems in your marriage." He said, "No, no, no. She was delighted by your conversation. She was thrilled because she had never heard this before." I think as the body of Christ, we can come alongside believers to help them share with their families.

Don't you sometimes feel that way about your own family? Sometimes it seems that other people can have a better entree into your family than you can.

Thinking through the Issues

1. *The author points out that the apostles seemed to have more a ministry of visitation than of hospitality, with the hosting family gathering curious neighbors and friends. Would this model be workable in your context? Why or why not? What cultural rules do you need to be careful to follow in your society to be a "good guest"?*

2. *The author speaks of "credit societies" in her culture wherein women form strong covenantal relationships. Do you have similar "surrogate family" structures in your society? Could any of these be used as evangelism networks or potential fellowship structures?*

3. *How have you seen other social gatherings become witnessing opportunities in your cultural context? Have you been able to use events like weddings or births or even Ramadan or the feasts?*

4. *Much of what women talk or worry about fits in with stories about or by Jesus or the prophets, or our own struggles. Have you found ways to introduce storytelling (perhaps as language practice) or Bible reading to common social gatherings in a way that is appreciated? Or have you been able to introduce prayer for needs into existing social gatherings?*

5. *Divorce, multiple wives, or fathers that work at a distance destabilize many Muslim societies. Have these, or other problems in your society, resulted in a number of those coming to Christ already having fractured social networks? It is not unusual for outcasts to gravitate toward Christ before others in the society do so. How can we respond rightly to these people, minister to their needs for fellowship, and still keep focused on network evangelism? How can we help overcome trust issues to integrate outcasts into larger church bodies that are based on existing family networks?*

6. *The author talks about the importance of our nonverbal witness. In what ways would viewing your whole community, instead of specific individuals, as your witnessing "audience" change not only what you say, and in which context, but also how you live with*

respect to the entire community? Think of examples of how ministering to a third party provided a powerful witness to watching eyes. Also, list ways you can be a servant and "do good" to your entire community, providing valuable community support for any seekers or believers. (Example: helping during crisis with transportation, telephone or childcare.)

For Further Study and Reflection

- *One advantage of house churches is that the host is still the authority, even though a foreigner or native believer from outside the family may lead the teaching. If the host is allowed to dictate the form and pace the introduction of controversial topics and questions, with his understanding of those he has invited, a more culturally relevant format and progression may develop. Also, what transpires carries the weight of his authority, even if he is not a believer. Jesus taught in the homes of both Pharisees and sinners. How can we take advantage of Jesus' pattern of evangelism in the Muslim world? Can we expand our view of emerging house churches so that they are not just defined as a group of believers who meet in a house (instead of a church)? Instead, could we view it is as home full of (mostly non-Christian) friends and relatives which nevertheless welcomes those who regularly come to share about Christ?*

- *How much discipling of new believers really needs to take place apart from non-Christians and how much can take place in these group settings? How much of Jesus' training of his disciples was segregated and private vs. integrated and public? Consider whether we need to alter not only our individualistic view of witnessing but of discipling as well.*

Building Community in a Muslim Background Believer Church: A Case Study among Uighur Women

Anne Jansen

I would like to share some insights on community building that I have learned while living among the Uighurs. I hope these will be helpful to others in similar situations. Uighur women, for the most part, have a strong sense of community among their extended families, neighbors, classmates and coworkers. I have learned much from them! I think it is very important that we look for what natural community structures are already in their culture and society and prayerfully use these as some of our vehicles to communicate the gospel.

Hospitality

Uighurs are very hospitable people. They see every guest as sent from God—especially at mealtime! No matter what time of day a guest appears, it is the norm for the woman of the house to prepare a meal. The guest is always given the best of whatever is in the house at the time. I believe it is important for me to have an open home as well.

To have an open home provides women with an opportunity to gather in a small group in a safe, nonthreatening environment. I have seen women share their struggles with one another in a much easier, more relaxed way than they would have at a church

Anne Jansen has spent nine years among the Uighurs of Central Asia. Seven of those years were in Northwest China, spent mostly in learning language and culture, sowing seeds and one-on-one discipleship. During two years in Kazakstan, she and her team were able to work with small groups of Uighur believers to plant a church in a Uighur neighborhood.

gathering. It also encourages women to get to know each other and trust each other. However, having an open home has meant that I have had to be willing to drop everything to make tea or a meal. It has meant being spontaneous and sitting and chatting or perhaps praying and having a Bible study.

Sometimes it is difficult, and I need to have some boundaries around our family and my own personal time in order to thrive in the Uighur culture. The key for me has been to find a balance between an open home and a closed home. Usually, when we need a break, we have had to leave the house. We go on lots of walks, to the parks or in the mountains. Or we go away for a weekend. One summer, we took three weeks in August to vacation at two lakes in the region. It was just what our family needed. Then we were ready to go again in September.

Ladies' Teas

Traditionally, in this society, women enjoy same-sex gatherings called *chais*, *gaps*, or *messraps*. Though their function is mostly social, they also have an economic aspect. First, the organizer decides on whom to include in the group. Some groups of ladies meet together for many years, but new groups are always being formed among women from the same work group, neighborhood or village. The host provides an elaborate feast. Each attending woman puts in an agreed amount of cash—usually between $10 and $50. The host gets the money, but then as she attends the other teas (which she is obligated to do) she must pay each member the same amount she received from them. Often, the members are of the same age group.

In Kazakstan, a group of Christian Uighur women of various ages from different churches started a tea. They invited another English-speaking missionary and myself to join them. During the first year of their tea, they practiced the traditional money exchange, but they later abolished it because it caused relational problems when some of the women who had the tea earlier could not afford to pay their dues when they went to another's tea. The other missionary and myself did not have any part in the decision-making processes; we sat back and observed them do this. When there was a decision to be made, everyone had her say. The final decision rested with the more mature (not necessarily the oldest). These teas were six-hour parties where we ate, sang, danced, told stories and testimonies, read from the Bible, prayed and ate some more.

The difference between the teas and a house church meeting was that they were women only, lasted much longer, and involved women from various churches in the city. Their purpose was so that women from the different churches could meet and fellowship together, as well as invite nonbelieving family members and friends. These gatherings built community because they provided an opportunity for Christian women to meet together in a socially acceptable manner. They could relax and enjoy one another's company as well as minister to one another on a spiritual level.

Church Planting

Community building and church planting need to go hand in hand. We need to create communities of faith that take following Jesus seriously. We will build healthy, growing communities only if we are healthy and growing. We need to make sure that we are working on our own spiritual lives with God.

Jesus said he only did what he saw the Father doing. We need to learn how to listen to the Father. Find out what he is doing, what he wants us to do, and do that. Spend time in prayer, asking for his direction for our communities. We need to be on our guard against busyness. We can get so busy with our ideas that either we miss what God is doing or we are too exhausted to do the things he wants. Keep it simple. A busy life does not build community.

I also think we would do well to keep our church plants small, simple and easy to reproduce. House churches that meet regularly are a good model. It does not matter which day or what time. Then these house churches can meet occasionally with other house churches for celebration services, if possible.

I believe we need to think of "pastor" more as a verb than as a noun or title. It is something we do. We do not need the title. There are many spiritual gifts. Create an environment in which everyone can use her spiritual gifts. We do this first by modeling as a team and teaching specifically on spiritual gifts. We are trying to stay away from the one-man show. If one man leads the church, what will happen if he falls? Why does he fall? Maybe it is because he becomes isolated, he is not accountable to anyone. This model may work in our home countries, but in our new fields, where believers are only a few years old in the Lord (if that), I think we are asking for trouble. I suggest we lean towards elders serving the body, equipping the saints for works of ministry. Plurality of leadership models a community working together, making decisions together. The group of elders needs to prayerfully consider each decision and make it together. In addition, keep in mind that our teams need to model what we believe is important for the churches we are planting. This builds community because everyone is learning to do his or her part in the body of Christ.

Kazakstan Examples

A mobile ministry team of nationals and missionaries worked well in our situation. Often, it is difficult for a woman to go to the home of someone she does not know—or even to a large gathering. This is especially true if she is a new seeker. She may not trust others, or perhaps travel is difficult for her. So if the women will not come to us, why not go to them? We found that people loved our visits. So we went to them, shared a meal, prayed, worshiped, read scriptures, blessed them and prayed for their needs. We then would continue to visit them every week or two. Then, as the family came to Christ, they invited those they felt comfortable with to join in our gatherings, and the house church grew. We saw this happen in various degrees.

At the beginning, we did not have a committed ministry team, so what could have been small house churches were not given the opportunity to grow. Later, we joined a different team made up of nationals and missionaries from different organizations and focused on church planting in a Uighur neighborhood. We had a meeting room in our back yard and some would come to that. I think it would be better not to have the meeting at the missionary's home, but in this particular circumstance there was no other place available. Other times, we visited different people and took the meetings to them. This encouraged them to take ownership of the meeting, with the view that someday the missionaries would be gone. Now, those meetings are continuing, and we no longer have the house with the room out back. They meet in two different Uighur homes now. The church is continuing to grow in this neighborhood, with only a small team of missionaries still present.

Our team also tried to model what we felt the church was to look like. We made decisions by consensus. We always worshiped and prayed before we made any "business" decisions. We studied the scriptures together. We tried to get a sense of where God was working in our community, so that we could go there and do that. We sometimes had nonbelievers come and ask us to pray for them.

I hope some of these insights can be helpful to others as we seek to share the good news with Muslim women and their families.

Participants' Discussion

Arab MBB working in USA—I believe hospitality and tea times are very important. But I have a practical question: How do you practice hospitality if you have a ministry partner who is not hospitable at all?

From Malaysia—I had a team member who did not even like the traditional foods of our culture. If you have a ministry partner who does not see the point of practicing hospitality, I think you have to teach by example. My teammate didn't even want to cook, so I had to cook extra dishes. For a while I complained, thinking, "This is not fair! She is here to minister, and now I have to minister to her, too." But I had to overcome that. I decided she must not really understand the importance of hospitality.

From the Caucasus Region—I don't know how good I am at hospitality, because I can't make the foods they make, but I have turned this to my advantage. I have said, "Will you help me?" They are so willing to come and help me, and it has knit us together. From my weakness has come a strength. They appreciate that I am trying.

From Southeast Asia—I like your idea about what to do if they won't come to your church or your home. Just go to them! In our culture, it seems that they are honored more for us to go to them than for them to come to us. We also honor them by allowing them to feed us.

I've been discipling a believer. Finding creative ways to get together was a challenge for us, until we realized it is best for me to go to her house. A lot of people gather around. It isn't as though we are in a private little room with the door closed, but we're still able to discuss what we need to.

From Central Asia—We are in a society that is strictly gender segregated. About a dozen believers get together weekly for fellowship, but we know of only three women believers in this tribe of 20 million. These women are not able to come out of their homes for fellowship. We have been praying that God will bring this community together for worship so they can fellowship. But I'm wondering, is this a Western idea or a biblical one?

Unknown—We held meetings separately until after our first baptism. After that, we started out with the men on one side of the meeting room and the women on the other side. After the first month, the men said, "We must have a curtain down the center of the room. We are getting men off the street who only want to see our beautiful sisters, and that is not right." So we have worshiped for years with a curtain down the center and men and women in the same room. When we have communion service or a teaching service, we have men and women meeting at separate times, but the worship service is together.

From the Caucasus Region—We tackled this issue the same way. We desired to have the men and women together for some activities. Yet in our area of the world, that was a novelty. We worked long and hard on this. The group was no longer brand-new Christians when we asked them what they thought about having men and women meet together some of the time. They agreed to try it. First, we had a dinner, with men and women eating in separate rooms. We followed the meal with a sharing time, during which the women stood in the background. Then we divided to study the Bible. At the end, we had dessert all together. In the beginning it was strange, but it developed into a very good community. This pattern provided a culturally acceptable way for them to fellowship—at least, more than any means we could think of. They look forward to these gatherings, which occur only once a month.

In our area of the world, when people get together socially, each one gives a toast to whatever is going on. (This usually involves alcoholic beverages in our former Soviet republic.) But in our times together as a church, we adapted this cultural pattern and used this occasion to express what God was doing or an answer to prayer. (And we used tea instead of alcohol!) It turned into a beautiful thing. And when newcomers visited the church, they saw us doing something so comfortable and right in their eyes. It was glorifying to God and uplifting and encouraging to the body. It built community quickly.

Thinking through the Issues

1. *What natural community structures have you seen in your culture, like the ladies' teas of the Uighurs, that you could use for outreach or fellowship models?*

2. *How could one introduce the biblical study and prayer necessary for the believers to sort out any worldly or godless elements from existing community practices? For example, was the decision to eliminate tea dues made solely on mature godly thinking or on group Bible study and prayer as well? How can gossip, or fashion and food one-upmanship, be eliminated, in favor of prayer, worship or Bible study? How can we ensure that the believing women, as well as the men, are discipled in godly decision-making, and develop healthy community structures?*

3. *The author notes that Uighurs love hospitality and feel more comfortable with hosting than with visiting others. How did the mission team make use of this fact? Is this true also in your area? How did this increase the chance of developing strong house churches along established relationship lines?*

4. *What community structures or practices do you see in your culture that can enhance the spread of the gospel or provide a possible form for house churches? What can we do if the leaders of these structures are not initially interested in the gospel?*

5. *In the Kazak example, mobile ministry teams visited homes where the hosts chose those invited. Jesus used a form of this method when he sent his disciples out two-by-two into outlying towns, to stay with whoever welcomed them. Wesley's followers also used "circuit riders" to plant churches and minister to them in early American frontier areas. Is this model usable in most parts of the Muslim world? Why or why not? How might this encourage the development of more house churches, stronger house churches, and ones better able to face persecution than the Western model of a local church or meetings in the home of the lead "pastor"? Why might this model work especially well in rural situations or multiethnic, multi-faction populations?*

6. *Would women need to visit homes with their husbands for women to be reached, or are women allowed to eavesdrop or be present when there are male visitors? Can women visit homes alone, or, if so, only when the men of the family are not around, or would men of the family be able to listen in to what a woman guest was saying?*

7. What types of "jobs" for the missionary world make this type of ministry seem reasonable to officials? (Examples: A pregnancy coach could visit pregnant women, English tutoring in the home could provide weekly visits, a backpacking tour guide could regularly take a few tourists through specific towns.)

8. Chronological Bible storying has great potential for being used in this ministry context on an informal basis. A story is told on each visit, but not formalized or prearranged. (See related article on that subject.) What other forms of outreach or discipleship could work in this model?

For Further Study and Reflection

*   Do you find community structures or events that actively undermine the faith or spiritual commitment of new believers—such as believers being forced to marry nonbelievers, group drug or alcohol abuse, occult practices required by all townspeople? What are these things? Are there dynamic equivalents (things that could meet the same personal or community need) that would be less spiritually debilitating? (For example, "soft drinks" were invented by Christians in America during the 19th century to provide a cheap recreational alternative to "hard" alcoholic beverages and beer that were draining working families financially as well as causing relational/marital problems in alcoholics.)

Developing Women Leaders in Muslim Background Believer Churches

Fran Love

I found this article difficult to write. Even though my husband and I established an MBB church [1] that continues to meet today, and even though I had the privilege of seeing women develop in ministry and leadership skills, what we left behind appears weak in the face of unfinished church planting challenges among Muslims. Another reason this article was difficult to write is that in it, I describe missionaries as the ones who "teach" believers, when often I was the learner—a learner who was humbled time and again by my lack of love and my willingness to accept superficial cultural understanding as good enough. The fact is that working among Muslims requires extraordinary grace and truth. May we be women full of both.

The article includes two parts: starting points and lessons learned. Illustrations from my own church planting experience and those of several other women I have interviewed are woven throughout.

Part One: Starting Points

Understand Leadership in the Context of a Persecuted Church.

Unimaginable suffering faced the church. Behind this suffering were the minds of powerful, evil officials, quick to authorize soldiers to impale, flog, and burn to death those who

Fran Love has worked for 16 years in an organization focused on planting churches among Muslims. This article was based on experiences she and her husband had among Muslims in Southeast Asia. They have three daughters.

[1] Throughout this article, the range of meanings for "church" can include any small group, fellowship, or denomination. Church with an upper case "C" refers to the Church of Jesus Christ universal; all references to church with a lower case "c" refer to a local congregation.

proclaimed Christ as their Lord. Families were torn apart as believers willingly went to jail and into exile rather than betray their new faith. Their religious beliefs inflamed sentiment against the believers, while also compelling others to know the source of their courage and hope.

This was the Church around the corner, from the Apostle Peter's point of view, when he wrote his letters around AD 63-64 on the eve of Nero's persecution of Christians. Peter, quickened by the Holy Spirit, poured his heart into letters to a Church already suffering and soon to experience intense persecution. The Church was under threat.

This parallels the Church of Jesus Christ in Muslim countries today. There is hardly any 10/40 window nation where Christians are not being intimidated or threatened or killed for their faith. While I cannot speak from my own persecution and suffering, I grieve to see my MBB women friends suffer. Indeed, there were times I could barely face going on in the ministry as I realized that bringing Muslim women to Jesus might bring them death. God sustained me during those confusing moments with the verses in Acts in which Luke tells us that both men and women were sent to jail for their faith (Acts 8:3; 22:4). Women suffered for their faith—it was true then, it is true today.

Because of the certainty of persecution (no matter how slight or severe), we need to plant dynamic churches that will endure long after missionaries are gone. When these churches go underground, they grow underground. They may be small, but they reproduce.

We read Peter's letter to the scattered believers, soon to face a malignant force unleashed against them, and from our perch in history we know the Church will take a beating, but it will grow. The Church Peter describes cannot help but grow. It is a Church that will stand strong in the faith and obey the teachings of Christ (1 Peter 1:2, 2:2, 3:15). It is a Church that will be sustained through suffering by God's power (5:10, 12). And it is a Church whose members will continue to be known for their love, their good deeds and their transformed lives (1:14-16, 22; 2:12).

But this is not all Peter mentions. He mentions elders who eagerly and lovingly watch over the flock (1 Peter 5:1-3). Good leadership is important to sustain the life and growth of a church in any situation. It is imperative when the churches are endangered. A common perspective about national leadership is reflected in the missionary's goal to "work myself out of a job." I have always thought the focus of that statement was more on the missionary than on the Church. So I would like to challenge us to think of turning over the work to national leaders with the goal that we would "prepare them to withstand persecution and reproduce."

Again, as I make that statement, I am deeply moved and humbled because of the incongruity of preparing someone to face persecution when I have known little of it myself. My respect for Muslim background believers deepened on numerous occasions when their courage sustained me through *their* suffering! They taught me.

The question "what kind of leadership will it take to keep the Church growing through persecution?" can best be answered by looking into God's Word. From this, we can work backwards to determine the who, the what, and the how of leadership development. This is a worthy call for any missionary working in MBB churches or fellowships.

The Goal Is to Make Disciples.

The Great Commission does not command us to "make leaders." Rather, we are to make disciples. Who is a disciple? The one who "obeys all that Jesus taught" (Matt. 28:18-20). In a leader, this obedience to Christ's teachings will be evident in her teachable attitude, her ability to teach others, and her faithfulness through suffering (2 Tim. 2:2).

Armed with this perspective, we begin at the beginning: *All leaders must be disciples of Jesus Christ.* By launching from this starting point, it is easier to integrate the practical, cultural and religious issues of selecting and training leaders. At this point, let me raise two issues which pertain to this:

A felt needs vs. a systematic approach to training. Two admonitions I repeatedly hear about working among Muslims are, "use friendship evangelism" and "use a felt needs approach." These were certainly helpful to me, but I now see that they were starting points for a ministry that should go beyond friendship and felt needs. I used to say that a missionary woman didn't need training manuals because they were usually Western in their approach and content and because they imposed a structure out of touch with the real and daily needs of women believers. A missionary corroborated this attitude by telling me about the women she was training: "I was the concordance. When they raised concerns over everyday problems, I would show them the scriptures that addressed those concerns." This "felt needs approach" can be helpful for the young believer. However, my colleague rightfully pointed out that it is even more important to provide a foundation by systematically teaching doctrinal truths about the Christian faith, an approach that benefits both the missionary and the MBB woman. [2] The missionary is reassured that important truths are not neglected, and the MBB woman has a tool that she can then use time and again when the leadership is turned over to her. Especially where no Bibles in the local language exist, MBBs should have a way to systematically train the next generation of new believers and leaders. The goal is to be relevant and reproductive.

In one very unusual case, missionaries gave a copy of the Serendipity Bible in English to an MBB church leader. This young man spoke and read English and was a gifted teacher. He teamed with his semiliterate father as the church leaders. The Serendipity Bible lists questions alongside scripture passages. The young leader took the questions he thought most relevant for his context and distributed translated copies to the small group leaders to use in their small groups, an excellent way to talk about scripture when there is no teacher in the group.

In our setting, I combined a systematic and felt needs approach through a study of Jesus and women. I told them the *Injil* contained a story about Isa that I was going to tell them. I opened the Bible to that passage so they could see my holy book, but instead of reading it, I would tell the story. Each story was designed to approach Jesus from the local Muslim woman's perspective: Jesus' power over the fear of death and evil spirits; Jesus' compassion for women in shameful situations; Jesus and his mother; Jesus and the women who were with him in his death and resurrection; and so on. I told the story; we discussed it, and then we closed with prayer and a big meal. (Food is very important!) Later, a colleague of mine printed the stories into an attractive booklet with appropriate Islamic artwork.

A systematic approach can be helpful and relevant. I also recommend that we supplement written materials with creative

---

[2] I know missionary women who struggle to choose the next teaching for MBB women's gatherings, with the result that the missionary can be anxious about whether or not she is teaching the right things, especially if this happens week after week. A helpful tool is the chronological Bible storying book, *God and Woman*, by J. O. Terry.

songs, drama, storytelling and memorization. Perhaps you may have to wait for indigenous forms to emerge from within an MBB group, but in our situation, we gave scripture portions to a Muslim musician, who set the words to music. We shared with him the intent of each passage of scripture, to make sure that he understood what the words meant before he found melodies to express their meaning. Other teams have used the Jesus film in their local language, used professional worship tapes, or created pregnancy calendars that give biological and spiritual facts about life and birth. All can serve to teach systematically.

Honoring both biblical and cultural standards of leadership. Even those who hold conservative viewpoints about the biblical scope of women in church leadership face imposing cultural barriers in the Muslim world. With the gender separation that is typical in most Muslim cultures, women most often meet without men. Thus, women must be trained to be leaders. They must learn to shepherd other women along the pattern set forth in Titus 2:3-5. They must learn to teach, admonish and guide the members of the flock according to Romans 12:8, Romans 15:14 and Colossians 3:16.

When I worked with women in our MBB church, as I looked for those with leadership potential, I initially looked for those who were teachable and faithful. I showed them scriptures that talked about these traits in order to encourage them, and then I would let them lead in some small way, never forgetting to give huge doses of affirmation and love. I did not rush to label them "leaders," because I knew that doing so would make them fearful. Over and over, they expressed their fears that they were not worthy of leadership. As these women heard God's Word through my words of encouragement, and as they saw me model that type of leadership, *they* began to take leadership. The dawning realization would come later, corroborated by biblical evidence and the confirmation of others, "I *am* a leader."

Yet sometimes a woman becomes a leader because she is the wife of the head elder or pastor. It was that way in our church, and I have observed similar situations in other MBB groups. But what if the wife (the assumed woman leader) is not able to lead due to her lack of skills or godly character?

The MBB church may choose its leaders because of the culture's value of age, status, or wealth, and one way to honor these people is to give them leadership positions. This works if the woman is a good woman. But sometimes, cultural values clash with spiritual ones. When such a woman is thrust into a leadership position, her role must be negotiated with great tact and delicacy. The missionary can show appropriate honor by allowing the woman to fill official and symbolic roles, such as giving opening greetings at a function, praying at a mealtime, reading a portion of scripture, and so on. She saves face, and the missionary acts honorably. Hopefully, the woman will not cause problems. If she does, the church may need to take firmer steps of church discipline.

But let us not assume that cultural values will clash with spiritual ones. New Testament churches honored older men and women, and Paul told Titus to teach the older women to train the younger ones (Titus 2:3-5). American women ask me, "Does Paul mean chronological age?" I believe that is exactly what Paul meant, and we would do well to help older women lead the younger ones. There are many cultural cues we can pick up about how older women do this in their culture, but because they are often subtle and different from what we value in women leaders, we miss opportunities to honor older women in our MBB churches. I struggled with this because older women were not as educated. They had more time on their hands and so were better gossips and meddlers. Further, they had had more years in which to sin and alienate themselves from the goodwill of family and community members. Paul talks about two types of older women: troublemakers (1 Tim. 5:6, Titus 2:3) and do-gooders (1 Tim. 5:9-10, Titus 2:3-4). We can choose the latter.

A missionary couple working in Central Asia took care to honor older women by pairing women leaders. If the gifted leader was a young single woman, she was asked to co-lead with an older married woman who would bring stability and experience to the group and credibility to the younger leader.

In one MBB church, two educated, single women were sent away to learn about Evangelism Explosion. Because it was not fitting for them to teach what they had learned within a public setting to MBB married men, these two women taught the principles to the married couple in leadership. The male leader passed on what he learned to the men in the church; similarly, the woman leader taught the women in the church. This honored both the spiritual gifts of the single women and the culture's values.

Part Two: Lessons Learned

William Beckham, a missionary in Thailand, has said, "Before the church can change, you and I must change. Simply changing materials, programs and activities is not enough. We must change how we perceive the church, how we see God expressing himself in the world through the church, and how we do church" (1997:13). The important phrase in that statement is "how we perceive." Perceptions guide activities; we do what we think.

My American church structure and activities gave me a picture of church life that didn't always connect with the reality of planting an MBB church. So I had to develop a new way of perceiving or looking at the Church and its ministries. From these new perceptions—or paradigms—I began to put together the cultural and spiritual pieces of an Islamic-context church, much as I would assemble a puzzle. [3]

These paradigms shaped how I "did church" and trained women:

1. The church scattered and the church gathered
2. A continuum from emerging church to established church
3. House church as the best structure in which to train women
4. Couples as ministry leadership teams
5. Ministry models from the New Testament
6. The fourfold training process

Paradigm 1: The Church Scattered and the Church Gathered

One of the most difficult goals to achieve in church planting is to gather MBBs into a body. Bringing them to faith in Christ and discipling them individually is a relatively easy task compared to getting believers to work together as a church. Fears of being betrayed and a cultural distrust of nonfamily members keep most believers from trusting one another long enough to become a church.

The goal of getting MBB women together threatened to undermine any joy I had in the work since I was often angry with them

---

[3] A very helpful look into a church meeting in the first century is from Robert Banks' book, *Going to Church in the First Century*, which is written as a first person narrative.

for not wanting to accomplish my desires! This is when I knew I had to shift my thinking about the church. At that point, I wasn't doing any good to anyone—them or myself! So each time I walked to the home of a woman to disciple her, I grilled myself:

Are you doing what the church should be doing by visiting her? *Yes.*

When you meet with her, are you the church? *Yes.*

What good will come out of meeting with her individually? *I am training her.*

How will training her help a church body—should one ever develop? *She will learn from me how to reach out, what true fellowship is, how to encourage through prayer, and how to share from the Word.*

I was ministering to the church scattered, but that didn't lessen the importance of what I was doing. Nor did it change what the church should be. At this stage in church development, the missionary (or any other believer who is taking the leadership role) is key. It was such a release for me to know that as I faced these women individually in their homes, and as they and I prayed and shared from the Word, we were the church. At this point, we were the church scattered, but we were on the way to becoming the church gathered. Never underestimate the power of ministering to one person. Until the church is an established body, you will minister to her so that eventually she will learn to minister to others. This means that you will use times with her to do all the things you would do in a larger meeting: pray, worship, study the word, share a meal. Thus, when the time comes for her to do this with others, she will be comfortable; it will simply be an extension of what she has already experienced. [4]

Paradigm 2: A Continuum from Emerging Church to Established Church

An effective church planter I know in Indonesia begins her church planting efforts by gathering neighborhood children into a Sunday school–type ministry. The mothers take an interest when they see changes in their children, so they begin to attend. Then the husbands get curious, and they also begin to attend. In this

---

[4] Three activities that probably should take place only in a larger gathering of believers (assuming that you have such a body) are baptism, the Lord's Supper, and tithing/giving.

way, the last time the missionary spoke with me, she had planted nine churches. When I asked her about the size and stability of these churches, she said, "When you go into the neighborhood where the church is located and ask people if they know where the church is, they reply, 'Oh, you mean the church of women.'"

The phrase "church of women" piqued my interest. Could a group of children and women be called a church? Apparently in the mind of the Muslim neighbors, it could! As it turned out, men were so slow to accept Christ and attend the church that these churches functioned for a long time with mostly women and children.

Getting families to accept Christ is a worthy goal, and ideally churches should be made of family units who reach out to other family units. So a church should have a good mix of men, women and children. But until that happens, and if all you have to work with is women and children, consider it a church—an emerging church on its way to becoming an established one. Why does it help to label it this way? I think if we give something a name and define it, it is easier to understand the activities that need to occur. For example, if you cannot call a woman's gathering a church because it lacks male leadership, then you might not think to train the women to do all the things a church does. You might not think to appoint women leaders. But if a women's group exists, someone has to lead. Even if that leader is you at first, you need to think about who will take over for you.

The New Testament itself implies stages of church development. For example, Paul and Barnabas appointed elders in every church (Acts 14:23). In other words, these communities were described as "churches" before elders were appointed. This is also implied in Titus 1:5; Paul exhorts Titus to set the church in order by appointing elders. The inference is clear: While the ideal is a church with trained leadership, you can have churches without duly appointed leadership.

Paradigm 3: House Church as the Best Structure in Which to Train Women

Many of us don't come from a house church tradition, and while a house church resembles a small group or a cell church, it is different. Thus, it can be difficult to understand and emotionally accept a house church as a "real" church until you have actually been part of one. I believe an experience in house church planting in our home country is an effective way to prepare for church planting in a Muslim context. Moreover, it is thoroughly biblical.

New Testament churches were house churches, often centered around one family. For example,

> Greet also Priscilla and Aquila and the church in their house [5] (Rom. 16:5).
>
> Aquila and Priscilla greet you ... with the church that is in their house (1 Cor. 16:19).
>
> Greet Nympha and the church in her house (Col. 4:15).
>
> To Philemon ... and to the church in your house (Phile. 2)

A house church is a small group of people operating as a genuine extended Christian family, gathering as a church in the security and warmth of homes. Going to house church, unlike going to a small group or a cell group, is not an introductory step to going to the main church. A house church has a high degree of informality. While meetings are religious, they are also genuinely social occasions. Every believer is expected to contribute, even when it comes time to study and discuss the Word. While there are clear leaders, these leaders act mostly as shepherds and not as teachers. Children participate in all the activities and separate only if they need teaching geared for their age levels. (I estimate that my children stay with the adults for the entire house church meeting half the time.) All the church sacraments are included in the house church activities.

A review of some of the words I used above to describe a house church—family, home, secure, warm, informal, social, shepherd—shows instantly that this is a place where MBB women can thrive and grow. Indeed, for a house church to succeed, the skills of women are necessary. The things Muslim women have experience in—hospitality, caring for family members, nurturing children, managing household finances, planning family activities, working in and out of the home—easily transfer over to the nurture of the spiritual family in the safe environment of a home. It seems to me then that some of the training of women for leadership roles has already been done for us!

---

[5] The NIV says, "the church that *meets* in their house." The word "meet" is not in the Greek. Its inclusion in the NIV displays our cultural prejudice. We tend to view church as a meeting rather than as a family. Yet the Bible uses the metaphor of a family and family relationships to describe church life. (We are brothers and sisters. God is our Father. See Gal. 6:10, Eph. 2:19, Heb. 3:6, 1 Peter 2:5, 4:17.)

Leadership is not some lofty position—it is most often right under our noses. It means taking the things that Muslim women already do and transferring those activities to spiritual matters and imbuing them with spiritual meaning (i.e., showing the biblical value).[6] St. Augustine once wrote to a group of men, "Oh you men, you are easily beaten by your women. It is their presence in great numbers that causes the church to grow."[7] An Iranian author, in her book comparing Islamic and Christian fundamentalism, commented that she thought Christian women of the early Church had great advantage over Muslim women in Islam's early years because they were taught in and learned how to minister in the context of their homes (Gerami 1996).

An important function of house church is hospitality. In early Christianity, hospitality was a factor in the gospel transmission. The Christian message had to be proclaimed; the proclaimers needed hospitality as they traveled around. And the families (adults and children) who hosted them also learned from them. In the beginning it was people, not documents, who spread the good news about Jesus. Women can significantly spread the gospel through involvement in hospitality.

Paradigm 4: Couples as Ministry Leadership Teams

MBB churches will benefit if they develop husband and wife ministry teams. I believe that's true for four reasons:

- First, since religious instruction usually takes place in segregated groups, the wife of the male leader can pastor the women and report back to her husband about what is going on. This will foster unity in the ministry.

- Second, married women have an honored status that is not always accorded to a single or a divorced woman. In mixed meetings of single or divorced men and women, scandal can occur unless married couples act as chaperons and guardians of the group's honor.

---

[6] A church that meets in a home is not necessarily the same as a house church. Meeting in a home won't automatically guarantee that an MBB woman will grow in ministry and leadership skills.

[7] A quote in *Houses that Change the World*, by Wolfgang Simson. This book is about house churches, and has a chapter entitled, "Developing a Persecution Proof Structure." The prepublication draft can be ordered via email: 100337.2106@compuserve.com.

- Third, when singles come to know the Lord, it helps to have a married couple or believing family reach out to his or her non-believing family members. The married couple brings stability and credibility to a young single's whereabouts. They provide a home to which the new believer's family can be invited.

- Finally, the couple in leadership can open their home for meetings and activities, which is an important factor in countries where public meeting places for believers are illegal or dangerous.

However, this is easier said than done. I realize that a huge need in MBB churches is for single men and women to find believing spouses. One thing we can do is to pray that God would provide such spouses. In our situation, my husband discipled the male leader, and I discipled his wife. As they read through Acts and studied the early church, this pastor and his wife came across the story of Priscilla and Aquila. This early church wife and husband ministry team provided an interesting model for them, so we thought through the process of what it would take for them to become a "Priscilla-Aquila" team. They adopted this model and later named their second son Aquila!

Another way we can work toward husband and wife leadership teams is to teach on marriage early in the discipling process. Single women should hear these teachings, too, so that they will receive a good foundation for marriage. One missionary woman took MBBs through a study of marriage in the Bible, including the lives of married women in scripture (Sarah, Rachel and Leah, Ruth, Proverbs 31 woman, etc.). The MBBs were required to study the passages together as a group, taking notes in their "marriage" notebooks. Later, the women were told to teach someone else (believer or not) about what they had learned. Marriage provides a good window into God, family life and godly character. Even if a missionary is unsure about the salvation of a Muslim woman, she may find that these studies convince the seeker of the truth.

Paradigm 5: Ministry Models from the New Testament

Being in a Muslim environment helped me appreciate New Testament passages on women. For example, I better understood admonitions about women's hair being uncovered and loose and the need for modesty. After observing mosque meetings with women behind partitions, I understood why Paul exhorts women to learn in silence. The courage Lois and Eunice faced in raising

Timothy to be a godly man in the absence of a believing father gave me hope for such mothers, grandmothers and children in MBB churches. Lydia, the female counterpoint of Cornelius, who was baptized along with her household, made me think of the increasing number of Muslim women heads of households and what could happen to whole households if the matriarch was a God-seeker like Lydia and if someone spoke the gospel to her. Married women who followed Jesus and gave financially to his needs (Luke 8:1-3) might have caused a scandal in a culture in which women were rarely active in public. And consider that Jesus says that being his disciple is more important than family and also commands us to honor mothers and fathers (Matt. 10:37, 12:49-50). I shiver to think about the implications of those passages for women who follow Christ apart from the consent of their family and their culture. I gained insights and hope by looking at scripture within an Islamic context.

But two passages of scripture primarily shaped a model of ministry I still use today: 1 Timothy 5:1-10 and Romans 16. These passages give me a continuum of ministry for women disciples and women leaders. In 1 Timothy 5, Paul reveals the value of ministry in the home and the lifespan of a woman who has ministered both inside and outside her home. Romans 16 reveals the value of women's ministry in the church as Paul commends various women—Phoebe, Priscilla, Mary, Junias, Tryphaena, Tryphosa and Persis. (The NIV provides a clearer translation than the NASB). I have written an article listing the numerous ministry activities in which the MBB women in our church involved themselves. I concluded, "I encouraged them in all these ministries, knowing that Romans 16 [working in the church] was just as important in their lives as 1 Timothy 5 [working in the home]" (Love 1997:27).

Paradigm 6: The Fourfold Training Process

The fourfold process of training is:

- I do it.
- I do it and you watch.
- You do it and I watch.
- You do it.

Before I go further, I want to emphasize my respect for both Muslim and MBB women. One reason I was able to train is because I also wanted to learn from them. They graciously taught me much about their culture, traditions and faith in God. In humility, the technique of stage three (You do it and I watch) should be a habit we cultivate throughout the span of our ministry with Muslims. For example, from them I learned modesty, courage in suffering, generosity in giving and simple trust in God to provide for the next bowl of rice!

Please note that I have selected the following examples because of their relevance to Muslim women. In so doing, I have bypassed large areas of training common to any other situation.

First stage: I do it. Here are two ways you can prepare yourself for the discipling and training of MBB women. (Perhaps you can think of other ways you are doing or have done it). While you can start these before you go to the field, I suggest you develop them within your context.

First, explore a response to the question, "What does the gospel (good news) mean for people who live in an environment hostile to the gospel?"

Second, think through this question, "What should the Church be and do in an environment hostile to the Church of Jesus Christ?" [8]

As you think through these difficult questions about the nature of the gospel and the Church in an Islamic context, you will develop the foundation for the type of ministry you will model for Muslims and eventually train them to lead. I suggest you study these in a group setting, spending weeks looking at these questions in light of scripture and what you know to be true about environments hostile to the gospel and to the Church of Jesus Christ.

Second stage: I do it and you watch. I touched on this earlier when I mentioned the importance of how you minister to an individual MBB woman. She is watching what you do as much as listening to what you say. In fact, much of what you say probably confuses her, so your actions and attitudes are very important. I believe the most important thing she is watching for is proof that you can be trusted. She won't want to imitate you if she believes

---

[8] John Travis (1998) has developed a helpful cultural and contextual overview of church structure in a Muslim context.

you to be untrustworthy. With Muslim and MBB women, I found these areas of trust crucial: Can she trust that you won't gossip about her or slander her name? Can she trust your friendship by having you visit her regularly? Can she trust your modesty around the men in her life? Can she trust your integrity by seeing that you do what you say you will do? Can she trust your love for her, as you hug her, pray for her out loud in her presence, eat with her, open your home to her, generously share your belongings with her? Can she eventually trust your judgment when it comes to her financial requests for a loan or a gift of money? This is a critical stage because friendships between you and the MBB women deepen into long-lasting bonds as trust is built. [9]

One missionary couple developed their women leaders in three stages. In the initial stage, MBBs spent weeks being grounded in the basics of Christian living (prayer, fellowship, quiet times, confession of sins, Christian witness) with the goal of producing Christian character. The intermediate stage took disciples through the basics of Christian doctrine (the nature of salvation, sanctification, heaven and hell, the church) with the goal of strengthening the faith of the believers. The advanced stage was training in Bible study skills, with the goal of producing leaders who could teach the Word. Each woman was given a notebook in which she would put all the lessons, her answers to the study questions, and her plans to apply what she had learned. She also recorded other women's insights. The women were then encouraged to teach other women, using their own notebook as a resource. In this way, each lesson would be retaught by the MBB woman with her own insights and cultural expressions. This approach is for women who can read and write, but even if they can't, the missionary can teach the lessons in story form, with constant repetition and review, thus helping MBB women remember the lesson.

Third stage: You do it and I watch. Don't assume that the MBB woman can automatically lead even the simplest forms of

---

[9] About this issue of trust among Muslim women, an Iranian author writes, "One must be careful not to interpret women's reliance on each other for child care or other supportive services as indications of trust necessary for group solidarity. Given the traditional hostilities between in-laws and fear of polygamous marriage, it is possible that practical dependence on other women does not eliminate lack of trust and fear of competition" (Gerami 1996:99). In other words, community does not necessarily mean intimacy.

religious expression. By now, you should have modeled for her all kinds of spiritual activity, but you will need to encourage her to do it on her own. The areas we needed to see them launch on their own were: praying out loud in a group context, ministering to children, and developing indigenous forms of worship. Praying out loud was a tall hurdle for our women because their Islamic prayer forms did not prepare them for the potential landmines of spontaneous prayers: How do I address God? Am I choosing the correct religious vocabulary? Am I using the right form?

Getting mothers to minister to their children provided a wonderful training opportunity because they weren't afraid to make mistakes in front of children. They learned how to plan children's meetings, teach songs and prayers, memorize scripture and have fun with crafts and games. Once they were comfortable with the children, we found it was easier for them to participate in adult meetings by praying and giving testimonies.

One missionary couple, after modeling and exploring with their national church planting team about the importance of contextualizing the ministry to an Islamic mindset, had them do "dress rehearsals" of an entire church service before they invited Muslim seekers. The team was thus prepared mentally and physically to be at ease in a situation that might otherwise have been a bit frightening. [10]

In this stage of reproduction, we constantly learn new things about ministering to Muslims. The weight of leadership exposes deeper spiritual bondages in MBBs. And the transference of spiritual forms from your culture into theirs sheds new light on ways to minister with more cultural sensitivity and spiritual authority. For example, in our situation, we slowly realized that a deeply ingrained fear of losing face stifled many in their Christian growth. They couldn't affirm people because they feared those affirmed would get arrogant. They couldn't ask forgiveness because that would mean they would have to acknowledge they were wrong! In another fellowship, after the death of a believer, the group had to determine what culturally religious

---

[10] This situation occurred in a Muslim country where an established Church exists. Fears of being persecuted by the Muslim majority make Christians afraid to witness to Muslims. To help a national church understand the mandate and the means to reach Muslims is a process that requires tenacious modeling by the missionary.

practices surrounding death and burial had to be changed. Conversely, issues arose in our own lives. When inquiring MBBs scrutinized our behavior, they rightly forced us to scramble for answers as to why we did what we did. We had to change some of our cultural habits and religious traditions.

Fourth stage: You do it. I had the privilege of returning to our field of ministry for a visit within two years after the end of our nine-year stay. One day during my visit, the woman leader in our MBB church drove up on her motorcycle and said, "Hop on! Let's go visit some women." A worker in Central Asia, when I asked her what she looks for as she trains MBB women, answered, "I want to know that she *got it*." My motorcycle-driving friend *got it*. How thankful I was that I had given so much time to model the ministry.

Conclusion

This article was not written to offer a "how to" approach to developing women leaders in MBB churches. I have instead shared with you my starting points and the lessons I learned along the way because I believe that it is our ideas that affect our behavior, and it is our theology that affects our practices. I wish I had known these things before I went overseas, but as I reflect now, I realize that much of what I have learned has come from my study of the scriptures and of the culture of the MBB women with whom I was privileged to minister. These parallel tracks of study take time.

Participants' Discussion

The author—Why is it important to develop women leaders in MBB churches?

From the Middle East—We need to fulfill the scriptural principle of older women teaching younger women.

From North Africa—Men and women in our situation have different vocabulary, because women relate to one another in such a different manner from men. So, of course, women need to disciple other women.

From Turkey—I saw a negative example in our fellowship. We failed to teach women to be good leaders. In Turkey, if you are a leader, you are like a queen on her throne, and people serve you. One of the key women should have been taught more clearly about servant leadership, but because I did not teach her scriptural principles of leadership, she never caught on. Her behavior was culturally correct, but not biblically correct.

The author—Have you seen a women's group start first and then seen men become interested in following Christ because of their example?

From Indonesia—That is what happened in my ministry. We got the women's ministry going before we got the men's ministry going. We found that it was so much easier with the women. Then, the men decided they were missing this special kind of fellowship.

The author—In my situation, after the women were full of life and vitality, we incorporated with the men. The male pastor was ordained, and a group of male elders was formed. One of the women who had been very actively involved said to me, "You know, since the elders took over leadership, the women have taken a back seat in ministry. They wait for the men to do everything. They lack the initiative they once had. I really miss the old days." I didn't know what to say to her then. Have any of you had that experience?

From a missions professor in the USA—It has happened in church after church and people after people.

From Central Asia—After our new church appointed male elders, women who had been actively involved in decision making and setting the direction for the church faded out. At first, the women had been quite involved in planting the church. Then they began to think that they could only be involved with the women's agenda. They lost a sense of ownership and authority. I'm not saying that they should have had authority over the men, but they lost the sense that they had a voice.

From the Middle East—What kind of affirmation or encouragement were the men giving to the women at that point? Was there any?

From Central Asia—There was probably a lack of affirmation from the male converts. All I know is that the women felt their role had been usurped. After that, attendance for the women's activities declined, too.

Unknown—In a pioneering situation, women are often full leaders. But when there is a consolidation, or when the church gets in order, women become those who make the coffee and casseroles rather than those who lead the Bible studies. The solution is to be always pioneering, so there is always room for the ministry of women.

Unknown—I'd like to propose that just because we are not in the active leadership or the official leadership, why should we abdicate leadership? Can't we leave leadership before the throne?

From Jordan—At the Evangelical Seminary in Jordan, students come from all over the Arab world. About one-third of the student population is women. The biggest question they face is where they fit in. If you are an Arab pastor's wife, you are the Sunday school superintendent, you are the hospitality queen, you are everything. Finally, several of the young women realized that there must be more that they could do in the church. Now women are taking courses on counseling, teaching, learning to study scripture, apologetics, Hebrew and Greek, as well as being a wife and mother. They have the vision of starting women's ministries in the churches, of teaching, going on for master's or doctoral degrees to teach in the seminary. They see that they are able to do more than just be a pastor's wife.

We also developed a program for the wives of the students who could not come into the seminary to study, so that they could study at home. Even if they are unable to attend the seminary, they are getting trained for their role as a pastor's wife.

The author—Does anyone have any experience with a systematic teaching and mentoring partnership among illiterate women?

Unknown—We did both. To use your terminology, we used both a felt needs and a systematic approach to training the women. All along the way, we reacted spontaneously to their needs, but the systematic approach took us about five years to complete, since the women were not time conscious. The systematic approach we used is an old-fashioned one. We adapted the visualized Bible.

However, our difficulty is how to hand the baton over to illiterate people. How can we help them see themselves as leaders since they know we are the educated ones?

The author—We did three things to pass the baton. First, our group met for periodic celebrations with other believers. They talk about the outreach to their people group, which helps them realize they are part of a larger, stronger group. Second, we asked another missionary couple to check in on them periodically. Third, we are still in letter and phone correspondence with them. We have also visited them on several occasions. They know we are still linked with them, that we have not abandoned them.

Missiologist from USA—Jacob and Ann Loewen were missionary anthropologists in Latin America. After they and their colleagues had established a church among a tribe, they felt it was time to move on. But they said they would be available to the tribe as consultants for the next 25 years. They promised to return every year or two for a couple of months, if the church requested it. They would talk about whatever the church wanted to talk about and teach about whatever the church wanted them to teach. He has recently written up what it was been like for those 25 years to be consultants (Loewen 1998).

From Kazakstan—Five years ago, who would have thought we would be discussing the problem of finding the right woman leaders? This is God's hand! Whether in North Africa, the Middle East, Central Asia, or Southeast Asia, what a beautiful problem to have! Look at how far we've come. Hallelujah!

Thinking through the Issues

1. *The author points out that the scriptural injunction is to "make disciples," not to "make leaders." One tendency Protestant missionaries have had, historically, is to focus on in-depth training or discipleship of only those deemed to be potential pastors or elders. In a situation where persecution and scattering of believers is probable, what are the pros and cons of a selection-then-training versus a training-then-selection view of discipling leaders?*

2. *In the West, we tend to think of training as one-on-one tutoring or mentoring, or as classlike group instruction. Have you seen other ways in which people or women in your culture are "trained"? How would having a systematic plan for Bible topics you need to cover (such as chronological Bible storying) enable you to make good use of informal settings or other forms such as song, drama, memorization or video? How does use of more forms encourage the development of leadership gifts?*

3. *A "felt needs" approach to training tends to be reactive. A "systematic approach" is more proactive, but it doesn't always teach people how to find answers to their current crises. How have you balanced these needs in your own life? What have you found to be effective in*

balancing these needs as you disciple Muslim women? How would you train illiterate women to find biblical answers to their problems?

4. Because Muslim men often play a distant authoritarian or negligent role in the lives of their children, Muslim women actually assume most of the day-to-day leadership in their homes. How can this dynamic help or hurt the development of strong house churches? In what ways does this make active discipleship of the women a key step in stabilizing the churches? How can we also move toward a more biblical role for men in the home and avoid further discouraging them from active involvement in the lives of their wives and children?

5. Both men and women often wield "leadership" in the Muslim world through the use of intimidation, polarization (us/them), control, shame, rejection, manipulation, and deception. These cultural characteristics are in stark contrast to the biblical characteristics of leadership described by the author: a teachable attitude, faithfulness, and servanthood. What specific training or modeling should you incorporate into your discipling to avoid the reemergence of these patterns in leaders? What are nonbiblical patterns of leadership in your own culture that you should avoid introducing?

6. The author also mentions cultural values of leadership, such as honoring older men and women, that agree with biblical values. How did some of the missionaries mentioned effectively use this in their leadership training models? What are other positive cultural leadership patterns? How can you make use of these to strengthen leadership in the church?

7. How might you need to change your perceptions of what "church" means in order to develop a strong church in an actively antagonistic culture? The author lists six paradigm shifts she experienced. What problems of the Muslim context do each of these paradigms address?

8. The author states: "Never underestimate the power of ministering to one person." She had to learn to train women in all the aspects of church fellowship, prayer, worship, study of the Word, when they met one on one, so the women would be comfortable when the time came to meet as a group. Have you been able to see each encounter you have with an MBB as a "church" function? Do you find yourself desiring the more institutionalized functions of Western churches? What aspects of fellowship do you find most difficult to incorporate outside a "church meeting"?

9. Do you believe a church that begins as a children's "church" can lead to a strong, multigeneration church? Why or why not? What about in the next generation when the children have grown? What could you do to help ensure strong male leadership in the next generation (so that it wouldn't remain a "women's church")?

10. Because of the diversity of age-segregated formal church functions in the West, we often neglect worship in our homes as family groups. We tend to think of Bible references to "the church in their home" as meaning adult Bible studies. How can we recapture the family-based worship/teaching/ fellowship model that has been lost? How has the loss of this function weakened the Western church in the face of persecution? How has "hospitality" in the West moved out of our homes?

11. How can you help increase the numbers of believing couples? Often, women and men will hide their Christian beliefs from each other. What do they fear? How can you help them overcome their fears? Can women's fellowships pray for and help "plant" male fellowships and vice versa? Have you ever seen this done? Have you developed effective ways for wives to reach their husbands or vice versa?

12. What ingredients do you feel are necessary for a strong combined (male/female) fellowship to exist? In your culture, do the sexes mingle on social occasions between families and neighbors or only with an extended family? In these gatherings, which leadership roles do men fulfill, and which do women fulfill?

13. You are being watched—Praise God! The "I do it, you watch" stage of the fourfold process of training is much easier in communities where not only the women you are actively developing friendships with, but the whole community, is watching you carefully. They also watch your relationships with other team members. What behaviors have Muslim women seen in you that they seem most struck by? Service, generosity, care of the sick, lack of fear, love for teammates, modesty, etc.? What acts best communicate genuine love?

14. Not all women will be able to copy all aspects of your ministry. For example, some husbands do not allow their wives to leave their homes. Are you modeling things they can't copy—like leaving the kids with your husband? How can you help each woman to grow into "doing it" themselves in areas where God has enabled or gifted them? How can you train the women to seek and recognize God's unique calling on their lives?

15.   *What have been your major areas of success or discouragement as you have discipled MBB women? What possible solutions do you see from this article or elsewhere? What areas of weakness do you need to work on to be an effective discipler of Muslim women? How has God specifically gifted you to reach out?*

16.   *When one spouse of a believing couple, often the husband, renounces his faith, it can be devastating, especially if he is a leader among the believers. Are there ruling spirits of lust or fear that you are not adequately combating? How can you and your team more effectively fight for the spiritual strength of our couples? How can you best help the hurting spouses or encourage other believers to persevere in spite of the example of one who recants?*

SECTION 3

The Missionary Woman

The Relationship between the Missionary and the Agency That Sends Her:

From the Perspective of the Agency

Mary Ann Cate

I remember it well. The summer of '74, my husband and I, our three-year-old daughter and all our worldly goods arrived at candidate school. We had accomplished all our pre-mission field goals: get a Ph.D. in Islamics, plant a church and have our first child. Expecting to leave within a year for Iran, we jump-started our departure by packing 55-gallon drums with all our household comforts and took them to a shipping company in New York—all this before we were accepted by the mission! Candidate school for me was a fog. After the first week, we women did all the shopping, cooking and childcare for the next two weeks. I remember some boring lectures, impossible financial procedures, sleepy slides and a visit to a "hallelujah" African American church for our cross-cultural experience. I don't remember many chats with a missionary woman or any women teachers. But there was lots of advice from men, and of course the frightening board interview by an equally frightening board of men. I didn't know what to expect, so I didn't know what was missing.

Sixteen years later, I knew! Two countries, two languages, one expulsion and two more babies began to awaken me to the challenges women face as we live overseas. After spending 30 hours a week in language study, trying to educate our daughters, helping to lead a new church planting team, coping with losses of father,

Mary Ann Cate is the Director of Women's Ministry in the U.S. headquarters of her mission. She worked among Muslim women in Iran and Egypt from 1974 to 1989.

teammates, health and converts—I felt driven and called to a ministry to help missionary women prepare for and prosper in overseas ministry.

The new missionary woman comes to a mission agency with a desire to serve God in a cross-cultural ministry. But I believe she is also looking for connection with individuals—not just men—in that agency who will affirm and guide her through the process of application, acceptance, pre-field ministry, leaving, and the delicate paces of her first term.

Contemporary women expect to be recognized for their educational background, career attainments and personal achievements. If the modern missionary woman is married, she views herself as a ministry partner, not just part of her husband's excess baggage allowance. The twentieth century has educated her to expect services—childcare in candidate school, conveniences and accountability. She has learned to appreciate her uniqueness—whether she is single, a mother, an administrator or a gifted learner. She also tends to express her needs—for a friend, a mentor or a ministry partner.

My experience as a learner and now as a coach to women in ministry has led me to see that missionary women have three basic needs that our mission agencies must help to meet. I would like to share how God has led our organization to attempt to address those felt needs through our Women's Ministry division.

The missionary woman, whatever her age or status, needs to know that she is viewed by the mission agency as **capable**. Her theology, culture and training tell her that she is highly valuable—the King's daughter, heir of the grace of life, a valuable team player, the best she can be, an asset to any organization, gifted to serve. The response she needs to sense from the agency and her coworkers is total acceptance and a belief that she can handle the rigors of missionary life and make a tremendous contribution to the cause of missions.

Second, our women need to see themselves as **significant**. "I am," they rightly say, "the object of divine love. Gifts of the Holy Spirit have been poured into my life in abundance. I have been blessed to be a blessing." They want to use their training, life skills and personality, whether single or married, to make a contribution to the evangelization of the nations. Our mission agencies must see that each one is placed in the right spot, on a team and in the ministry for which she is gifted.

Third, the missionary woman needs to sense that she is immensely **influential**. Because of who she is and the gifts and talents she has been given, she can have tremendous power over the minds and behavior of others around her. As a ministry partner, mom, grandmother, teammate, mentor, pioneer church planter, discipler of women, neighbor to a Muslim woman, or mission administrator—in every area of life, she is leaving a legacy imprinted in the lives of those she touches. Our agencies would diminish by more than half if all our women disappeared. Our agencies will suffer if we act as though women are not really essential to the life and work of the mission. History haunts us with the memory of great ladies in mission work who formed sending societies, pioneered outreach to tribal peoples and temple children—women who sacrificed marriage and childbearing and other cherished dreams in order to bring the good news to some far corner of the world. Here with us today is Iliam, one of my mentors, who took the opportunity God gave her to see 646 Muslims trust Christ and many to be planted in a church. This took place in a dirty village in Pakistan while the mosque next door denounced her presence and ministry over the loudspeaker as women poured into her clinic. She, and women like her, leave their mark, written on the hearts of men, women and children around the world.

In 1989, when I knew that my husband was selected for mission leadership and we would be returning to the States, God began to call me to this vision to develop a Women's Ministry program in our mission. This vision was also fueled by my own sense of what missionary women need as I looked back on 25 years of serving with some wonderful missionary women. We have designed our Women's Ministry program to address the three felt needs we all have: to feel *capable, significant* and *influential*, by providing programs to help support, encourage and train our missionary women.

Missionary women, whatever their age or term of service, need support from other women. When they are on campus at our agency, a future missionary woman needs to make soul contact with a woman recruiter who can paint a realistic picture of what her life will be like and how she can be used by God to reach Muslim women. Our training sessions, now, are staffed with women teachers who use personal life experiences that women can appreciate. Healthy teams should reflect men and women working together as partners—complementing each other's gifts and submitting to one another. In our agency, we have given the field leader's wife the special role of encouragement and support to the women on her team. We have offered her suggestions for how to help the women in her care in different areas of life and ministry. A variety of women at our headquarters and on the field mentor our women informally in the areas of personal holiness, prayer, child nurturing, finding her niche in the team, language learning and ministry to nationals.

All missionary women need encouragement. Ministry to Muslims is tough work! Living in some of the great Muslim cities or hidden Muslim villages is no picnic. Working year after year with no visible results can be plain discouraging. Feelings of isolation, discrimination by Muslim men, the drudgery of language study, raising a family overseas and poor team dynamics—all these factors tend to beat down on our women. So they need other women to come alongside: to listen to their cries during culture shock, to laugh and pray with them on weekend retreats, to sort through schooling options for the MK, to encourage them in their marriage, and to help them not to give up the task of missions. Our agency provides medical advice for women in all seasons of life. We provide an MK coordinator, on-field visits by experienced women missionaries, and a woman administrator/friend during all interviews with men. Through our newsletter for women, Heart to Heart, we share with each other from field to field on topics like stress, juggling priorities, marriage, and ministry to nationals. Through it, we are mentoring from a distance but intentionally trying to help our women move forward in all areas of life. When a woman comes home on furlough, she is debriefed by many in the headquarters. At least one of these debriefers will be a woman who lets her tell her story and share her frustrations and joys. Over lunch, she receives counsel and affirmation.

The agency can also provide our missionary women with ongoing training. Prefield training in Islamics and apologetics, seminars on furlough to upgrade skills, retreats, correspondence courses, graduate work, relationship-building seminars—anything we can do to enhance a woman's abilities will contribute to her mental and emotional health, longevity and impact on those around her.

Most of the seminars and conferences that I attend have few missionary women participants. Whether it is an issue of budgets, oversight on the part of administration, or lack of priority by the women or their husbands, we women who care must urge our agencies to consider the support, encouragement and training of member women as a top priority.

Because missionary women are capable, significant, and influential, all our missionary programs and agencies should experience the continual touch and influence of women at every level. Care of missionary women, the gentle influencers among us, should be on the heart of every mission agency.

The Relationship between the Missionary and the Agency That Sends Her:

From the Perspective of Field Missionaries

Group Discussion

Editor's Note: This article is the record of a large group discussion.

Question—As you look back on your missionary career thus far, what do you think would have better prepared you for the situations you have faced?

- We went to the field as team leaders, and I was unprepared for the many problems we would have with team members—interpersonal problems, marriage problems, and the like. I could have used Counseling 101 or something. I had never had experience with dealing with other people's problems. Since we were team leaders, we were responsible for helping people sort through a lot of these things, and we were just lost.

- We went overseas when our kids were small—5, 3 and 6 months. The only advice we got about raising MKs was, "Don't worry, because children adapt quickly. They will pick up the language. As long as you are happy and content, your children will be, too." Maybe that's true for most families, but it wasn't for us. To watch my children go through culture shock, to see them struggle with language, to see that they didn't know the cultural cues …

   Once, my son was playing with a man. After a while, the man gave him the cultural cue that he did not want to play any more. But my son didn't recognize that cue, and the man just slapped him across the face. My son came up to me with this big red imprint on his face, and I didn't know what to do.

I was so angry at the man. At that point, I didn't care the man was lost!

I think we need to be more aware of how we can prepare our children—whatever their ages are. I was adequately prepared for my own culture shock. I had read the books. But our kids will go through culture shock, too. As a parent, my first reaction was guilt. It is my fault my children are suffering like this. I wasn't prepared for what my children would go through.

- I can suggest a resource to prepare kids for culture shock. Missionary Training International has a week-long, hands-on program called Splice that prepares both children and adults for cross-cultural ministry.

- As a single person, I was unprepared for being such a marriage target. Because I am single and an American citizen, I am often sought for marriage in ways that make me uncomfortable.

Question—What advice would you give to a young candidate woman today?

- I found it really helpful to go visit the field before we moved there. I know sometimes the cost of such a trip makes it infeasible, but it helped me to see the missionary women that I'd be working with and to establish some friendships. To see what the ministry would be like day-to-day helped me establish realistic expectations.

  I would also suggest that candidate women start getting to know Muslim women in their area and start practicing hospitality. Although some of us don't feel gifted in hospitality, it can be learned. It is helpful to start learning things like that before you go.

- I suggest you interview your team leader as to his philosophy of leadership. There is so much variation out there. Your personality may gel very well with a certain kind and not gel with another kind. I tried that and it worked. I had a team leader that was able to articulate everything, and I agreed with it. We were both happy that I did that before I went.

- That helped me, too. I knew the curfew issues—that I would have to be home by dark—and the contextualization issues. I would also encourage others not to wait to have fellowship on the field. Take the initiative and set something in motion.

Finally, I recommend that you get a mentor, someone who can hold you accountable.

- I think we need to be careful about our attitudes. With all the material and information that is available to us, we can be so trained and ready to go overseas, I think we need to remember to go as learners. We need to be humble and let the nationals teach us their culture. Don't go thinking we know it all.

   I also encourage new missionaries to expect that a lot of what God is going to do is going to be in yourself. You may be dealing with a lot more issues of character and personal holiness than you expected. A lot of your ministry will flow out of what God does in you.

Question—What advice to our single women?

- Before she even moves overseas, I would suggest that she make a plan for her father to come visit her soon after she moves there. She can take him around to her place of employment and to meet her friends. I knew someone that did. She was having a hard time getting some official papers, but after her father visited, she immediately got the papers. She was much more respected. Her father had told her friends that he expected his daughter to show them the love of God.

- If your father can't make it, you can wing it. I used to pass around letters from my father to a couple of the English speakers. This provided a similar validation.

Question—Any advice we should be giving to our married women?

- My biggest mistake was that we moved to our field when I was six months pregnant. Then I faced the task of learning the language with a newborn. I faced so much language shock—it has taken years for me to get past that resentment I had. I would tell women that there is no rush to get to the field. If you have something that may be holding you for a few more months, take a few more months. You've got the rest of your life overseas if you are going as a career missionary.

- My husband is a linguist, so I dealt with a lot of jealousy. He was so much better than I was in language learning. My advice for married women is to hang in there with the language. Think of it as a lifetime activity, and don't be resentful of it.

- I think we mothers often wrestle between language study and our children. There is no point in feeling guilty if you have to put off language learning because you have to be there for those kids. God has given them to you. I didn't even start studying classical Arabic until I'd been there about 10 years. I don't regret that at all.

- As a single woman, it seemed to me that every married woman in my language school got pregnant while they were in the school. I quit drinking the water! I know that babies are precious, and we want them. I'm not saying, "Don't have babies." It just seems to me there it takes such a short time span to learn language. I don't know what mission agencies tell their married women, but maybe they could be encouraged to delay having babies for just a little while, so that they can get the language under their belts.

Question—Describe a struggle you are facing in ministry today.

- My biggest struggle is making a language change. After studying Arabic all my adult life, I have now moved to a different country and must start all over again because the dialect is so totally different.

- My problem isn't the language, it's changing locations. We have had to move and start all over five or six times. After the last move, I went through a year of depression—I lost faith in God; I lost faith in my husband. I felt as though nothing would ever happen in this new city. It is very difficult for me to start all over.

- My biggest struggle is getting the team to understand the vision. We each have our own vision. My vision is working with Muslims in a protective atmosphere. But then a teammate says, "No, we need to go into the courtyard and shout, 'Jesus! Jesus! Jesus!'" So we have such different approaches to our ministry.

Question—What has surprised you in your work among Muslim women?

- When I went to the field, I was clueless about living in the Middle East. I told people I felt called to work with Bedouin people. My biggest surprise came when I went out for a walk and they shouted to me come on in and drink tea. And it was so easy. God is gracious to make it so easy.

- The interpersonal conflicts between missionaries surprised me. I was around outwardly secure people who underneath it all were very insecure. That caused us all a lot of pain.

- For that, I can recommend a study guide called Peacemaking (Rick Love, 1995).

Question—Describe something that has weakened you in your ministry.

- My pride ... and giving up what I know. I make all these plans about the tools I will use and the women I will teach to reach my goals. But that's just my pride. I want to do what I know how to do. Instead, I need to let God do what he is doing. I am only doing the things that I want to do for God. My early years in ministry were all about what I could do for God. And it was also about my pride: What I can give! But I need to watch what God is doing and join him. Learning that lesson has changed my whole perspective about ministry. I don't feel guilty anymore. I don't go out searching for opportunities. God brings opportunities when I'm watching. In the past, when I have made appointments with friends, I have approached each encounter with some agenda in my head. Now, I'm learning to just be with the person. I am not using this as an excuse to avoid sharing the gospel, but I am learning to watch and see what God is doing instead of just developing my own agenda.

Question—Where have you found joy in your ministry?

- After a number of years in one country, we had to move to a new place. When we got to our new country, the temperature was 125 degrees Fahrenheit. I spent the whole first year checking the temperature, and that didn't help at all. It just seemed to get worse, seemed to get hotter. And it never got cool, all year long. The Lord showed me from his word, "God is at work in you to will and to work for his good pleasure. Do all things without grumbling so that you may prove yourself to be blameless and innocent children of God above reproach in the midst of a crooked and perverse generation" (Phil. 2:13-15). I made a promise to the Lord that I would not grumble and complain. I can't tell you what a change that made in the level of joy in my life.

- I found joy in worshipping and fasting alone in my house. But I also had so much fun in making meals with Uighur women, as they talked about their lives and their husbands.

- My joy is talking with my people and sharing the gospel. Such joy comes when they say, "Oh, I never thought about it that way."

- I never thought about it being a joy, but God has given me and my husband six different ministries.

- I have found joy in approaching conflict correctly.

Question—When you think of the future, what are your dreams? Not just your plans—what has God revealed to you? What are you believing God for? Has he given you a specific vision that keeps you going?

- When I was 16 years old, I first saw what I wanted to do with my life as a missionary overseas. When I finally got to the field, I was a mother with two small children, and I knew that the dream of ministry I had wasn't going to be the first thing that I got to do. I'm really grateful that I'm here at this Consultation, but I feel very unqualified to be here. I have worked for 15 years in ministry with three young ladies. They are my three daughters. The majority of my ministry has not been with Muslim women, which was my desire when I was 16 years old. Earlier in this Consultation, someone said, "The Lord is working more in me than through me." He knew he wanted me to be a mommy to these girls in an Arab Muslim culture, where our neighbors were going to watch our family and me as a mommy. At times, it was hard not to be with my teammates, visiting all the ladies. I had to keep telling myself not to be guilty because I wasn't doing it but to realize that caring for my family was the ministry God gave me at this time. It is a tremendous honor to be the mother of three daughters and to have the opportunity that we had to show Christ's love to the families in the community. Now, my girls are older. I won't be doing as much home schooling, so I'll finally be able to spend some time with the local ladies. We have been home on furlough for the past year, and I'm hoping that when we return to our home, I will be able to get to know my neighbor ladies and use a lot of the information we have talked about here to start a ministry time with them. So this is a long-ago dream that God has seen fit to give to me again.

- First, our mission is to see a church planted in our own village. And then to see ourselves replaced by nationals.

- I have spent a few years in Tunisia. This is a special year of prayer for Tunisia. People around the world are praying for the country; churches are sending teams of people to pray there. For years, the people of this country have been very slow to respond to the gospel. As a part of this prayer movement, someone has produced a video that suggests some of the reasons (apathy, etc.) why so few Tunisians have come to Christ. People around the world are praying against these things. I recently heard someone report on how the Lord is beginning to answer those prayers. New people are coming to know Christ in various ways. My dream and vision is to see the church built—and it is beginning to happen!

- Revelation 21:3-4: "And I heard a loud voice from the throne saying, 'Now the dwelling of God is with men, and he will live with them. They will be his people, and God himself will be with them and be their God. He will wipe every tear from their eyes. There will be no more death or mourning or crying or pain, for the old order of things has passed away.'" This is the vision that fuels my passion.

Why Am I Here?

Elizabeth Learner

I am grateful for the opportunity to answer this question—but maybe not for the reasons that you may think. My husband and I are presently living in the United States. We will be here for two years total, God willing. This is the first time that we have been in the US for longer than three months since 1986.

Let me clarify that the question "Why am I here?" does not refer to "Why am I in the United States?" but rather "Why am I among Muslims?" This is precisely the question that I packed to bring back to the USA with me, determined to find an answer. When I was asked to speak on the subject of "Why am I here?" I wanted to scream, "*I don't know!*" However, I suspected, and my husband agreed, that there was divine purpose in this assignment. Because I had the responsibility of presenting an answer in integrity, I was forced to struggle to think through the subject.

Why Am I Here?

I was raised in the United States. My local church not only failed to teach me anything about missions but also failed to teach about the redemption available to us by Jesus' blood. There were, however, occasional visiting groups or pastors who proclaimed that we are sinners and invited those who had a need to salvation in Jesus. I resisted these invitations each time, despite the pull on my heartstrings. It wasn't until I was 17 I felt that pull again.

Elizabeth Learner has lived in North Africa for 14 years, working as an evangelist and discipler among Arabic-speaking women.

Along with that pull was a thought that I'd better quit trying to boss God. (I look back at that attitude amazed that God didn't just send a ball of fire to consume me.) I gave in and admitted that I was a filthy one who was in need of cleansing by the living and holy God through Jesus Christ. God forgave me, cleansed me and gave me a strong desire to see others understand the reality of new life in God's family.

My parents were the first ones who sent me to the mission field. At age 18, I went to work with a family who lived in Bolivia, South America. This family showed me that God is interested in our physical being as well as the spiritual. There, I took some of my first steps toward understanding faith. (*Faith*—a heart-felt and head-thought knowledge that God is not necessarily limited by the physical factors that we see.)

Four years later, I married my husband, who was heading to the Arab world. My first criterion in husband-choosing was that he was going to be a missionary, for it was clear to me by this time that God was calling me to present the mystery of the good news to a culture other than my own. However, at the time, I had *no* idea of who a Muslim even was. And I have never been specifically "called" to work with Muslim women.

So, why am I here?

(*Culture*—generally, a set of unwritten rules of how people in a society act and interact with each other. The rules seem to the members of that society to be absolutely correct and indisputable, although they will often appear illogical and absurd to members of a different society.)

My culture tells me to be happy, comfortable, fulfilled and successful.

I am not happy. I am not comfortable. I am not fulfilled or successful.

I am an American. "Go home, ugly American!" Even Christian brothers and sisters imply this. That hurts.

Why am I here?

My apartment is small. I sweat in the summer. I am cold in the winter. My children have no yard to play in. City life is aggressive. Sometimes the other children are mean to mine, steal from them, hurt them.

Why am I here?

I struggle with the language. The deep things from my heart

still don't flow easily. I am handicapped. How can a handicapped person aid the church in its growth?

Why am I here?

I have to constantly watch how I dress, what I say, how I act. Did I insult her? Was I too bold with him? Are my children acting appropriately? Did we greet everyone? Did we remember to say goodbye to everyone? Have we left someone out in our attention or affection? Do I ever quite get it right?

Why am I here?

What is home? This is not home. America is not home. When we are here, we all have to adapt to the local system of thought and expectations. When we are in the USA, we have to adapt to those systems of thought and expectations. We do not belong to either culture, yet we want to adapt to the culture of our location for the sake of being bridges to Christ. Being a missionary is not something that I do. It is someone who I am. Being in a culture unfamiliar to me requires continual adaptation. This is painful. Why go through the pain?

Why am I here?

I have come to care about my neighbors. They have become a part of my life. Their struggles are impossible. There is only One who has authority over the impossible. Why can't they see him? Why can't they submit? Why do they not fall down in repentance recognizing Jesus' Lordship? Why do my words seem powerless?

Why am I here?

My soul yearns to hear, "Good job, servant! That's the way it is done." Maybe God has said it. I haven't heard it.

Why am I here?

The church needs the gifts in order to grow. In a place where the church is more established, there are more brothers and sisters, each with their gifts. However, in a place where the church is tiny, who makes up for the shortage of gifts? I am not multi-gifted!

Why am I here?

I am not in control. I have not mastered discerning where to invest my limited energy.

Why am I here?

In so many ways—ways too personal to share here—I am not adequate for the task before me.

Why am I here?

This has been very difficult to write. From the time I was first adopted into God's family through the work of Jesus Christ, I have been learning what it is to be Jesus' disciple. Verses about the costs of following Christ, such as Luke 14:25-35 and Matthew 10:37-39, have always scared me, yet I would not ignore them. When I left the USA 16 years ago, I was willing to pay the price, but I had a hidden motivation. I was willing to pay the price, but I wanted results in direct proportion to the cost. I wanted a "good deal." I could not answer my question today—*Why am I here?*—until I had pinpointed that hidden motivation. The dissatisfaction evident in the pain, discomfort and lack of success in the above arguments tells me that I did not get a "good deal." I realize that many of these were just superficial costs, their difficulty lying in the consistency with which I have to pay them. But there were dearer costs, and I'd had enough. My reasoning was that if you paid a lot, there would be a lot of results. I continued to reason that I had paid enough, and I no longer wanted to pay the price.

God, however, never promised comfort, success, or lack of pain. As I prepared this paper, I have been forced to look at the ugliness of these culturally based goals that attack my peace. Do I actually forget that God is faithfully in control?—that he never promised me a false "good deal"? The falsehood was based on the lies of my culture that I unknowingly accepted as truth. Our history as children of God is filled with God asking his people to move in faith beyond circumstances and cultural goals.

I see this in the story of Esther, who went before the king on possible penalty of death. I see it in Sarah, who because of her husband's lack of faith was placed squarely in the hands of the pharaoh. I see it in the Hebrew midwives, who feared God more than pharaoh and let the Hebrew babies live; in Mary, the mother of Jesus, who faced the loss of her reputation as well as that of her family when she became pregnant before the wedding; in Mary Magdalene, who received wonderful freedom from sin from the Lord but at the same time lost her source of income; and in the women in the book of Acts, who aren't even mentioned by name but who were dragged off to prison because they dared openly to be followers of "the way."

So why am I here?

Or rather—Why are we here—both you and I?

We are here because these women were faithful to trust God despite the cost, and God's will was done.

We are here because we are challenged by the example of present-day sisters with that same faithfulness.

We are here because closeness to the holy God is an exquisite banquet that we cannot keep to ourselves. We will not eat and let others starve.

We are here by the authority of the Holy Spirit.

We are here by God's grace.

We are here because God is the potter, and we are the clay.

We are here because Peter walked on the wavy sea when his eyes were on Jesus.

We are here because being Jesus Christ's disciple is worth utter, total failure in all the ways we presently understand success.

My culture tells me to be happy, comfortable, fulfilled, "successful."

What are the lies that your culture is telling you?

Being a member of God's family puts me in a new culture.

Romans 12:1-2: "Therefore, I urge you, brothers, in view of God's mercy to offer your bodies as living sacrifices, holy and pleasing to God—which is your spiritual worship. Do not conform any longer to the pattern of this world, but be transformed by the renewing of your mind. Then you will be able to test and approve what God's will is—his good, pleasing and perfect will."

Ephesians 4:22-24: "You were taught, with regard to your former way of life, to put off your old self, which is being corrupted by its deceitful desires; to be made new in the attitude of your minds; and to put on the new self, created to be like God in true righteousness and holiness."

John 12:26-28: "Whoever serves me must follow me; and where I am, my servant also will be. My Father will honor the one who serves me. Now my heart is troubled, and what shall I say? 'Father, save me from this hour?' No, it was for this very reason I came to this hour. Father, glorify your name!'"

Psalm 115:1: "Not to us, O Lord, not to us but to your name be the glory, because of your love and faithfulness."

This is why I am here.

How Can I Thrive Here?

Karol Downey

It was only after I left the Middle East that I realized how much stress I was under while I lived there. It was not just the general stress of living in a different culture, or of explaining my husband's tentmaking job. It is true that I felt tremendous stress and fear when my husband went in for several police interviews. But I think there was a specific, continual, underlying type of stress in just being an American woman living in an Islamic culture. Of course, it wasn't a totally negative experience. There are many aspects of an Islamic culture that are helpful and positive in helping us to share our faith with Muslim women.

The separation of the sexes is great. While the men sit on one side of the room, the women are on the other side, and have more freedom in their discussion. If we are in a separate room, we are even more able to share than if men were present and controlled the conversation. The women would be afraid to ask questions with their husbands or fathers listening. They feel freer to really interact with just women. When I took my kids to the pool, I didn't swim. The culturally appropriate thing for women at the pool was to sit and watch their kids. So, I would always sit with the other moms and we would chat together. Subject matters ranged from dinner plans, to marriage, to religion.

In an Islamic culture, there is a great deal of openness in talking about religion. It comes up almost immediately in conversation. This is very useful to a missionary in sharing her faith.

Karol Downey lived in the Middle East for 12 years, helping to plant cell fellowships and provide leadership training. She now works in the U. S. headquarters of her mission.

In an Arab culture, everyone loves children. It follows that if you have children, people will like you and want to get to know you and your children. Children open doors to building friendships.

Nationals are curious to get to know foreigners and how they live. They ask many questions, and as we answer them, we are able to share more than just our cultural differences. We can also share our personal testimonies of God's work in our lives.

As foreigners, we can interact on all social levels. We can visit our maids, neighbors, teachers, doctors and shop keepers. We can move through the classes without stepping on toes, simply because we are foreigners and have freedom that nationals may not have.

We can use these positive aspects in the culture to share our faith on a broad scale in society as we meet people, sit and share with women and go where men cannot go. As we live moral and upright lives, women will want to know us. They'll be curious about the reason we are so different from their expectations. Then we can tell them about our deliverance from sin because of Jesus Christ.

There are, however, some aspects of Islamic culture that can negatively affect women missionaries and their work. Later, I will offer some suggestions about how to deal with these issues, making them not obstacles but opportunities for our own spiritual growth and evangelistic outreach.

One of the most difficult aspects for a Western woman living in an Islamic culture is that she is living in a male-dominated society. Women are not seen as equal partners in the adventure of life. We are seen as inferiors who need men to guide us. Women are sexual beings with an insatiable desire for physical relationships and could damage the family honor through their immorality at the drop of a hat. Men feel they have to keep control over women family members. Therefore, their women relatives need to be covered, possibly circumcised, watched, and even killed if there is just a hint of immorality. A Muslim man doesn't bring as much dishonor to his family by his immorality. A Muslim woman brings much shame through her immorality, even if it is only a rumor. A Muslim man is freer to pursue his sexual interests. So when he sees a Western woman in his culture, he assumes she is open to his advances, as national women would be if they weren't controlled! He sees this Western woman and automatically believes she is like the movie stars on TV—loose, immodest and ready for relationship with any man! This results in foreign women getting pinched, propositioned, proposed to, talked to and about—even more so than national women. Even if a Western woman dresses modestly, she is seen as easy prey.

It is not easy to live in a culture that doesn't respect you as a woman and doesn't approve of you as an individual person. Missionary women from the West, who are taught to look a person in the eye when talking, must learn not to look into the eyes of men. We may feel rude as we don't talk to men who try to start up a conversation with us. We may feel dirty as we do nothing to encourage men yet draw them to us like magnets. This can lead to guilt, shame, fear, and unhappiness.

Then there are the security issues for Christians working with Muslims in an Islamic culture. What if I get into trouble for being a missionary? How will I handle it? What will I tell my national friends? What will happen to the work? Where would we go? What if my husband is imprisoned? These are all the "what ifs" of missionary life within this context. Then, when there is trouble, there is the reality of "What do I do now?"

Keep in mind that if you are a mother, you carry the load if your husband is imprisoned or taken in for questioning. You answer the kids' questions if they are old enough to know what is going on. If they don't understand what is going on, you try not to let them know you are scared so they won't be afraid. You keep things going smoothly on the home front and try to be a support for your husband in what you know is truly difficult for him. When he is gone for a police interview, you wait, not knowing where he is, whom he is talking to, or when or if he will return. There is a certain freedom, in that a foreign woman is rarely taken in for questioning—especially if she has children. However, if the husband is deported, the wife is left to do all of the packing and preparing to leave the country. She may have to do this all alone if other team members are wary of helping—as she may be under observation to see who else is involved in their mission. So it can be a lonely time as well.

We have looked at both positive and negative aspects of living in an Islamic culture and how it can affect us and our work. I would like to close with nine tips for thriving in this culture as missionary women.

Adapt to the culture where possible. Since making eye contact with men is suggestive, don't make eye contact. Since dressing modestly is appropriate, as well as biblical, please dress modestly. Hospitality is key, so learn from your national friends how to show hospitality. You can make other adaptations as you learn more about the culture. My friend and I went to a Quranic study. When one woman suggested that we believe in three Gods, my friend jumped up and said in a loud voice, "God forbid that we would ever believe such a thing!" She continued to voice loudly her belief in one God. A national friend talked to me the next day and said, "Your friend has a stronger faith than you do, doesn't she?" I didn't know how to answer, so I countered with another question, "Why do you ask that?" She said it was because my friend defended her faith so vehemently. When it is culturally appropriate to raise your voice to show you really believe strongly, I would recommend learning to raise your voice!

When a cultural practice goes against scripture, don't adapt but stand firm against it. In the Middle East, people can be extremely class-oriented. When my maid came to clean, we welcomed her little boy as well. He also came at other times just to play with our boys. This wasn't easy, as he urinated on our floor, stole toys, etc., but we did our best to make him and her feel welcome. One national friend commented that she couldn't believe I let our children play with the maid's children. I remember struggling with this issue—should I adapt here so that I fit in better with my friends? But scripture is clear: we are not to be prejudiced; we are to be kind to the poor. I continued welcoming them into our home. Some time later, this same national friend told me that this attitude of love and kindness amazed her. Then I was able to share with her God's love for each one of us, no matter where we are in society. It is imperative that we know what scripture says about our role: who we are, what we as women are to do, how we should live. Then we need to stand firm in these scriptural principles so that we can be light that shines in a dark world.

Make sure you have enough time alone for relaxation and rest. Take time for yourself so you will be able to handle the demands placed on you by a different society. You know your energy level—when you need to say "no" and stay home or escape to a five-star hotel to swim or read a book. Be aware of your limitations and needs.

Aggressively forgive the wrongs you see and experience in your host country. Don't let grudges build and bitterness take root. When you are offended, work through your anger and forgive. In dealing with sexual harassment, I believe it is important to deal with anger and then forgive these poor, lost men. One day as I was walking down the street, a man walked close by me and was feeling himself and making an obscene gesture toward me. I was so repelled, disgusted and angry that I began talking to myself, saying what a jerk he was. It was true. He was being a jerk. But as I continued walking and fuming, I realized that man was walking into a Christless, hopeless eternity. I was so blessed to be forgiven by God for all my sins. I was like that man once, hopeless and Christless, but when I became a believer, all my sins were totally forgiven. I didn't want that man to have to face eternity without Christ. I knew I had to, and even wanted to, forgive him and pray that he would come to know the Lord. He, too, could be forgiven and know the love of Jesus Christ. This was an activity I practiced regularly. As often as I was offended by men, I would remember their future, what my future could have been, work through my anger, and then forgive them and ask God to work in their lives. It is freeing. I don't have to live under the wrongs of another human being. I am free to forgive and go on.

As I came to know the culture better and learned the ins and outs of life, this type of sexual harassment happened less frequently. Or it could be that I just got older, so men lost interest!

Deal with fear. Face it. Plan for the "what ifs" so you will know what to do when the "what ifs" become reality. Memorize scripture and stay strong in your relationship with God. Don't borrow tomorrow's pressures. Trust God for today and leave tomorrow in his hands. In dealing with fear, there is no quick, easy, one-step way to overcome it. It is best to be prepared for the "what ifs," but not continually daunted by them. You can achieve this by having a plan as a person, couple and/or team. What is Plan B if we get kicked out of the country? What is the plan if your husband is imprisoned? What will the team do to help? Once there is a plan, a lot of the fear will dissipate. It is the unknown that is most frightening. We need to be sure we are growing in our relationship with Christ and praying to him regularly. It is as we entrust small crises and troubles to him on a regular basis that we are ready when a major trial comes.

We must always remember that God is sovereign and will lead us where he wants us to be. When my husband was asked to come in for questioning, I was afraid and wanted to run "home" where I could feel safe. But we stayed and committed ourselves to the Lord. As time went on and we were still in the country, we thanked God. We left for furlough unsure of what would happen on our return. Many times, they let the wives in but sent the husbands away. We had a Plan B. When we arrived, we went through customs with no problems. We stayed in our country for another year. It turned out that a little piece of paper was hidden from view so that my husband's file never made it to the national security office when it was supposed to. As a result, we had that extra year and saw a cell church established during that time! God is in control—not the police authorities. God moved us, when he wanted us moved.

Don't be afraid to try new things. Don't be so embarrassed by cultural and language mistakes that you quit trying to learn.

Expect respect from others and give respect to each person you meet. It is important to counteract the loss of respect we experience in an Islamic culture by remembering who we are in Christ, not just who we are in our own culture. It is necessary to base our value, our sense of worth, on how God sees us, not how other people see us. As we make mistakes both in the language and in the culture, it is easy to feel stupid. This, compounded by the society's view of us, can be devastating. But not if we are secure about who we are in Christ. We need to respect other women, too. We listen to their ideas and learn from them. As they feel respected, they will be encouraged to think and to listen to us, as well.

Be creative in ministry opportunities. Go to an aerobics class. Teach English. Have a craft club or a baking club. Establish a children's summer club. Host birthday or holiday parties. Go to a Quranic study. Visit neighbors. Invite neighbors over for Christmas. Have an Easter egg hunt while you explain why we celebrate the holiday. Use your own gifts and abilities to find a way to fit in where you are.

Know the culture and language well. Study hard and practice the language. Read books on the culture. Ask many questions. Never stop learning.

As Christian women serving God in an Islamic culture, we can do more than survive. Yes, it is hard. As we face these challenges, we come to realize that we cannot handle this life on our own. We become more sensitive to our sinful attitudes and character weaknesses. We know what it is to be an "alien" and not fit in with a society. We know fear. However, it is exciting that we also know the one true God who conquers fear, gives victory over sin, and is at work developing within us the character of his Son. It is only as we face these struggles in his strength, relying on him for guidance, and depending on his power that we can do more than survive. We can thrive.

Who Is with Me Here?

Cookie Liverman

As we think through the questions "Why am I here?"and "How can I thrive here?" we may rightly conclude that the most valuable resource we have with us in our field of service is our relationship with our heavenly Father. After all, he is the one who drew us into this ministry, gave us the tools we needed to live abundantly and provided us with a significant role serving his kingdom purposes. If we are able to rejuvenate this truth, we will find comfort and help to sustain us through the difficult and weary times in our life of ministry. But for those times when we need a practical solution or feel overwhelmed with the magnitude of our struggles, we may ask the question, "Who is with me here?"

This topic is dear to my heart. My husband and I are in transition. After working overseas and then at our mission's US office for a number of years, we are headed back to the field. I am preparing, once again, to be a team leader's wife in a new work in Central Asia. Between our early years in South Asia and the new work ahead, the Lord has led us to a ministry of visiting the fields, working with teams, giving oversight and pastoral care, helping with strategies, problem solving, and just being there as someone to come alongside. I feel it is a ministry close to God's heart.

One of the more difficult aspects of missionary life is the feeling that we are helpless to change a situation. Often, when we are working through a difficult issue, we get so focused on the

---

Cookie Liverman and her husband lived in South Asia for about four years and have worked in missions for about 14 years. Among her many roles, she has been a missions mobilizer, a team leader, a church planter, a trainer and a coach. She has two grown children.

problem that we fail to see solutions that may be available to us, and this makes us feel helpless and lonely, which in turn often leads to ineffectiveness. We begin to feel we don't have anything to contribute. Sometimes, we even feel worthless. It grieves my heart when I find my colleagues in such a state.

After Paul's dramatic conversion, Barnabas introduced him to the leaders of the church in Jerusalem. He came alongside Paul in order to validate his new life in Christ. In the same way, we often need someone to enter our situation to bring fresh perspective and walk us through to a workable solution. People involved in this type of ministry, whether as a part of their everyday lifestyle or as an intentional ministry role, are valuable resources for workers on the field. They are resources we often overlook and need when we've been robbed of the joy of doing the work for the Lord. When we fail to take action, we rob the Lord of being able to use us as he wants.

> And my God shall supply all your needs according to his riches in glory in Christ Jesus (Phil. 4:19).

Sometimes we aren't living as though we know this to be true. Sometimes we fail to see the "glorious riches" the Lord has right before us. Perhaps you need to realize that these resources are available to you. Perhaps you might even be a resource that God wants to use as glorious riches in someone else's life! When I consider "Who is with me here?" I find there are five major types of *glorious riches* available to us: God, other missionaries, sending agents, pastors or church representatives, and coaches.

God

We often spiral down as we look inward, thinking that we can supply our needs instead of trusting the Lord to do that. So the first, most valuable and foundational resource we have is, of course, God himself. He is the *why, what, how,* and *who* of our lives. When I forget that my purpose is to give God glory and to worship him—that's when I struggle. My purpose is not to do translation work or to plant churches, or any of the other tasks we often list.

> Now to him who is able to do immeasurably more than all we ask or imagine, according to *his power* that is at work within us, to him be glory in the church and in Christ Jesus throughout all generations, for ever and ever! Amen (Eph. 3:20-21).

According to *his power*—not my power, not my ability, not my strengths, not my fretting, not my worrying—none of those things! The reason his power is available to us is so that we might bring God glory.

Have you ever lost your passion for what you are doing? Have you ever found yourself just going through the motions? God can be a resource for you. Take a personal spiritual retreat. Take a day or a weekend to go away somewhere. If that is not possible, then ask your family to help you set aside a morning or a day all alone so that you can dive into God's word and spend time in prayer, rediscovering God's grace. Have extended times of worship. Even a few hours of extended worship and music can get you back into the presence of God so that you can seek his perspective on your situation. You might need to get out of your situation to see what spiritual attacks you have been under, and then equip yourself for returning to the situation. It may be helpful to reread a journal you wrote about God's leading you to enter a life of service to him. That will help you remember why you ever came to this place. It is important to remember those moments that you know that you know that God has spoken to you. Keep a record of how he speaks to you during these times of renewal.

Sometimes it's enough simply to remind yourself of the truth and dispel the lies that we so often believe when we are discouraged or hurting. After you set yourself back in line with the truth and have God's perspective on your situation, you may need some practical help to move on to the next step. Just remember that God is the one who has provided all the other resources at your disposal. Trust him to know what you need and then thank him for his provision. Once you've set that foundation in place, you can say to the Lord, "Now I need some of those other glorious riches you have for me. Show me what can change and what I need to do differently so that I can give you the glory for why I am here."

Other Missionaries

You may be a part of a large, close-knit team, you may be in a city where dozens of missionaries from different agencies work, or you may be in a remote village and have little contact with other Westerners. No matter where you find yourself, you are still within reach of other missionaries. I have found that most missionaries are resilient, innovative, self-sufficient people who try to work through problems on their own in an effort to keep from burdening others. Sometimes missionaries don't even share their problems with their spouses or teammates. Although taking responsibility for our own issues and seeking to work things out with God alone is a worthy method, it is sometimes necessary to seek the help of other members of the body of Christ. This interdependency is also a worthy method, especially if a problem goes unresolved.

Among many resources you might choose are your teammates. This may seem to be an obvious solution, but I have found that many women refrain from sharing their struggles with teammates. They're often afraid that no one else struggles with the same issue or would understand. Sometimes they have been offended by a teammate and can't bring themselves to talk about it. Sometimes they feel that they have nothing to contribute to the team, and they don't want to be a burden.

Your teammates are a part of the resources God has given you. You are neglecting God's provision if you fail to involve them in your situation. When one person on the team is hurting, others are hurting also, even if they don't know what the problem is. Actually, working through problems bonds communities together. You may be keeping your teammates from growing or your team from progressing by not including them. They are your most accessible, and probably your most empathetic human resource, and they can offer the best follow-up and accountability.

The second group of other missionaries that can be a resource for you is what our mission likes to refer to as "God's team." This can mean others with whom you share some sort of partnership because they work in the same city or have the same type of ministry. Sometimes, when you are not comfortable to talk about your struggle with a teammate, your heart might open up more to someone from another agency who is there on your field. That is one of the reasons God put her there. We are not only to be developing our relationships with local women, God wants to work in us and through us so that we can help others. "God's team" people are likely experienced and may be able to point you to resources you hadn't considered. I don't recommend that you become a burden to people from other agencies, but we do need to rely on the body of Christ.

Imagine a missionary family with small children. They have been in their new country only one year. The wife is not fitting in. She keeps herself busy solely at home, is withdrawn from her team, is often sick, and misses team meetings. Yet she projects a positive attitude, saying, "Everything's fine!" After months like this, the wife will likely become less and less involved in the work of the team. She'll find some reason that convinces her husband to take their furlough early. Her reasons may be valid, but she has exaggerated their impact. If she goes home in this kind of defeated condition, she's likely to stay there.

On the other hand, consider what might happen if, after a month or so, she opens up to a determined teammate, who discerns that she needs help and looks with a suspicious eye on her cheery "Everything's fine!" Under the loving scrutiny of her caring teammate, our first-termer might admit that she has lost all sense of value in the culture and wonders if she made a mistake. She doesn't understand the language and can't seem to learn it. Everything she does seems to be wrong, and she's certain she's the only one who ever felt this way. The teammate does some creative problem solving with her, gets others involved in meeting practical needs, finds ministry opportunities that suit her, suggests changes in her schedule or home situation, reminds her that feeling lost in the language is expected at first, gives her bite-size pieces to learn, volunteers to help her learn how to visit and shop in this new culture, and reminds her why she came. "This is a God-sized task. Of course you can't do it all alone!" It may be that all she needs is someone to come alongside her and help her walk through this time of transition.

Sending Agents

Most missionaries are sent from an organization, a church or a group of supporters. The resources available to a missionary from her sending agent vary from an occasional encouraging letter to a full structure that stipulates ministry, furlough, budget, location and education.

Common to most sending agents is that they give leadership to missionaries. They can help us make responsible decisions, especially if we are so involved in our situation that we can't see the big picture properly. We can easily get involved in a worthy cause—preaching in an expatriate fellowship, teaching Sunday school, helping with a homeless shelter, or herding along some other project—that takes us away from the work we were meant to do. We women typically face a lot of practical decisions at home—such as how to school the children, whether to have house help, or what type of schedule to keep—that need input from those outside our situation.

Let's say a mission leader visits a first-term missionary family in a remote area. This family has three children, ages 4, 6, and 9, whom the mother is homeschooling. The wife is frustrated by her lack of progress in the language, still feels out of place in the culture, and has only shallow relationships with the local women. On first consideration, it may seem that the solution is for her to develop a better language learning system or to get out in public more. She has talked to a few other missionary women in the area, and they all seem to feel the same way. The more they talk, the worse the situation seems. She keeps thinking if she did more, it would get better. But "more" is never enough.

When the mission leader comes to visit, he is able to review the family's goals, plans and language learning program. He is also able to evaluate the personality of the couple, their ability to help one another, and their willingness to make things work. Considering the needs of this family and other families in the area, the mission leader offers to recruit and send someone to be a school-teacher for all the children, in order to free up the mothers to study language and develop deeper friendships. The leader asks the couple to write up a job description for the new teacher and promises to give this need a high priority on his return to the home office.

This mission leader's response validates the family's ministry because he entered into their situation and did not assume that he understood their needs from a distance. He involved them in the solution by having them write a job description and think about what they were willing to promise a teacher in terms of support and help when she or he arrived. Promising to give this prompt attention, he encouraged the family and gave them new enthusiasm for their work. The mission leader and sending agency also blessed the other workers by causing them to work together to solve a problem relevant to many. It needs to be noted that if the family said they were unwilling to work with an outside teacher, the resource offered would have been useless and the field director might have hesitated to offer help in the future.

Professional member care is another significant aspect of the resource that sending agencies can offer. Sometimes needs are beyond the scope of our team leader, teammates, or even our mission leadership. Sometimes, problems in our lives have deep, tangled roots that need to be unraveled by a professional member care provider, such as a psychologist or licensed therapist. In considering a person's need for member care, we need to realize she may not be able to articulate her need adequately, which diminishes her ability to get help. Imagine a missionary who has seemed to be depressed for three months. No matter how much you pray with her, encourage her, or involve her in worship, you don't see any changes. That may signal that she needs to seek outside help. If she is not responding to the resources at hand, help her find more resources. If that describes you, let me encourage you to ask for help. Plenty of psychologists know how to work with missionaries and would be willing to travel to the field to visit you. There are also many places missionaries can go to receive help from professionals in a setting suitable for our line of work.

Pastors or Church Leaders

Some missionaries come from strong, missions-minded churches that have sent them out in the style described in Acts. Others come from churches that do not support them emotionally or spiritually, houses of worship that never even mention missions from the pulpit. In either case, most missionaries have a relationship with someone in a pastoral role or a lay person with spiritual authority and input in their lives.

Let's imagine a model in which a supporting church has a missions coordinator and a pastor who shows interest in the needs of the missionaries the church supports. One of the reasons why this resource can be of such comfort to us is that a pastor or someone from our home church has a history with us. They know where we came from and who we were before we arrived in this strange place. Just their proximity can bring real comfort and draw struggles out of us because we know they have our needs close to their hearts. Their ministry is to us and not to the community we are there to serve. Pastors also bring the resources of the entire church body with them.

Imagine a family with two teenagers. They have been living in their Muslim country for more than five years. No one from their church or family has ever come to visit them. Because their church's missions coordinator has an interest in Muslims, he and the pastor come for a three-day visit. The wife is thrilled to host them, pummeling them with questions about church members and news from home. The visitors bring gifts from the women's

Bible study for her and CDs from the youth group to the teens. The connection to the church and to the home culture is renewed, and it meets a felt need for the family.

On the second day of the visit, the wife apologizes to the visitors because she has some local women coming for her weekly lesson. The local women are teaching her to do fine embroidery. The pastor is able to see firsthand how this woman welcomes her local friends, slips into their language and culture with ease, and is obviously loved by her local friends. After the women leave, the pastor asks the wife about the embroidery and the obvious opportunities for ministry this opens up with the women. As the wife shows the pastor samples of the embroidery, he asks if he can purchase some items for his wife and other women in the church. In fact, he thinks the women's Bible study could sell the products at their boutique next month. In the transactions that follow, the missionary develops a handicraft business with the local women, providing them with much-needed money and involving the local church in ministering to Muslims through the work of their missionary. Not only is the missionary woman's role on the field strengthened, but it is also broadened, and her husband and children take a part in making it happen. The members of the local church might have been slow to take on this project without the endorsement of the pastor. His enthusiasm for the missionary family's activities spreads new vision in his church.

Pastors and church leaders can also be a great resource in the event of an emergency or crisis. Sometimes, they can be available to fly out for a visit, contact sending agencies, act as an advocate on our behalf, or raise prayer and financial support quickly. Keeping a close, intimate relationship with our home church will also help us continue the relationship when we return for furloughs. It can enable the pastor to come alongside us if we should have a crisis and need to leave the field.

Coaches

This last resource happens to be my role in our mission agency. Although many of the people I've already described can serve as coaches, our missionary colleagues, sending agents, and pastors usually have other agendas if they visit us on our field. For this reason, I place coaching in a separate category.

A coach is someone whose role is to help and care for

missionaries in both their personal lives and public ministries and encourage them to keep pressing toward a desired goal. A leader gives an assignment and manages personnel toward its completion. A coach, on the other hand, focuses on someone else's desired goal and helps her achieve it. Coaching can take on a variety of forms.

Issue-Specific Coaching

One type of coaching is issue-specific. This type of coach is an expert on a given topic, such as schooling, language learning, entry strategy, micro-enterprise or team dynamics. This coach would come to the field to address that one issue and work with a person or team to improve in that area. Such a person may serve as a resource on this issue for the entire mission agency.

When my husband and I led a team, we invited an issue-specific coach to a team retreat. He administered and interpreted various personality tests, staying long enough to help us apply some team dynamics exercises and evaluate how we needed to grow. He gave us tools. Later, since he was familiar with the dynamics of our team makeup, we were able to call on him to help us resolve specific problems. We didn't have to leave our field or work. Help came to us.

Ongoing Coaching

Another type of coach enters an agreement or covenant to provide an ongoing relationship. This is not a one-time exchange of information and resources. Such a coach helps a team or individual to walk through a given period of ministry to reach specified, God-given goals. The missionary team gives this type of coach the freedom to point out their areas of weakness and make suggestions for growth. Such a coach offers overall checkups and regular accountability in areas such as goals, problem solving, spiritual life, marriage/singleness issues, team life and ministry strategies. In order to succeed, these coaches must regularly visit missionaries on the field.

My husband and I serve several teams in this role. On one annual visit, we met with a family who were separated from their team, had a change in team leadership, and were wondering what to do about a rebellious teenage daughter away at boarding school. Their rugged conditions were worsening as a result of heightened Islamic control. While the husband loved his role in the city, the wife felt as though she had nothing to contribute and too many restrictions and concerns to make it worth trying. It would have been pointless for us simply to check up on their language learning and personal devotions. We needed to address all the areas of concern and help them arrive at solutions they could live with and carry through after we left.

We discussed strategies for pulling the team together and having the husband assume the leadership role. He needed lots of coaxing and assurance that we would be there for him later. We listened to stories about what their daughter was doing and offered compassion and encouragement. God is in control and would accomplish his work in the daughter's life. We evaluated their description of the recent surge in religious restrictions and their reactions to it, exhorting them to focus on the truth and ignore the rumors.

Then I asked the wife, if there were no barriers, what would she most like to do with the local women or in her setting. "Just dream," I told her. After careful thought, she said that even though she hadn't done any nursing in many years, she would like to develop some materials to help mothers with breast feeding and caring for their babies. I was thrilled. I had no idea that she was interested in doing something like that, because at first glance, she looked overwhelmed and out of energy for almost anything. We then talked with her and her husband about the feasibility of her idea. What would need to change in their lifestyle to accommodate a project like this?

After we left, we wrote to check on their progress. I encouraged the wife, telling her how valuable I considered her ministry with the local women. We also put this idea into possible long-term goals for the team. My desire is not to have this family meet our mission's criteria for activities, but to help them achieve their own well thought-out goals for reaching their Muslim friends.

Urgent Need Coaching

A third type of coach addresses urgent needs. This type of coach has a personal responsibility to respond in the case of an urgent situation, such as a burglary, an attack or threat, a discovery of moral failure or an imminent expulsion from the country. Often, a mission leader helps in this type of situation, but a coach who lives nearby, knows the team or has lived through a similar experience may be the one the team prefers to lean on.

This type of coach may be able to guide and comfort the team during traumatic times through e-mail and phone calls, but he or she needs to be ready to visit the field if necessary. This coach walks the team or the individual through the crisis and helps to manage it from the big picture perspective, bringing in outside help when needed, informing all the involved parties (family, pastor, personnel director, counselor), and helping everyone handle the aftermath of the crisis. This coach will see the issue through, help the team or individual evaluate the crisis as a learning experience, make appropriate changes as a result of what they've learned, and encourage the team to move on toward their next goal. Crisis management rarely is a long-term relationship; often, this coach's task is complete when the team seems to have recovered.

Conclusion

Here are five practical steps to follow whenever you find yourself asking the question, "Who is with me here?"

- See your situation in light of your purposes.
- Articulate your need.
- Look at resources already available to you.
- Ask for help; don't keep the need all to yourself.
- Believe God to provide what you need.

Finally, remember the promise we find in scripture:

> And my God shall supply all your needs according to his riches in glory in Christ Jesus (Phil. 4:19).

And be sure to apply it to your situation. No matter what your situation looks like, this is the truth. You need to believe this first, and then see how God will supply your needs.

Reference List

A. H.
> 1999 *Producing Mature Fruit*. Church Strengthening Ministry, CSM Building, Pascor Drive, Sto. Nino, Paranaque, Metro Manila, Philippines 1704.

Akbar, Ahmed S.
> 1992 *Postmodernism and Islam: Predicament and Promise*. New York: Routledge.

Anderson, Neil T.
> 1990 *Victory Over the Darkness*. Ventura, CA: Regal Books.

Banks, Robert
> 1980 *Going to Church in the First Century*. Beaumont, TX: Christian Books Publishing House.

Beckham, William
> 1997 *The Second Reformation*. Houston: Touch Publications.

Bible Storying: Chronological Bible Storying Newsletter.
> A quarterly newletter. Contact: Bible Storying, 2 Marine Vista, 20-75 Neptune Court, Rep. of Singapore 449026.
> E-mail: biblestorying@iname.com.

Bourdieu, Pierre
> 1977 *Outline of a Theory of Practice*. New York: Cambridge University Press.

Brubaker, Roger
> 1985 "Rethinking Classical Theory: The Sociological Vision of Pierre Bourdieu." *Theory and Society* 14, 6:745-775.

Colgate, Julia
> 1997 *Invest Your Heart: A Call for Women to Evangelize Muslims*. Available in English or Spanish from Frontiers, 325 N. Stapley Dr., Mesa, AZ 85203; Phone: (480) 834-1500. E-mail: info@us.frontiers.org.

Coody, Ron
> 1988 *Fields of Gold: Planting a Church among Muslims*. Available from Ron Coody, Union Chapel Ministries, 4722 N. Broadway Ave., Muncie, IN 47303.

Deen, Hanifa

    1995 *Caravanserai: Journey Among Australian Muslims.* Sydney: Allen & Unwin.

Durkeim

    1998 A Study Guide for "Introduction to Culture and Control: Boundaries and Identities." Deakin University, Australia.

El Sadawi, Nawal

    1980 *The Hidden Face of Eve.* London: Zed Press.

Fiske, Alan Page and Nick Haslam

    1997 "Is Obsessive-Compulsive Disorder a Pathology of the Human Disposition to Perform Socially Meaningful Rituals? Evidence of Similar Content." *Journal of Nervous and Mental Disease* 185, 4:211-224.

Foucault, Michel

    1977 *Language, Counter-Memory, and Practice: Selected Essays and Interviews.* Ithaca, NY: Cornell University Press.

Gerami, Shahin

    1996 *Women and Fundamentalism: Islam and Christianity.* New York: Garland Publishing.

Gray, John

    1992 *Men Are from Mars, Women are from Venus.* New York: HarperCollins Publishers.

Kendrick, Graham

    1981 "One Shall Tell Another." Quoted from *Songs of Fellowship.* Eastbourne, U.K.: Kingsway Music, 1991.

Kraft, Marguerite G.

    1990 Reaching Out for Spiritual Power: A Study in the Dynamics of Felt Needs and Spiritual Power. Ph.D. Dissertation, Fuller Theological Seminary.

Loeffler, Reinhold

    1988 *Islam in Practice: Religious Beliefs in a Persian Village.* Albany, NY: State University of New York Press.

Loewen, Jacob A.

    1998 "My Pilgrimage in Mission." *International Bulletin of Missionary Research* 22, 2:69-72.

Love, Fran

    1997 "What the New Testament Taught Me about Ministry Models." *Evangelical Missions Quarterly* 33, 1:22-31.

Love, Rick

    1995 *Peacemaking: A Study Guide*, 2nd edition. Available in English or Spanish from Frontiers, 325 N. Stapley Dr., Mesa, AZ 85203; Phone: (480) 834-1500. E-mail: info@us.frontiers.org.

Macleod, Arlene Elowe

    1991 *Accommodating Protest: Working Women, the New Veiling, and Change in Cairo*. New York: Columbia University Press.

Mallouhi, Christine

    1997 *Mini-Skirts, Mothers and Muslims: Modeling Spiritual Values in Muslim Culture*, 3rd printing. Spear Publications, STL Distributors, P.O. Box 300, Carlisle, Cumbria, CA3 0QS, UK.

Musk, Bill

    1989 *The Unseen Face of Islam: Sharing the Gospel with Ordinary Muslims*. East Sussex, UK: MARC.

    1995 *Touching the Soul of Islam: Sharing the Gospel in Muslim Cultures*. Crowborough: MARC.

Muzaffar, Chandra

    1987 *Islamic Resurgence in Malaysia*, 2nd edition. Petaling Jaya, Malaysia: Fajar Bakti.

Otis, George, Jr.

    1997 *The Twilight Labyrinth: Why Does Spiritual Darkness Linger Where It Does?* Grand Rapids, MI: Chosen Books.

Patai, Raphael

    1983 *The Arab Mind*, revised edition. New York: Macmillan.

Peristiany, J. G., ed.

    1970 *Honor and Shame: The Values of Mediterranean Society*. Chicago: University of Chicago Press.

Riddle, Donald Wayne

    1938 "Early Christian Hospitality: A Factor in the Gospel Transmission." *Journal of Biblical Literature* LVII:141-147.

Sadat, Jihan

    1987 *A Woman of Egypt*. New York: Simon & Schuster.

Schultz, Del

    1984 *God and Man*. Manila: Church Strengthening Ministry. Available from New Tribes Mission, 1000 East First Street, Sanford, FL, 32771-1487. Phone: (407) 323-3430 or (800) 321-5375. Internet: www.ntm.org.

Spradley, James P.

    1979 *The Ethnographic Interview*. Fort Worth: Harcourt Brace Jovanovich College Publishers.

Steyne, Philip M.

    1989 *Gods of Power: A Study of the Beliefs and Practices of Animists*. Houston: Touch Publications.

Terry, J. O.

    1998 *God and Woman: Bible Lessons for Oral Communicators*. Richmond:

International Mission Board, Southern Baptist Convention. To order, write to Mark Snowden, International Mission Board, Southern Baptist Convention, Box 6767, Richmond, VA 23230.

Terry, J. O. and Jim Slack

1999 *Chronological Bible Storying: A Methodology for Presenting the Gospel to Oral Communicators*. Richmond: International Mission Board, Southern Baptist Convention. To order, write to Mark Snowden, International Mission Board, Southern Baptist Convention, Box 6767, Richmond, VA 23230.

Thompson, LaNette W.

1996 *Sharing the Message through Storying: A Bible Teaching Method for Everyone*. Ouagadougou, Burkina Faso: Burkina Faso Baptist Mission. To order, write to Mark Snowden, International Mission Board, Southern Baptist Convention, Box 6767, Richmond, VA 23230.

Travis, John

1998 "The C1 to C6 Spectrum." *Evangelical Missions Quarterly* 34, 4:407-414.

Young, William C.

1996 *The Rashaayda Bedouin: Arab Pastoralists of Eastern Sudan*. Fort Worth: Harcourt Brace College Publishers.

Index

abuse, 21, 22, 23, 28, 29, 30, 31, 32, 40, 51,
 101, 114, 122, 137, 198, 200, 209, 246
adultery, 5, 23, 83, 115, 161
Afghanistan, 13, 15, 21, 22, 24, 25, 26
Akbar, Ahmed S., 72, 117, 261
alcoholism, 13, 28, 82, 110, 196, 198
amulet, See also charm, 26, 39, 47, 48, 52,
 60, 61, 62, 63, 88, 102
ancestor spirit, 38, 44
Anderson, Neil T., 84, 261
animism, 89, 91, 92, 97, 146, 162
Arab, 5, 12, 13, 66, 69, 71, 95, 102, 103,
 105, 112, 164, 195, 217, 235, 238, 243,
 263, 264
Arabian Gulf, 13, 60, 61
arrest, 18, 161, 165
baby, 24, 29, 34, 40, 41, 42, 45, 46, 47, 61,
 80, 81, 83, 84, 85, 88, 108, 114, 140,
 164, 225, 233, 240, 258
Bourdieu, Pierre, 66, 261
Brubaker, Roger, 66, 261
Caucasus, 73, 74, 75, 195, 196
Central Asia, 28, 30, 95, 135, 187, 191, 195,
 204, 215, 216, 218, 249
charms, 19, 40, 61, 121, 165
childbirth, 41, 80, 81
children, 6, 12, 13, 20, 22, 23, 24, 25, 29,
 30, 34, 39, 40, 42, 45, 51, 56, 63, 70,
 81, 82, 85, 87, 88, 89, 91, 92, 93, 103,
 104, 106, 108, 109, 112, 113, 114, 115,
 116, 119, 121, 137, 143, 144, 154, 158,
 160, 162, 163, 165, 174, 175, 182, 183,
 185, 186, 206, 207, 208, 209, 211, 213,
 214, 219, 220, 225, 227, 228, 230, 231,
 233, 234, 235, 238, 239, 240, 243, 244,
 245, 247, 249, 252, 253, 254, 256
China, 13, 29, 191
chronological Bible storying, 32, 55, 146,
 150, 151, 156, 158, 163, 166, 167, 168,
 169, 202, 218
church, 2, 3, 6, 18, 28, 33, 35, 50, 65, 70,
 73, 74, 75, 91, 96, 107, 108, 109, 110,
 112, 118, 120, 137, 138, 142, 144, 145,
 148, 149, 167, 168, 169, 170, 174, 175,

177, 181, 183, 184, 186, 187, 189, 190,
 191, 192, 193, 194, 195, 196, 197, 199,
 200, 202, 203, 204, 205, 206, 207, 208,
 209, 210, 211, 212, 213, 214, 215, 216,
 217, 218, 219, 220, 225, 227, 235, 236,
 237, 239, 247, 249, 250, 253, 255, 256
church, emerging, 181, 205, 206, 207
church, established, 205, 206
church, home (of the missionary), 139, 255,
 256
church, house, 167, 181, 190, 193, 194,
 197, 207, 208, 209, 219
church, women's, 207
Colgate, Julia, 33, 180, 261
communion, 105, 111, 196
community, 15, 30, 33, 38, 41, 47, 51, 53,
 57, 66, 70, 72, 81, 83, 86, 87, 90, 91,
 92, 93, 94, 97, 101, 103, 117, 119, 121,
 136, 139, 140, 141, 142, 143, 145, 175,
 181, 182, 185, 189, 191, 193, 194, 195,
 196, 197, 198, 204, 213, 220, 235, 255
contextualization, 48, 136, 181, 214, 231
conversion, 15, 73, 74, 76, 96, 122, 135,
 174, 216, 226, 250
culture, 3, 5, 12, 13, 16, 17, 20, 22, 27, 29,
 30, 31, 32, 35, 37, 39, 40, 55, 58, 61,
 62, 63, 65, 66, 67, 71, 74, 75, 76, 83,
 93, 94, 96, 97, 103, 116, 120, 121, 122,
 139, 140, 144, 149, 156, 164, 176, 177,
 179, 180, 181, 183, 189, 191, 192, 195,
 196, 197, 199, 201, 203, 204, 205, 208,
 211, 212, 213, 214, 215, 218, 219, 220,
 225, 226, 228, 230, 231, 232, 235, 238,
 239, 240, 241, 242, 243, 244, 245, 246,
 247, 253, 254, 256
cursing, 19, 26, 43, 47, 48, 58, 62
daughter, 23, 24, 26, 37, 43, 56, 70, 89, 91,
 101, 114, 161, 179, 185, 186, 188, 199,
 225, 226, 232, 235, 257, 258
death, 3, 4, 7, 18, 22, 24, 25, 26, 27, 29, 35,
 38, 41, 42, 44, 46, 48, 55, 80, 82, 83,
 84, 88, 92, 101, 103, 105, 106, 111,
 136, 141, 144, 155, 158, 161, 165, 183,
 199, 200, 202, 214, 236, 240

265

men, 3, 4, 14, 16, 17, 22, 23, 24, 27, 30, 31,
  32, 48, 58, 64, 66, 67, 68, 71, 72, 76,
  77, 78, 81, 83, 86, 88, 90, 94, 95, 97,
  103, 113, 114, 116, 122, 144, 145, 149,
  158, 159, 174, 180, 183, 186, 188, 196,
  197, 200, 203, 204, 207, 209, 210, 213,
  215, 216, 219, 220, 225, 226, 227, 228,
  236, 242, 243, 244, 245, 246
Middle East, 64, 70, 71, 73, 75, 79, 92, 94,
  146, 170, 215, 216, 218, 233, 242, 245
midwife, 21, 81, 84, 86, 88, 89, 91, 97, 240
modernism, 11
Muhammad, 65, 113, 118, 169
Moroccan, 149
Morocco, 17, 72, 74, 75, 95, 97, 113, 149
mosque, 19, 33, 68, 92, 210, 227
motherhood, 5, 22, 23, 24, 25, 29, 45, 46,
  51, 70, 81, 83, 84, 92, 95, 101, 102,
  106, 109, 112, 115, 150, 162, 179, 185,
  186, 202, 206, 211, 214, 217, 226, 233,
  235, 240, 244, 254, 258
Musk, Bill, 33, 37, 61, 79, 81, 85, 87, 90,
  94, 98, 263
Muslim background believers, 4, 5, 6, 7, 23,
  31, 63, 69, 70, 73, 75, 76, 84, 86, 95,
  96, 97, 98, 106, 136, 139, 140, 141,
  142, 145, 146, 148, 150, 151, 158, 166,
  167, 168, 169, 174, 175, 176, 177, 178,
  179, 180, 181, 182, 183, 184, 186, 187,
  188, 190, 191, 193, 195, 197, 198, 199,
  200, 201, 202, 203, 204, 205, 206, 208,
  209, 210, 211, 212, 213, 214, 215, 217,
  218, 219, 221
Muzaffar, Chandra, 72, 263
neighborhood, 13, 24, 33, 34, 38, 39, 41, 42,
  44, 45, 47, 48, 51, 52, 54, 62, 66, 68,
  83, 92, 93, 140, 141, 142, 144, 159,
  170, 178, 179, 187, 189, 191, 192, 194,
  206, 207, 220, 227, 235, 239, 243, 247
networks, 109, 142, 174, 175, 177, 179,
  180, 181, 186, 187, 189
North Africa, 13, 28, 29, 95, 96, 136, 169,
  174, 188, 215, 218, 237
occult, 19, 32, 33, 35, 36, 40, 44, 46, 48, 54,
  55, 56, 57, 61, 63, 76, 77, 90, 95, 96,
  97, 102, 106, 165, 198
oral communication, 146, 147, 149, 151,
  153, 154, 164, 166, 167
Pakistan, 11, 21, 22, 23, 26, 137, 138, 227
Parshall, Phil, 187
Pashtun, 22
Patai, Raphael, 69, 71, 263
Peristiany, J.G., 71, 263
polygamy, 17, 21, 24, 31, 213
power, 2, 5, 17, 18, 19, 20, 26, 27, 29, 32,
  34, 35, 37, 38, 39, 40, 41, 42, 43, 44,
  45, 46, 47, 48, 49, 50, 51, 52, 53, 54,
  56, 57, 58, 61, 62, 63, 67, 72, 77, 85,
  86, 87, 88, 90, 94, 95, 96, 97, 101, 102,
  103, 106, 108, 117, 122, 138, 141, 143,
  144, 155, 160, 161, 162, 164, 165, 178,

186, 200, 202, 206, 219, 227, 248, 250
power encounter, 62, 87, 94, 96, 102, 106
prayer beads, 74
prayer, see also intercession, 3, 7, 17, 27,
  29, 34, 35, 38, 42, 43, 44, 45, 46, 47,
  48, 51, 53, 56, 58, 62, 63, 66, 67, 68,
  73, 74, 75, 76, 84, 85, 86, 88, 90, 92,
  95, 104, 108, 110, 111, 112, 113, 115,
  117, 118, 119, 120, 121, 136, 138, 139,
  142, 143, 144, 145, 165, 167, 169, 174,
  178, 180, 184, 185, 186, 187, 189, 192,
  193, 194, 195, 196, 197, 202, 204, 206,
  213, 214, 219, 228, 236, 246, 251, 256
pregnancy and childbirth, 6, 11, 19, 23, 24,
  34, 40, 41, 45, 46, 55, 80, 81, 84, 89,
  111, 113, 114, 160, 161, 165, 189, 198,
  203, 232, 233, 240
purdah, 15, 22, 23, 25, 26, 90
Quran, 3, 18, 19, 25, 29, 70, 71, 72, 73, 77,
  81, 86, 102, 104, 110, 117, 118, 120,
  140, 155, 162, 163, 245, 247
Ramadan, 68, 73, 81, 92, 118, 119, 189
rape, 28
refugee, 11, 13, 21, 25, 26, 32
rejection, 15, 40, 81, 91, 92, 93, 94, 97, 219
rites of passage, 38, 140, 145
sacraments, 208
sacrifice, 39, 42, 53, 73, 121, 155, 158, 159,
  160, 163, 170
saint, 5, 61, 95, 97, 194
Satan, 35, 40, 42, 44, 45, 46, 47, 48, 50, 51,
  52, 53, 55, 57, 62, 96, 113, 140, 159
savior, 155, 158, 166
Sayyed Qotb, 140
seminary, 108, 217, 262
shamanism, 38, 39, 41, 43, 91, 94
shame, 5, 22, 25, 27, 30, 51, 69, 70, 77, 81,
  82, 83, 94, 96, 219, 243, 244
sheikhs, 19, 95
shrine, 26, 95, 98, 102
sickness, 19, 20, 22, 39, 46, 85, 140, 161,
  165
sin, 50, 83, 84, 85, 139, 144, 158, 159, 160,
  161, 162, 164, 165, 167, 169, 204, 240,
  243, 248
single women, 28, 179, 204, 232
Son of God, 163, 165
spiritual power, 19, 37, 38, 39, 40, 58, 62,
  63, 88, 97, 109, 121
spiritual warfare, 31, 35, 47, 48, 51, 54, 57,
  62, 63, 85, 96
stereotype, 12, 14, 17, 69, 90
Steyne, Philip M., 79, 92, 263
suffering, 4, 5, 11, 29, 48, 135, 136, 137,
  199, 200, 201, 212, 227, 231
tea, 3, 117, 119, 178, 188, 192, 195, 196,
  197, 233
team, 2, 28, 62, 63, 73, 74, 79, 83, 93, 175,
  176, 179, 180, 184, 185, 186, 187, 191,
  193, 194, 195, 197, 202, 203, 205, 209,
  210, 214, 220, 221, 225, 226, 227, 228,